Presenting invaluable guidance, *Sharing Jesus with Hindus* emerges as essential reading for individuals delving into the contextual interpretation of the Gospel within Hindu communities. With profound insight, the book not only underscores the critical significance of diaspora studies but also sheds light on the remarkable prominence of the Hindu diaspora within our interconnected global landscape.

Jose Abraham, PhD
Associate Professor of Islamic Studies, Fuller Theological Seminary

Energetic Hindu agitators, organizers, and thinkers will seize upon this book to help them understand why so many Hindus in the diaspora are becoming Christians and will find here scholarship and analysis that is careful, thoughtful, systematic, and comprehensive—and which, to their surprise, will also lead to surprisingly numerous flashes of self-understanding.

Prabhu S. Guptara
Retired Professor and Publisher, Salt Desert Media Group UK

This book is a must-read for all who are engaging Hindu people around the world. It makes a wonderful contribution to the contextual methodologies employed to effectively communicate the gospel.

Godfrey Harold
Principal, Cape Town Baptist Seminary, South Africa

An invaluable resource for gaining a good understanding of the belief systems of your Hindu friends, neighbors, and colleagues. More importantly, learn how to share your Christian faith with them that is meaningful and impactful.

Dr. Ravi I. Jayakaran
President, Medical Ambassadors International

Hindus in diaspora now constitute a community come of age and draw the well-deserving attention of the larger society. Christian thinkers and practitioners featured in this volume challenge the followers of Jesus Christ to sympathetically understand the psyche, concerns, religiosity, and aspirations of millions of Hindus scattered all over the world. A must-read for all who take seriously their Christian faith and Hindu friends in their neighborhood.

Bishop Dr. C. V. Mathew
Former Deputy Chair, Lausanne Committee for World Evangelisation

Jesus selflessly sacrificed his life to grant us forgiveness for our bad karma. For those who believe in him, he provides a fresh start, with God guiding us as our inner guru. This profound act of love and redemption is an extraordinary gift. *Sharing Jesus with Hindus* offers pragmatic insights to help us unwrap this mystery and present Jesus as homage to our Hindu friends worldwide.

Yeshu Samaj

Dr. Sam George and Dr. Ashok Kumar, and the chapter contributors need high commendation for making this volume available to the global Church. They have highlighted biblical principles, ministry insights, and helpful bridges to enhance and expedite the reaching of Hindus in diaspora. May the Spirit of God freshly awaken and catalyze the global Church to embrace the evangelization of all Hindus everywhere.

Dr. T. V. Thomas
Chairman, Global Diaspora Network

Since 2020, India remains the country with the largest diaspora population in the world. The globalization of Hinduism, largely driven by this Indian diaspora represents a profound challenge to the long-held view that Hinduism remains isolated to the Indian sub-continent. Sam George and Ashok Kumar are widely connected with Christian leaders of the Global Indian diaspora and their prolonged engagement has served them well to bring together their collective wisdom for missional engagements with Hindus everywhere. This remarkable set of essays highlights the challenges and promise of reaching this growing diaspora with the gospel of Jesus Christ.

Timothy C. Tennent, PhD
Professor of World Christianity and President
Emeritus, Asbury Theological Seminary

I recommend reading another excellent product of the Global Diaspora Institute at Wheaton College Billy Graham Center, the very informative new book, *Sharing Jesus with Hindus*, which has been edited by two very well-known Indian diaspora thought leaders, Drs. Sam George and Ashok Kumar. They have brought together reputed writers and published on a variety of topics that address the issues related to Indians living around the world but continuing to love and stay to some degree or another, culturally enmeshed with their ethnic traditions.

Junias V. Venugopal, PhD
Associate Dean and Associate Professor, Wheaton College

Sharing Jesus with Hindus

Global Witness Among Hindu Diaspora

Sam George & Ashok Kumar
Editors

visit us at missionbooks.org

Sharing Jesus with Hindus: Global Witness among Hindu Diaspora

© 2024 by Sam George. All Rights Reserved.

No part of this book may be reproduced, stored in a retrieval system, or transmitted in any form or by any means—electronic, mechanical, photocopy, recording, or otherwise—without prior written permission from the publisher, except brief quotations used in connection with reviews. This manuscript may not be entered into AI, even for AI training. For permission, email permissions@wclbooks.com. For corrections, email editor@wclbooks.com.

William Carey Publishing (WCP) publishes resources to shape and advance the missiological conversation in the world. We publish a broad range of thought-provoking books and do not necessarily endorse all opinions set forth here or in works referenced within this book.

The URLs included in this workbook are provided for personal use only and are current as of the date of publication, but the publisher disclaims any obligation to update them after publication.

Scripture quotations marked ESV are taken from the ESV® Bible (The Holy Bible, English Standard Version®), Copyright © 2001 by Crossway, a publishing ministry of Good News Publishers. Used by permission. All rights reserved.

Scripture quotations marked NIV are taken from the Holy Bible, New International Version®, NIV®. Copyright © 1973, 1978, 1984, 2011 by Biblica, Inc.™ Used by permission of Zondervan. All rights reserved worldwide. www.zondervan.com. The "NIV" and "New International Version" are trademarks registered in the United States Patent and Trademark Office by Biblica, Inc.™

Scripture quotations marked NLT are taken from the Holy Bible, New Living Translation, copyright ©1996, 2004, 2015 by Tyndale House Foundation. Used by permission of Tyndale House Publishers, Carol Stream, Illinois 60188. All rights reserved.

Published by William Carey Publishing
10 W. Dry Creek Cir
Littleton, CO 80120 | www.missionbooks.org

William Carey Publishing is a ministry of Frontier Ventures
Pasadena, CA | www.frontierventures.org

Cover and Interior Designer: Mike Riester

ISBNs: 978-1-64508-588-1 (paperback)
 978-1-64508-590-4 (epub)

Printed Worldwide

28 27 26 25 24   1 2 3 4 5   IN

Library of Congress Control Number: 2024909292

Contents

Introduction by *Dr. Ashok Kumar* — vii

1: Witnessing to the Hindu Diaspora in North America — 1
   Dr. Atul Aghamkar

2: Constructive Interfaith Encounters in Diaspora — 19
   Dr. Wilson Paluri

3: Pollution and Cleansing from *Kala Pani* Crossings: — 37
   Sin and Salvation for the Hindu Diaspora
   Dr. Sam George

4: Modi, Hindu *Rashtra*, and India's New Internationalism — 51
   Mr. Rahil Patel

5: Challenges of Pastoring Hindu Converts — 67
   Dr. Martin Alphonse

6: The Home Church among Hindu Households in the Diaspora — 77
   Dr. Danny Sathyadass

7: Understanding Hindu Neighbors — 87
   Rev. Ashwin Ramani

8: Christocentric Satsang: Contextualized Worship for Hindus — 99
   Mr. Anil Yesudas

9: Dealing with Family after Conversion — 109
   Dr. P. T. Subrahmanyan

10: Ministering to Hindu Families — 121
    Mr. Srinivasa Moorthy

11: Ministering to Hindu Students in Western Universities — 133
    Dr. Kamesh Sankaran

12: Ministry among the Indian Diaspora in the Philippines — 145
    Rev. Mark Sudhir

13: Malaysia's Tamil Women: Agents of Change — 155
    or Guardians of Tradition?
    Mrs. Anita Lazarus

14: Virtually Possible: Digital Outreaches to Hindus — 165
    Mrs. Chandra and Mr. Naveen

15: Ministry among Hindus in the Caribbean — 177
    Dr. Krishna Ramsundar

16: Sense, Sensibility, and Sensitivity: — 189
    The Case of Evangelism to Hindus in South Africa
    Rev. Louie Naidoo

17: Conclusion: Christian Witness in Pluralistic Contexts — 197
    Dr. Sam George

Acknowledgments — 207
Bibliography — 209
Author Profiles — 225

Introduction

Dr. Ashok Kumar

I recently had lunch with a friend in Davao, a bustling city of 1.6 million residents in the southwestern part of the Philippines. Our restaurant was packed with medical students from different parts of India, and the streets were filled with Indian students wearing white medical lab coats. As we ate together, I could overhear four distinct Indian languages spoken around our table—namely Hindi, Telugu, Tamil, and Marathi. I almost forgot I was in the Philippines, as it felt like I was in a southern or western Indian city.

It is estimated that around twenty-five thousand Indian medical students live in the Philippines, which has become a viable alternative on account of its affordable, high-quality medical education. Additionally, the medium of instruction is English, and this place is closer to India and more comparable in culture than other options in the Caribbean or Eastern Europe. Moreover, these students have prospects to continue their medical training or to seek employment in Western nations, while those who return to India are able to build lucrative careers and become movers and shakers in the country. These students come from close-knit families in the middle and upper classes, many of whom are from Hindu backgrounds.

As part of God's marvelous plan, many Hindus are being brought closer to the gospel in foreign lands. They get unshackled from their inherited sociocultural and religious beliefs and practices when they go abroad. But although this represents an incredible missional opportunity for Christians worldwide, most have not realized this reality. Since many are reluctant to go to them and it is increasingly difficult to enter India for mission activities, God is bringing a record number of Hindus to our doorsteps globally.

They are more open to the gospel when far from home, and new environs lead them to question their long-cherished views and beliefs. We don't need to learn a new language and culture or to cross any geographical boundaries to reach out to them. There are practically no external barriers to overcome in reaching out to the global Hindu Diaspora. It is encouraging to note that many Hindus have become followers of Jesus in foreign lands, in some cases without any concerted efforts to reach them by Christians in their host nations.

A brief introduction about myself: I was born and raised in a Hindu family in Kerala, India, and became a follower of Jesus in my college years. I have lived in many different states of India, and I currently make my home in the island nation of Singapore. Over the last couple of decades, I have met thousands of Hindus who have become Christians in different parts of India and around the world. I have been involved in full-time Christian work in India and Singapore for over thirty years; and I have served in different capacities, mostly with Operation Mobilization but more recently with the SIM Intl team based out of Singapore. I have also served with the Missions Commission of the World Evangelical Alliance and now serve as a Catalyst of the Lausanne Movement. I have had formal seminary training in Singapore, the United States, and the United Kingdom in order to secure graduate and doctorate level theological degrees, with a special focus on ministry to Hindus worldwide.

Hindus and Diaspora

Defining Hinduism is not easy. One simple definition is *sanatan dharma*, meaning "eternal religion." Most Hindus believe in God and are very religious, even though their definition of *god* differs from the Judeo-Christian understanding. Most Christians in India and abroad have a shallow understanding of the Hindu faith, while only a very few maintain regular or sustained contact with Hindus around them. *Hethne* is a composite word made of *H*, standing for Hindu, and *ethne*, meaning "peoples" or "nations" in Greek. Lately, the term *Hethne* has become popular in mission circles to describe the Hindu people of the world.

Hinduism is often considered one of the oldest religions in the world, with customs dating back more than four thousand years. There are over 1.2 billion Hindu people in the world, which amounts to about fifteen percent of the world's population and makes it the third-largest religious group in the world, after Christianity and Islam. The word *Hindu* is derived from the Sanskrit name for the Indus River (*Sindhu*); and foreigners, such as the Persians, used the term *Hindu* for those who lived beyond the Indus River. Hinduism is generally considered to be a polytheistic religion with thousands of gods and goddesses, although it also allows for a monotheistic interpretation, with all the *gods* seen as different aspects of a single, universal spirit called *Brahman*. Hindus adhere to many different traditions, teachings, and belief systems; and a Hindu individual may have his or her own separate set of creeds, rituals, and practices. One might describe Hinduism as a culture rather than a religion, although it contains many faith movements that are more than just religious markers.

Introduction

A Hindu is born a Hindu; they don't become one by professing any particular set of beliefs, worshiping any specific god, or initiating any act of conversion. There are no commonly accepted ways for a Hindu to cease being a Hindu or for someone who wasn't born a Hindu to become one. Further, it must be noted that "Hindi" is a widely spoken language of North India, and it should not be mistaken for "Hindu," which denotes an adherent of Hinduism.

Diaspora is a widely employed word across many disciplines nowadays to describe people on the move. It is a Greek biblical word that means to disperse or scatter. Traditionally, *Diaspora* is associated with the Jewish dispersion following their expulsion from the land of Israel, culminating with the destruction of Jerusalem and the temple in 586 BC, and was generally associated with pain, tragedy, loss, and exile.[1] Steven Vertovec put it this way:

> The term diaspora is derived from the Greek word *diaspeir* meaning "to disperse or distribute." It is a compound of *speir*, meaning "to sow to scatter," like the seed, and *dia*, meaning "from one end to the other."[2]

It is an agricultural expression that depicts a farmer walking around to sow seeds by hand in order to spread the seeds over a wide area of tilled soil. The term became associated with the Jewish historical experience and hence was associated with being a dispersed people sharing a common religious and cultural heritage.

While most Hindus still live in India, there is a steady surge in their migration across the globe. Nepal is another nation with a majority Hindu populace and was the only Hindu nation until very recently. More Hindus now live outside of India and Nepal than ever in history. The reasons for this dispersion are many. Three of the leading factors for the growing outmigration from India and Nepal are a) educational opportunities, b) lucrative employment abroad or lack of employment opportunities in their native lands, and c) to support family back home. These immigrants are further aided by related push-and-pull factors of migratory propensities, resulting in unprecedented outmigration to destinations outside of the Indian subcontinent.

---

1 Kalpana, *Global Hindu Diaspora*, 9.
2 Vertovec, "Religion and Diaspora," 1.

A record number of the growing Indian urban middle class is looking for education and training in specialized fields, with the hopes of securing high-paying jobs that are often unavailable in India. Moreover, there are not enough colleges or universities that offer adequate vacancies for as many educational aspirants. Similarly, the lack of employment in their homeland or finding employment commensurate with their education or skill levels has forced many to look abroad for the prospect of securing career advances. Furthermore, many sense a deep sense of responsibility to support their siblings, parents, and extended family members with better financial returns for their work in foreign lands than what is available locally—especially with the rising cost of living in their native land.

The Global Hindu Diaspora can generally be divided into three eras: The first era, which I call the Ancient Hindu Diaspora, involves the spread of Hinduism through Southeast Asia, mostly via trade and cultural exchange. The second era, which I refer to as the Old Hindu Diaspora, was dispersed mostly through the actions of colonial powers prior to India gaining independence from the British Empire in 1947. The third era, which I call the New Hindu Diaspora, has largely evolved over the seventy-five years since Indian independence. The majority of this era includes the economic immigration by Hindus to other parts of the world.

Indian Diaspora

A noteworthy and sizable emigration from the Indian subcontinent can be traced back to the 1830s, although some people from certain pockets of the Indian subcontinent had migrated earlier, as well, to a few select destinations. Sam George divides the Global Indian Diaspora into two broad categories around the year 1947, when the modern nations of the Indian subcontinent were granted independence from the colonial rulers.[3] The pre–1947 dispersion of people from the South Asian region took place when many were taken as indentured laborers to work in the plantations of the colonial rulers. The post–1947 emigration from the Indian subcontinent were largely volitional migrants who sought either economic or educational avenues overseas or to escape from the drudgery and struggles of newly independent states.

Over the last seventy-five years, Indian migrants have spread to nearly every country in the world. The indentured migrants were not very religious and did not maintain any contact with the land of their forefathers, and

---
3 George, *Desi Diaspora*, 3.

their religious practices were relatively simple. The latter group of skilled professional and economic migrants were involved in trade, were semi-skilled workers, or were highly trained specialists who maintained regular contact with people back home and were found to be very religious—sometimes more religious after moving to a new place to preserve their culture and community in their places of settlement.

In 2022, 281 million international migrants were scattered around the globe, with the largest share—18 million—coming from India. Over the last few years, migrant flows out of India have been the largest in the world. The growing demand worldwide for highly specialized software, science, and technology careers, along with professional managerial jobs, continues to attract many millions of middle-income professionals in India to explore foreign assignments and upward economic mobility. This trend is likely to grow steadily for the next several decades and surpass all other categories of outmigration from India. Although permanent residency and citizenship have become difficult in many Western nations, the skilled younger generation is willing to venture out for a few years to foreign lands rather than settling for what is available locally and backbreaking work culture, in order to make some quick bucks and gain experience in global companies with the hopes of returning for better career prospects back in India.

Recent years have seen a noticeable surge in Indian student migration abroad—most going to English-speaking nations—surpassing 750,000 in 2022.[4] Before the COVID pandemic student migration stood at 590,000 in 2019, but it shrank by half in 2020 due to pandemic-induced lockdowns, travel restrictions, and the closure of foreign embassies. The most desired destination for international students out of India is undoubtedly the United States, which received a record level of nearly 190,000 in 2022, up from 120,000 in 2021. The next largest destination is Canada (180,000 in 2022), nearly doubling from the previous year. The United Kingdom received 130,000 in 2022, as compared to 77,000 in 2021 and 25,000 in 2018.

The new educational policy to attract Indians in STEM fields by British universities and their prime minister being of Indian origin has fueled the Indian student migration to the UK. After a slight drop in student migration to Australia during the COVID years, it rebounded to 59,000 in 2022, while in New Zealand intake fell steeply to 1,600 in 2022, as compared to 10,200

---

4 Rajan and Kumar, "India's Great Student Out-Migration."

in 2019. In 2022, Singapore took 17,000 students from India, while 11,200 students went to the Philippines. Other countries that have attracted Indian students include Germany, Russia, Kyrgyzstan, Kazakhstan, and China. The Gulf nations, such as UAE, Saudi Arabia, Qatar, and Oman, are also becoming destinations for Indian students.

Marriage migration is another major reason for young Indian men and women to go overseas these days. Marital alliances from well-settled grooms and brides in foreign lands are highly sought after by Indian parents and are featured prominently in matrimonial advertisements and by certain community matchmakers. The practice of arranged marriages is still prevalent, so many young people who are well-employed abroad look to their parents to do preliminary screening for suitable marriage partners. The numerous online matrimonial sites and social media platforms have become attractive alternatives in the marriage market.

Many qualified women and men prefer overseas alliances and are bolder to venture out to unknown faraway lands than their ancestors. However, this does not work out well for many, since there is much deception and exploitation in long-distance matchmaking. Recent years have seen multiple incidents of dowry extortion and sexual exploitation in migrant-sending Indian states like Kerala, Punjab, Gujarat, and Andhra Pradesh under the guise of marriage by the trafficking of poor, uneducated women to foreign lands.

An interesting trend to notice is that many Indians are relinquishing their citizenship after settling abroad. Some 225,000 Indians gave up their citizenship in 2020, and it is all but certain that most of them are from *Hethne* backgrounds. Since 2011, more than 1,750,000 people have renounced their Indian citizenship for foreign passports.[5] Many of them have taken foreign citizenship, though some of them may maintain the Overseas Citizen of India (OCI) status to keep their access to their ancestral land. While some have maintained close ties with diasporic Hindu establishments, many have renounced their inherited religions as well to become religious "nones," or in many cases, they have become Christians in their foreign lands.

Another measure of the growing influence of the Indian Diaspora is the remittances sent by global Indians back to their ancestral homelands, which hit a record high of almost $108 billion in 2022.[6] For more than a decade, India continued to be the top remittance-receiving nation in the world, largely from

---

5 Mohan, "Surge in Indians adopting foreign citizenship."
6 *The Economist*, "India's diaspora is bigger."

single workers in the Middle East and high-income professionals who send part of their earnings to support family members back home. Some construct homes, get their siblings married or invest in businesses to diversify their income streams and hope to return to India in the future. Besides helping their kith and kin, some of these monetary transactions are earmarked for religious activities and sociopolitical projects which have drawn some criticism and come under greater scrutiny by Indian government officials, as permits to receive foreign donations by Christian organizations were canceled for many Indian churches and mission organizations.

Hindu Diaspora Challenges and Opportunities

The global Hindu Diaspora is a highly successful community. They are well educated, work in professional fields as dual-income households, and are highly motivated to succeed. Indians are the highest-earning migrant group in America and many other Western nations. The perception sometimes arises that successful people do not need the gospel, but this is not true. If anything, there is greater urgency to reach out to the Hindu Diaspora precisely because it has amassed wealth and influence.

The Hindu Diaspora is a political and influential lobby. It has successfully lobbied for textbooks and school curricula to be modified in favor of their versions of history. Driven by *Hindutva* ideology (that India should be a Hindu nation), it has produced several pseudo-scholars who have attacked academics seen as hostile to the Hindu nationalist project. The list of victims is long and includes such eminent scholars as Wendy Doniger (*The Hindus: An Alternative History*), Paul Courtright (*Ganesa: Lord of Obstacles, Lord of Beginnings*), and James Laine (*Shivaji: Hindu King in Islamic India*). The *Rashtriya Swayamsevak Sangh* (RSS) is a far-right-wing Hindu nationalist volunteer paramilitary organization behind the current ruling political party and proponent of Hindutva and has now spread its wing to many overseas locations by creating *shakhas* (chapters) of its global operations in dozens of other countries, including the United States. The goal of the RSS is to redefine India according to its majority Hindu faith, although India was established as a pluralistic democracy based on secular principles—embracing all forms of diversity, including religions.

> The RSS's strategy of reaching out to the diaspora consisted in reproducing abroad the modus operandi of the organization in India. This voluntarist approach explains the rise of the Hindutva movement outside India at least as much as the diaspora's alleged long-distance nationalism. . . . The political positions of the long-distance nationalists serve to protect an ethnic identity that is threatened either within their country of origin or sometimes in the host society.[7]

The influence can be traced back to every area. Saffron diplomacy is a contemporary reality. The appointment of people in a diplomatic circle is a drive to replace the Anglophone class with pro-Hindi and pro-Hindutva Foreign Service recruits and it is taking its toll on Indian diplomacy and national interest. There have been urgent whispers about the saffronization of Indian foreign policy ever since Narendra Modi became the prime minister in 2014.[8] The large-scale violence against minority religions, particularly Muslims and Christians, has continued unabated since Modi took over the reins, and the growing populism and fascist ideologies are threatening the very fabric of Indian democracy.

All of this serves to remind us of that long-distance nationalism—a term first coined by Benedict Anderson—remains alive and well among at least some of the Hindu Diaspora. A change of passport does not make these emigrants less Indian or less Hindu; they have not changed their culture or allegiance to their motherland. Hindu people still refer to India as *mathru + bhumi* (motherland) with a sense of great pride and belonging.

For many of these individuals, religion and culture are inseparable. Many families keep the religious element alive through personal devotional acts, such as by setting up a *puja ghar* (literally, a "worship room")—a personal household temple—in their homes. Many parents in the Diaspora consider it essential to pass religious knowledge on to their children. The *puja ghar* also holds communal significance, as it brings families together for shared festivals and rituals. Many Hindus in the Diaspora harbor a prejudice toward Christianity, at times animated at the root by an understandable but unfortunate conflation of Christianity with colonial injustice. The clearest statement of this might be found in Swami Vivekananda's speech in the Parliament of World Religions in Chicago in 1893:

---

7 Jaffrelot and Therwath, "Sangh Parivar and Hindu Diaspora," 285.
8 Raman, "Ambassadors of Hindutva."

> We who have come from the East have sat here day after day and have been told in a patronising way that we ought to accept Christianity because Christian nations are the most prosperous. We look about us and we see England, the most prosperous nation in the world, with her foot on the neck of 250 million Asiatics. We look back into history and see that the prosperity of Christian Europe began with Spain. Spain's prosperity began with the invasion of Mexico. Christianity wins its prosperity by cutting the throats of its fellowmen.[9]

We can see the influence of *Hethne* people worldwide—from prime ministers of many nations to cabinet members to local elected officials, CEOs of major global corporations, venture capitalists, bankers, lawyers, media personalities, celebrities, and the like. Some of them are very public about their religious beliefs and practices to make Hinduism attractive in a post-Christian West and resurgent India. This creates some form of confusion among Christians in the West and makes them unsure of how to engage Hindus in the West.

It is time for us to think of the Hindu Diaspora differently. God has sent them to our doorstep in foreign lands for a purpose. Most are educated, well-off, and hold high positions in the marketplace. They are movers and shakers in societies around the world. Yet this does not mean that they are beyond the reach of the gospel or that they do not need its message—quite the opposite. There is an opportunity here to induct them into the family of Christ and make them allies in furtherance of the Great Commission. For this, we need to disciple and mobilize Christians globally to engage the Hindu Diaspora for a credible and sustained Christian witness.

I say *opportunity*, but perhaps the better word is *command*. God showed his love for us best when Jesus obeyed the Father unto death so that the world might be saved and be set free. In turn, Jesus commissioned all who believe in him to "go and make disciples of all nations" (Matt 28:19). Reaching the *Hethne* is not an option; it is a command: "Go into all the world and preach the Good News to everyone" (Mark 16:15 NLT), which includes 1.2 billion *Hethne* people. *Going* does not necessarily mean going to India or Nepal anymore, but only crossing the fence or street to reach Hindu neighbors and colleagues. He has brought these people from around the world to our doorstep. So what are we doing? How do we equip our fellow Christians to understand the Hindus next door? What works in witnessing to Hindus?

---

9 Bhattacharya, "When Vivekananda Reconstructed Hinduism."

What are common misconceptions? What mistakes are commonly made? These are the questions Sam George and I have set out to answer in this book, with the help of a set of leading scholar-practitioners who are involved in Christian ministry among Hindus around the world.

Book Outline

This book comprises sixteen chapters, with each having a distinctive focus and location. They could be read independently of other chapters, and readers could jump from one chapter to another depending on their interests. Each is written from a particular geographical location and deals with a specific issue of the author's distinct vantage point and expertise. Each author tends to jump directly into the assigned topic, as there isn't adequate space within the limits of a chapter to deliberate on the history of Hinduism or the Indian Diaspora community in that part of the world.

Readers are advised to acquaint themselves with other materials cited in the footnotes, bibliography, and related texts on sociocultural and historical literature. The chapters in this volume are not laid out in any critical sequence, and thus readers are free to read them in their order of choice. Moreover, Sam and I, as editors, will be the first to admit that this volume does not cover every aspect related to ministry to Hindus; but we hope that this resource spurs you to explore other resources and dive deeper into issues raised by this book. More importantly, we encourage readers to connect with other practitioners and scholars in the field in other parts of the world who could further assist you in ministry to the *Hethne* peoples of the world.

The first chapter was written by Dr. Atul Aghamkar, a professor of missiology who has taught at the leading evangelical seminaries in Pune and Bangalore, India, and many diasporic sites of the Global Indian Diaspora. This chapter provides a broad overview of Hindus in North America, including the latest statistics on the spread of Indians in American cities and states. He enumerates four distinctives of the Hindu Diaspora and advocates for partnership using the Apostle Paul's model to take on the challenge of engaging North American Hindus. He calls on Western churches to recognize the neglected people of the Diaspora Hindus living in their vicinities and to leverage the witness of Indian Christians among them.

The next chapter, written by Dr. Wilson Paluri, a leading Christian religion scholar on Hinduism, deals with interreligious dialogue in diaspora. Originally from Andhra Pradesh, he has taught in North and South Indian theological institutions for over two decades. He currently serves as a Catalyst for Hinduism for the Lausanne Movement. In this chapter, he analyzes some traits of diasporic Hinduism by exploring religious preservation and modifications taking place at diasporic sites before formulating some pointers on interfaith encounters with global Hindus.

The third chapter is by my coeditor Dr. Sam George. He lives in the suburbs of Chicago and directs a research center at Wheaton College Billy Graham Center while teaching global human migration, diaspora mission, and World Christianity at several seminaries in North America and around the world. In this chapter, he explores the historic Indian resistance to migration in terms of the Hindu scriptural prohibition of *kala pani* (black waters), specifically analyzing the notions of pollution and cleansing arising from sea crossings. Subsequently, he compares this worldview with Christian theological understandings of sin and salvation for Hindus in the Diaspora.

The fourth chapter was written by Mr. Rahil Patel, a former Hindu monk based in the United Kingdom who has recently become a follower of Jesus and now serves as an educator, coach, and adviser to churches and policymakers. In this chapter, Patel investigates the faith of the current prime minister of India, who is backed by radical Hindutva ideology to make India into a Hindu *rashtra* (nation). Patel explores how the prime minister's Hindu faith shapes his leadership style, governance ethos, and international relations. Though not a conventional chapter one would find in mission literature, this is a very insightful essay written by someone who has been part of the Hindu sect and will help readers understand the mindset of modern Diaspora Hindus and how transnational religious linkages are vital to the global Hindu Diaspora.

In the fifth chapter, Rev. Dr. Martin Alphonse draws upon his rich experience of over four decades of being a pastor in Chennai, Singapore, and the US, as well as a theological seminary professor teaching missions and cultural anthropology. He delves into some real challenges faced by new Hindu converts to Christianity, specifically examining issues related to worldview, caste, ostracization, and demonic oppression.

In the sixth chapter, Dr. Danny Sathyadass makes a compelling case for the house-church model to disciple and evangelize Hindus in the diaspora by advocating the strengths of the house church movement ecclesiology.

He served as a pastor of a traditional church before serving as a chaplain at a seminary in Bangalore, where he began to host a home fellowship which grew to become a network of home churches. More recently he has been based in Dallas, Texas, where he has trained many to host home churches to engage Hindus, in particular, who may not be keen to visit a Western-style church or an Indian church in the West but are more comfortable to explore faith matters in the intimate setting of a home.

The seventh chapter was written by Pastor Ashwin Ramani, who comes from a Tamil Brahmin background and is now pastoring an evangelical church in Calgary, Canada. He is currently doing doctoral research in the United States on reaching diaspora communities in Canada. He offers an astute and very practical challenge to all Christians everywhere to build relationships with Hindus in our neighborhoods. He calls everyone to share the gospel of Jesus with the Hindus whom God has brought to live in our localities all over the world.

In the eighth chapter, Mr. Anil Yesudas, who is based in Chicago and currently doing his doctoral studies in India on contextualized mission practices, offers a model of contextualized Christian worship in the form of Christ-centered *satsangs* (worship gatherings). He calls upon all Christians to be more sensitive to the context Hindus bring with them to their diasporic locations and to why incorporating ancestral cultural elements in worship is a powerful approach to communicating the truth about God to our Hindu friends, neighbors, and colleagues.

The author of the ninth chapter, Dr. P. T. Subrahmanyan, comes from a reputable Hindu priestly lineage and now serves as a religion professor at a Pentecostal seminary in Kerala. He presents the dilemma faced by many converts to Christianity from a Hindu background in regard to dealing with their family members. Drawing from his ongoing personal struggles, as well as having lived in the Netherlands and the United States while doing advanced theological studies, Dr. Subrahmanyan offers new believers practical help and clarity in navigating through the quagmires of the relational world and the rupture caused by their decision to follow Jesus as their Lord and only Savior.

The tenth chapter was penned by Mr. Srinivasa Moorthy who, along with his wife, hails from a Tamil Hindu background and is now in full-time Christian family ministry. Earlier he worked for multinational firms and lived in several European, North American, and Asian cities. As a family coach and speaker, he examines the notion of the family system from a Hindu perspective and provides helpful pointers on how to minister to uprooted and nuclearized Hindu families in the diaspora.

In the subsequent chapter, Dr. Kamesh Sankaran—who pursued a college education at a prestigious American university, where he met Jesus, and who now works as a university professor himself in another American university—makes a compelling case about the power of ministering to international students in college settings. The growing number of young people from India going abroad for studies—most of whom are young Hindus who often are open to caring fellowship, seriously evaluating their inherited belief systems, and comparing them with other worldviews—presents an unmatched opportunity to share the gospel of Jesus Christ with Hindus in global college campuses.

The twelfth chapter was written by Rev. Mark Sudhir, who is from Orissa and now serves as the pastor of the oldest Indian Christian church in the Philippines and has planted several new churches among the Hindus and Sikhs in Metro Manila. Mark is a musician, songwriter, and evangelist, who is doing his doctorate in that country. He is extensively involved in outreach ministry among Indian students, families, traders, and others across the Southeast Asian region. He presents the history of Indian migration to the Philippines and explains the religious beliefs and cultural practices of the Indian people there, before unpacking some ministry opportunities and challenges in reaching Hindus there.

In the subsequent chapter, Mrs. Anita Lazarus, who was based in Melaka, Malaysia, conducted a study among the Tamil women of that country who trace their ancestry to southern India or Ceylon many generations ago. She analyzes the psychosocial dynamics of a double-minority community in a Muslim-dominated nation and showcases the ministry of empowering women to help women become changemakers in society.

The fourteenth chapter was written by two non-Indians who are based in Australia and Africa and have been involved with ministry among Indians for many decades. Their names appear as Chandra and Naveen, which are pseudonyms for security reasons and present the power of the internet platform for engaging global Hindus online. They investigate the online faith journeys of Hindu seekers and explain the online ministry process. They encourage all churches and ministries to develop digital strategies to engage the growing global Hindu populace who may be more comfortable with faith explorations online.

The next two chapters come from the Old Indian Diaspora of historic indentured labor migration to the Caribbean and South Africa. The fifteenth chapter was written by Dr. Krishna Ramsundar, whose ancestors were taken as indentured laborers to the island nation of Trinidad in the Caribbean, while Krishna himself has been privileged to take advanced theological studies in the United States. He has served as a church planter in Mexico and pastored Spanish-speaking congregations in the United States. Dr. Ramsundar provides a brief history of the Indo-Caribbean community and his conversion from Hinduism to Christianity. He deliberates on the complexity of identity after generations and the vital importance of building genuine relationships in ministering to Indians. He advocates for strategic priority for reaching children and youth of Diaspora Hindus and not to present Christianity as a Western religion.

The final chapter was written by Rev. Louie Naidoo, who serves as the pastor of an evangelical church in the city of Durban, South Africa. In this chapter, he takes on a recent controversy created by a young pastor about Hindus and calls for the need to develop more cultural competency toward diasporic Hindus. He situates the scandal within the sociopolitical history of apartheid in South Africa and encourages pastors, evangelists, and missionaries to remain committed to the Great Commission mandate to win our Hindu friends with love and cultural sensitivity.

Finally, in the concluding essay, Sam George examines the meaning of Christian witness in pluralistic contexts from a biblical and missiological perspective to tie together varied themes and viewpoints from divergent locations of the global Hindu Diasporas covered in this volume.

Witnessing to the Hindu Diaspora in North America

Dr. Atul Aghamkar

The Hindu Diaspora is one of the most neglected and unreached peoples in the world, even though they live in close proximity to traditionally strong Christians in Europe and North America. Although the modern history of Christian missions to Hindus goes back to the arrival of the Danish missionaries in India in the early sixteenth century, the real impact of Christian missions during the past four centuries has primarily been seen among the outcaste (Dalit) and tribal populations. The caste Hindu people[1] have either been ignored or were only a peripheral focus of the missionary endeavors in India. In North America, where the majority of Hindus were derived from caste Hindu society, they appear to be marginalized by the Christian churches and mission agencies.

As the process of globalization continues to grip the world, upwardly mobile Hindus are increasingly emigrating to Europe and North America and penetrate Western culture. This brings immense pressure on the North American church and mission agencies to think strategically about their role in witnessing to Hindus who are now part of their society. Truly, the uttermost parts of the world have come to the doorstep of the North

---

[1] Caste Hindus are those who fall into one of the four major caste categories: Brahmin, Kshatriya, Vaisya, and Shudra. In each linguistic region, there are about two hundred caste groups, which are further subdivided into about three thousand smaller units, each of which is endogamous.

American church. The process of migration, settlement, adaptation, and eventually assimilation of the Hindus provides the North American church a significant opportunity to witness to them.

In this chapter, I will critically reflect upon the emergence and spread of the Hindu Diaspora in North America, with the specific aim of providing insights and guidelines for possible partnerships for Christian witnesses among them, in the light of Paul's model of partnership. Here a *partnership* is defined in terms of sharing information, equipment, personnel, strategic mobilization, and prayerful planning for Christian witness among Hindus in the Diaspora. While this applies to many diasporic settings globally, my primary focus is North American Hindus.

Toward an Understanding of the Diaspora

The term *diaspora* was at one time a concept referring almost exclusively to the experience of the Jews, invoking traumatic exile from a historical homeland and dispersal throughout many lands.[2] Both biblical and non-biblical sources indicate that the word *diaspora* has to do with people scattering from their homeland to an alien land, mostly by compulsion. It was deemed a negative experience because people living in the diaspora were believed to long for their original homeland, to which they wished to return.[3]

More recently, however, the notion of *diaspora* is increasingly employed to denote ethnic, linguistic, national, or religious communities settling outside their homelands. Broadly speaking, the *diaspora* term is often used today to describe any population that is considered "deterritorialized" or "transnational," and whose cultural origins are said to have arisen in a land other than that in which they currently reside, whose social, economic, and political networks transcend the borders of nation-states or spans the globe.[4]

As far as the modern Hindu Diaspora is concerned, in most cases, Hindus have sought opportunities to move out of India for their overall betterment. Normally, Hindus do not see themselves as in Diaspora; rather they call their diasporic situation *Desh Pardesh* (in Hindi), which "can equally well be translated both as 'home from home' and as 'at home abroad.'"[5] For most Hindus in the Diaspora, India (Bharat) not only is their motherland

---

2 Vertovec, *Hindu Diaspora Comparative Patterns*, 141.
3 Ter Harr, *Religious Communities in the Diaspora*, 4–5.
4 Vertovec, *Hindu*, 142.
5 Baumann, "Hindu Diaspora in Europe," 87.

and home but the holy land of their spiritual forefathers, *Punya Bhumi*. Another term used to differentiate them from Indians who live in India is "Non-Resident Indians" (*Anivasi Bhartiya*). In this chapter, the term *Hindu Diaspora* refers to the migration and settlements of Hindus outside of the Indian subcontinent, especially in North America.

Hindu Diaspora in North America

History shows that segments of Hindus constantly left the shores of India and impacted the surrounding nations. This Hindu presence can be traced in Burma, Bali (Indonesia), Fiji, Sri Lanka, Mauritius, Malaysia, Surinam, Guyana, and Trinidad. However, the contemporary wave of Hindu migrants to Europe and North America is quite significant, and the speed with which it is taking place in recent decades is unprecedented.

The early waves of Hindu migration were linked with temporary trade and business. The second wave was related to "indentured workers," taken as cheap labor for plantation and construction work to British, French, and Dutch colonies. "During the period from 1834 to 1917, about 1.5 million Indians signed five-year contracts and shipped to Mauritius, East and South Africa, South America, and the Caribbean and Fiji Islands."[6] Many eventually preferred to settle down there, thus becoming the early Hindu Diaspora.

Then there was a large influx of immigrants, especially to Britain due to a labor shortage, most of whom were male workers from the northwestern part of India. Then, in the mid-1960s, family-based immigration began to take place. Consequently, most of those earlier migrants who had intended to earn some money and return to India began to put down roots in their adopted land by investing in properties. This was probably the beginning of the real Hindu Diaspora in Europe. In the latter part of the 1970s, many East Africans of Indian descent started moving to Europe and North America due to political unrest in Zambia, Tanzania, Kenya, and Uganda. These were well-established and experienced business and professional people.

Migration to North America was earlier confined to European people; however, the repeal of the Asian Exclusion Act in 1965 resulted in opening the North American shores to Asians and Indians. During this time a number of Hindu professionals from a largely urban middle-class background started arriving in North America.[7] These included teachers, professors, scientists,

---

6 Baumann, "Hindu Diaspora," 88. Also George, *Desi Diaspora*, 4–5.
7 Coward, "Hinduism in Canada," 151.

medical doctors, and a large number of nurses and other professionals. Those who came after 1965 were among the best educated and most professionally advanced and successful of any population.[8]

In recent years, students and software professionals who came to North America found good jobs and remained there rather than returning to India. It is important to note that most North American Hindus tend to settle in major metropolitan areas. Thomas Wolf estimates that at least 38 percent of medical doctors, 36 percent of NASA scientists, and 34 percent of Microsoft employees in the US are Indians, most of whom are Hindus.[9] Estimates differ as to how many Hindus[10] are found outside India, but it is clear that the figure is significant and will continue to increase in the decades to come.

To ascertain the exact number of Hindus in the United States is particularly difficult because the 1957 Congressional Prohibition Act safeguards religious privacy. However, the steady growth in recent decades has swelled the Indian American population significantly. According to the US Census Bureau 2020, the growth rate of the Indian American population between 2000 and 2020 was 56.9 percent.[11] By 2022, that number grew to 4,606,000 and is currently estimated to have crossed 5 million.[12] The Pew Research report of 2012 found that 51 percent of Indian Americans are Hindus, 18 percent are Christians, and 10 percent are Muslims.[13] In addition, there are Hindus from the Caribbeans, Africa, Fiji Islands, and elsewhere. Putting these approximate figures together, we can assume there are nearly three million Hindus in the United States and Canada. Here is a list of the top ten cities of settlement for Indian Americans.

---

8   Hodge, "Working with Hindu Clients," 31.
9   Wolf, "Wrinkled Wired Elephant." These figures are consistent with the 2020 US census report, "American Community Survey 1-Year Estimates. Table DP05," 2020. https://data.census.gov/table?q=DP05.
10 *Hindu* generally represents Jains, Buddhists, and Sikhs, though these are distinct religious communities in India. The term *Asian Indian* includes Hindus, Muslims, Christians, Buddhists, Parsees, and other religious communities whose origin can be traced to India.
11 US Census Bureau, "2020 Indian Americans," https://www.census.gov/library/stories/2023/09/2020-census-dhc-a-asian-population.html.
12 Fact Sheet about Asian Americans, https://www.pewresearch.org/social-trends/fact-sheet/asian-americans-indians-in-the-u-s/.
13 Pew Research Center, "Asian Americans: A Mosaic of Faiths," 2012, https://www.pewresearch.org/religion/2012/07/19/asian-americans-a-mosaic-of-faiths-overview/.

TABLE 1: TOP TEN METROPOLITAN AREAS FOR INDIAN AMERICANS
(SOURCE: US CENSUS 2020)

Rank	Metropolitan Statistical Area	Population	Indian American Population	% of Indian Americans	% of Indian Americans in the US
1	New York	19,617,869	528,329	2.7	11.9
2	Los Angeles	12,872,322	295,448	2.3	6.7
3	Chicago	9,441,957	192,827	2.0	4.2
4	Dallas	7,943,685	163,657	2.1	3.4
5	Houston	7,205,819	142,105	2.0	3.0
6	Philadelphia	6,120,703	124,381	2.0	2.7
7	San Francisco	4,740,472	95,400	2.0	2.0
8	Washington	6,319,631	115,878	1.8	2.4
9	Atlanta	5,741,025	105,028	1.8	2.2
10	Boston	4,928,234	80,913	1.6	1.7

Hindu Diaspora Distinctives

While there are many similarities between Hindus in India and Hindus in the Diaspora, some of their differences need to be acknowledged. Though they are minor deviations from traditional Hindu society, they distinguish Hindus in the Diaspora from those in India.

Multilingual and Fragmented

When considering Hindus in North America, one must remember that these are not homogeneous people. India has thousands of castes, tribes, and ethnic groups[14] with different languages and religions, and only a small segment of these is represented in North America. The prominent groups of Indians in North America are the Gujaratis and Punjabi Sikhs, who have come either directly from the northwest part of India or via East Africa. In Britain, they make up about 70 percent of the Hindu population,[15] whereas in North

---

14 The Anthropological Survey of India documented 4,635 distinct people, caste, tribal, and ethnic groups in India.
15 Baumann, "Hindu Diaspora," 95.

America they comprise about one-fourth. Prominent among the Gujaratis are the Lewa and Kadwa Patidars, Lohanas, Kanbis, Prajapatis, and Mochis.[16] Except for the Mochis, the others are primarily trading and business castes; therefore, most of them are involved in business in North America.

Although most Sikhs perceive themselves to be a distinct community, they share many similarities with Hindus, including caste distinctions. Roger Ballard points out that among the Diaspora Sikhs the Jats (farmers) form a majority but include smaller local communities of Ramgarhias (craftsmen), Ramdasis (leather workers), Jhirs (water carriers), and Valmikis (sweepers).[17] Most of the early migrants from Punjab came as laborers or farm workers. Then there are Sindhis, who represent a strong business community. Also, there are Bengalis, Marathis, and other Hindi-speaking states of Uttar Pradesh, Madhya Pradesh, and Bihar, most of whom are educated professionals and skilled workers. Then there are many South Indian Hindu groups: Malayalis, Tamils, and Telugus, who are found in various professional, educational, and administrative sectors, and are primarily from one of the higher castes, if not Brahmin.

One thing is clear: the Gujarati, Punjabi, Sri Lankan, Surinamese, and Indo-Caribbean Hindus have created their own homes away from home, bringing with them a diversity of ethnic styles and cultural patterns.[18] While recognizing this diversity of ethnic styles, it must be kept in mind that there is no uniformity or unity in the Hindu Diaspora.

Educated and Open to Change

Those who immigrated before 1965 made substantial progress, especially financially. But those who came after 1965 were among the best educated and most advanced, partly because the US immigration regulations were favorable to educated professionals.[19] Table 2 shows the educational attainment of Indian Americans as compared to others as of 2020.

---

16 Baumann, "Hindu Diaspora," 88.
17 Ballard, "Growth and Changing Character," 133.
18 Baumann, "Hindu Diaspora," 88.
19 Williams, "Asian Indian and Pakistani Religions," 178–95.

TABLE 2: EDUCATIONAL LEVELS OF INDIAN AMERICANS
(SOURCE: US CENSUS 2020)

Educational Attainment	US Population	Asian American Population	Indian American Population
No schooling	3.2%	1.1%	0.4%
High school	88.9%	92.9%	93.8%
Bachelor's degree	33.7%	50.3%	61.0%
Master's degree	11.1%	12.4%	14.6%
Professional degree	4.6%	5.0%	5.7%
Doctoral degree	7.5%	10.3%	12.3%

Culturally Clashing

Life, culture, religion, and society in North America are different for Diaspora Hindus. This is especially seen in religious and social values and worldviews. Tension arises when Hindu cultural values conflict with American cultural values. At times, they develop mechanisms to resist changes to retain their Hindu culture and values. To cope with such tensions, concerted efforts are being undertaken by first-generation Hindus to reorient the new generation to the Hindu faith by inviting Hindu gurus and spiritual teachers to their homes and social gatherings.

Another way of safeguarding and strengthening their religious and cultural presence in North America is by establishing Hindu temples. These temples have become centers of Hindu faith and culture. Currently, there are over one thousand Hindu temples and religious centers in the United States. Diana Eck claims, "For Hindu immigrants to America, the process of building a temple is simultaneously the process of building a community."[20]

Apart from establishing temples and caste-based associations, a number of *ashrams* (monasteries), spiritual discourses, summer camps, and festival gatherings are arranged to institutionalize, preserve, and transmit Hindu values.[21] However, having been exposed to more free, critical, and objective thinking in North America, many youths critically assess their Hindu practices before retaining them. They are more exposed to the non-Hindu, American perspective of life, which they want to adapt to and assimilate with as much as possible. This leads to a deep clash of worldviews, since traditional

---

20 Eck, "Negotiating Hindu Identities in the US," 221.
21 Hodge, "Working with Hindu Clients," 33.

Hindu values, which most American-born Hindus find difficult to adhere to, are expected to be accepted without question.

First-generation Hindu migrants normally manage to maintain their own value systems, while slightly adapting to American culture. However, the second and third generations of Diaspora Hindus experience value-related stresses and at times give in to American culture. They are more inclined to be assimilated into the dominant culture while affirming their basic Hindu norms such as arranged marriages, modesty, and respect for others.[22] This process of assimilation creates a huge sociocultural and spiritual vacuum. Consequently, many are confused or frustrated because they cannot make clear sense of the traditional Hindu values and practices in their contemporary American context.

Family/Community Oriented

For most Diaspora Hindus, American society contradicts Hindu society, partly because Hindus are generally more accustomed to community, interdependence, and divinity in every aspect of human life and nature. "Consequently, for most Hindus, there is a great awareness of, and respect for, human interdependence and interconnectedness, which is understood to be the foundation of well-being."[23] "In keeping with the community ethos of Hinduism, the individual is understood to be embedded in a family that is embedded in an extended family, which in turn is embedded in an even wider kin and network."[24] This network is evident, especially during times of festivals, celebrations, and death.

Paul's Model of Partnership

When it comes to reaching the Diaspora Hindus, the New Testament gives us a great model of partnership via the Apostle Paul's life and ministry. A significant part of Paul's ministry was undertaken in the context of the Jewish Diaspora, and with significant partnership at various levels. Paul demonstrated a keen sense of partnership with God since he was fully aware that his work involved fulfilling God's plan of salvation for all. This collaboration at the vertical level is not an equal partnership; at best it indicates the "bipolarity of

---

22 Miller, "Cultural Diversity in Morality," 3–19.
23 Hodge, "Working with Hindu Clients," 27–38.
24 Reddy and Hanna, "The Lifestyle of Hindu Women," 386.

ministry."[25] However, Paul implied that as a coworker with God, he had the authority of God himself. Because of this sense of coworking with God, Paul developed a strong commitment to a team approach to ministry.

Partnership with the Church

Paul's basic approach to missions was strongly church-centered. He planted churches and established meaningful networks and partnerships between them (Acts 11:27–30; 21:17–19). Roland Allen observes, "Paul did not set out on his missionary journey as a solitary prophet … he was sent forth as the messenger of a church, to bring men into fellowship with that body."[26] According to Allen, Paul's mission was strongly anchored in the church, and he maintained a strong sense of commitment and accountability to the sending church while working among the Gentiles (Acts 14:26–27). Such commitment to the churches enabled him to develop meaningful partnerships for his ongoing mission and ministry to both Jews and Gentiles.

Partnership with Fellow Ministers

Paul's approach to networking was similar to that of Jesus, who taught how to do ministry while doing it. "Paul was a trainer and coach as much as he was a church planter."[27] He depended on many coworkers who were supportive of his efforts.

Initially, he partnered with Barnabas, an established leader of the churches in Jerusalem and Antioch, but later he began choosing his partners. His preference for them was part of his strategy as an expert builder (1 Cor 3:10). Hence, we see a variety of fellow workers who, with different gifts and commitments, played their parts in fulfilling the task.

Recognizing that each member of the team had different gifts and abilities, Paul mobilized them for the effective communication of the gospel. Acts 14:21–23 describes the sequence of activities of Paul's teams. These teams were mobile and independent. They were economically self-sufficient, although open to receiving funds from local congregations.[28] Explaining this team ministry, Manjaly states,

---

25 Manjaly, *Collaborative Ministry*, 109.
26 Allen, *Missionary Methods*, 126.
27 Greenway and Monsma, *Cities: Missions' New Frontier*, 22.
28 Glasser, "Paul and the Missionary Task," 27.

> The travels of Paul and his associates (1 Thess 2:17–20; 1 Cor 16:5–12; 2 Cor 1:15–2:4; Phil 2:19–30; Philem 22) were part of his missionary strategy and constitute an important mode of collaborative ministry, and not an ad hoc arrangement for crisis management. Regular personal contact with the communities to encourage, to support and to strengthen them, to prevent them from falling away from faith, and to help resolve problems when they arose were of high priority in his pastoral plan.[29]

Paul demonstrated his commitment to partnering with those who were committed to his missionary vision. The composition of his team itself shows how he was committed to multiethnic, multicultural, and multilingual ministries. Paul did not feel threatened by those who were senior Christians. He had many coworkers who functioned as his partners in his missionary work. Priscilla and Aquila (Acts 18:1–3), who were already Christians before Paul met them at Corinth. They instructed Apollos (Acts 18:24–26) and commended him to the Corinthians (Acts 18:27). Though they had begun ministry independent of Paul, they became his close associates.[30]

Interestingly, Paul's networking included prominent women who proved to be a great source of encouragement and support to his ministry; not only Lydia and Priscilla, but Junia, Euodia, and Syntyche, as well as Chloe, were women actively involved in ministry under the direction of Paul and his associates. Paul effectively administered people's gifts, experiences, and capabilities. Some of his coworkers were involved in the direct proclamation of the gospel with him; others served as his travel associates, providing needed support; others helped him in his correspondence and networking with churches; and yet others represented him in different churches that he was instrumental in planting. Consequently, Paul accomplished much because he was able to recruit, train, and mobilize diverse peoples for the work of ministry.

Partnership with Families

Paul worked exclusively in the urban context, where individualism tended to be elevated against the family or community, but he quickly recognized that the individual was inevitably a family member. Therefore, to reach an individual with the gospel, Paul often relied on the family network, since

---

29 Manjaly, *Collaborative Ministry*, 339.
30 Manjaly, 339.

isolating an individual from the family was almost impossible, even in an urban society. We notice that Paul established churches that were clearly centered on family networks.

> The success of the early Christian mission and the life of the new churches were closely connected with the private house. The Greek term *oikos* described the "house as living space and familial domestic household," and as such it became the base of missionary work, foundational center of a local church, location of the assembly for worship, lodging for the missionaries and envoys, and at the same time, of course, the primary and decisive place of Christian life and formation.[31]

Paul demonstrated a comprehensive understanding of the family structure so that he could use it in reaching the Jewish and Hellenistic societies of his time. Recognizing the role of elders in decision-making, he influenced whole households by dealing with the family decision-makers. In other writings, I have argued that "The gospel moved across cities and spread from family to family. When the families were united and formed into churches, they began to exert tremendous influence on their relatives and friends. These households became centers of Christian faith and evangelism."[32] Paul kept in mind the dynamics of family decision-making and used them to win the whole family (though not always), equipping and mobilizing them to be involved in reaching other families for Christ.

Becoming a follower of Christ inevitably brought shame, making it difficult for people to commit themselves to Christ. "Since honor is linked to the family and depends heavily on the way it defends its honor status, the result is an exclusive loyalty toward the family."[33] Knowing this reality, Paul made conscious efforts to instruct these new believers and their families, strengthening them in their newly found faith and encouraging them to be the bearers of this faith among their own extended families. The demonstration of life changes sometimes earned significant honor. This is particularly seen in Macedonia, where Lydia and her household became instrumental in spreading the gospel beyond their own family (Acts 16:12–15).

Paul saw the importance of families in building bridges with contemporary society. "The households of newly converted believers were

---

31 Schnabel, *Early Christian Mission*, 1302.
32 Aghamkar, "Family Coherence and Evangelization of India," 26.
33 Moxnes, "Honor and Shame," 28.

important centers of Paul's missionary work, and they were centers of the life of the newly established communities of believers, who met in 'house churches.'"[34] Most of his letters were to the house churches, functioning almost as an instruction manual for the Christian families that met in the houses to live their faith out in daily life. We find among these Christians a powerful combination of inwardness and outwardness.[35] In Paul's thinking, the house church was an important means of spreading the gospel.[36]

This approach was effective in winning large segments of different societies for Christ. Thus, Paul could boast of preaching the gospel to the whole of *Asia*—i.e., the ancient Roman province of Asia on the western end of modern Turkey, not the massive modern continent of Asia—although he only went to some strategic cities. Paul's secret was that he preached to family units, and these families, probably through their networks, spread the gospel to their own kin and clans.[37] Partnership with families was one of the most effective ways of reaching contemporary society in Paul's time.

Partnership in Witnessing to the Diaspora Hindus

The Diaspora Hindus in North America are largely neglected because the church has not perceived their significance. Ministry to Hindus in the Diaspora requires different, innovative, and contextually relevant approaches, with the backing of research and prayer. Keeping in mind the partnership model of Paul in light of the present reality of Hindus in the Diaspora, the following guidelines are presented for effective Christian witness among them.

Partnership with the Church

American churches may not necessarily have the expertise or people to witness to Hindus in the Diaspora, but the existing church networks can help to develop plans for witness.

---

34 Schnabel, *Early Christian Mission*, 1303.
35 Banks and Banks, *Church Comes Home*, 48.
36 Green, *Evangelism in the Early Church*, 207.
37 Aghamkar, "Family Coherence," 26.

Recognize the Centrality of the Church

The church is central to God's plan and therefore needs to be taken seriously while establishing a base for witness among Hindus in the Diaspora. As the Jewish church in Jerusalem sent their leader, Barnabas, to minister to the multiethnic church in Antioch, leaders of integrity, expertise, experience, and willingness should be sent to minister among the Hindus in North American cities.

Initiate Global Partnership

In this era of globalization, conscious efforts are needed for partnerships between the East and the West. It is time to explore the possibility of sending short-term, long-term, and even lifetime missionaries to work among Diaspora Hindus. Many North American denominations have had ministries in India for years and possess a pool of experienced leaders, theologians, evangelists, and pastors who have had exposure to and expertise in working with Hindus in India. Exchanges could be initiated to bring Indian experts to work with the American church leadership. Similarly, North American leaders can be sent for exposure trips to India and other diasporic settings where they could observe ministries among Hindus.

Further, churches and mission agencies that are involved in ministering to Hindus in the Diaspora should be encouraged to come together for mutual understanding, support, strategy development, and actual working out of effective Christian witness among them. The increasing number and the influence of Hindus in the Diaspora need to be researched and studied, for which partnership with mission bodies that have the expertise is essential.

Develop a Broader Network of Churches in North America

Reaching the Diaspora Hindus can never be done by one single church. Hence a larger partnership with the churches of North America is required. Learning from Paul's model, such partnership should be explored both at the local-church level as well as at city/state, regional or denominational levels. Knowing that strong pockets of Hindus are concentrated in certain cities of North America, partnerships should be initiated with those churches that have a strong Hindu presence in their vicinities. Conscious and deliberate efforts are needed to establish a strong support base of prayer, training, and finance.

Joint ventures should be undertaken to assess the progress, growth, and direction of the ministry, and measures ought to be taken to make them effective. There are large churches with sound financial bases, while other churches have good human resources; and these can connect for meaningful partnerships. For this to happen, proper planning, procedure, and accountability structures must be established.

Utilize Indian-Christian Networks

Several regional and language-based Indian-Christian groups and fellowships meet regularly across North America. These have great potential in establishing rapport with the Hindu community in North America. Many Indian Christians live in close proximity to their Hindu counterparts or work with them. This naturally provides a good point of contact with the Hindu community. Different ways should be explored to equip and mobilize the Indian-Christian Diaspora and collaborate with American churches to develop meaningful and sustained Christian witness to Hindus.

Encourage House Church Fellowships

Plans for follow-up and nurture of new believers with the concrete aim of forming worshiping communities of new believers should be undertaken. Since most Hindus are very family and community-oriented, efforts should be made to keep their family structures intact, as much as possible, even after their conversion. So different ways of establishing home fellowships should be explored, and through these fellowships of Hindu believers deeper penetration into the Hindu Diaspora community can be established.

Partnership with Fellow Ministers

There is a need to develop a team ministry to reach Hindus in Diaspora—i.e., teams of multiethnic and multilingual, as well as multiregional, missionaries, researchers, evangelists, pastors, and others working together. Seasoned missionaries with substantial experience in ministry among Hindus should be encouraged to team up with American leaders interested in working with Diaspora Hindus in North America.

Attempts should also be made to include women and youth in the team. Women have better access to and rapport with the Hindu community than men for sociocultural reasons. Christian youth could be good instruments in building bridges with Hindu youth. Building multiethnic and intergenerational teams to reach Diaspora Hindus will yield good results.

Partnership with Families

Any ministry among Hindus in the Diaspora will have to take the centrality of the family into consideration. To make any breakthrough into the Hindu community, we must leverage existing family relations.

Recognize the Importance of the Family

The importance of family, caste, and community should be kept in mind when developing strategies to witness to Hindus in the Diaspora. Upper-caste Hindus value their family as their religion, and any threat to it is vehemently opposed. Becoming a Christian means renouncing not only the religion of the forefathers but also the age-old caste structure that is strongly woven into the fabric of the Hindu family. Therefore, few caste Hindus, even after moving to North America, tend to renounce their caste and religion to become outcastes.

Taking Paul's example of partnership, we can gain several insights. He strongly focused on the family as a total unit. Learning from his family-centered approach, special care may be taken in developing family-based approaches to Christian witness among the Hindus. This would entail not only mobilizing families for Christian witness but also forming house churches in line with the Hindu extended-family structure. This approach has the potential of penetrating Hindu communities and triggering a family-based house-church movement.

Equip and Mobilize Christian Families

Perhaps the most effective way of reaching Hindu families for Christ is through Christian families. For the effective penetration of the gospel, Christian families need to be nurtured, equipped, and trained systematically to undertake Christian witness with Hindu families. Though this is a natural and effective way of witnessing, it is rarely taken seriously, since traditional approaches to evangelism tend to be more individualistic and male-dominated. Families with women and children could become effective instruments in witnessing to nuclearized Hindu families in the West without any social pressure from their extended family members or caste obligations.

Can the American church take this issue seriously and develop a strategy that would provide ongoing training programs for Christian families in order to make them effective witnesses among the Hindus? This unexplored area of ministry should be given urgent consideration in view of ministry among Hindus in the Diaspora.

Understand the Decision-Making Process

With a family-based approach to Christian witness to Hindus, the issue of decision-making has to be dealt with carefully. Focusing on the decision-makers has great potential for the natural spread of the gospel among other Hindu families. Many Diaspora Hindus have become more comfortable with individualistic decision-making. But it must not be forgotten that most crucial family decisions, and especially religious decisions, are still taken by the elderly male or at least processed through him. Understanding and respecting the decision-making process is crucial in witnessing to Hindus.

Be Sensitive to the Reality of Honor and Shame

Most Hindus come from a "shame and honor" culture, in which social acceptance and harmony in interpersonal relations are carefully balanced with the need to protect and enhance one's self-esteem. The issue of shame in Hindu culture acts as a potent social control. In most cases, individual conversion to Christ is considered by the Hindus as something that brings shame upon the entire family. When a Hindu decides to renounce his or her religion and become a Christian, heavy pressure is brought upon him or her from the family, extended family, and caste association.

Ways and means should be explored to present the Christian message in such a manner that accepting it would make people feel proud and honored by their decision to become followers of Christ. Since most Hindus consider it honorable to become a follower of Jesus Christ, there is a great possibility of triggering a Christian movement among them.

Conclusion

Until recently, Christian theologians and mission thinkers have rarely given any serious consideration to a systematic study of the Hindu Diaspora in North America. Traditionally, India and her people have been a mystery for most Western Christian theologians, and no serious attempts have been made to develop theologically informed and missiologically appropriate approaches to reaching upper-caste Hindus in and outside India. Some attempts were undertaken by the early missionaries in India to reach the upper castes, but within a short period, these were abandoned due to a lack of substantial results. Those approaches are now outdated and irrelevant for reaching Hindus in the Diaspora.

The failure of Indian and Western Christian theologians to deal with the issue of witnessing to Hindus in the Diaspora is partly because they are generally from a higher caste background and are financially better off, in contrast to most Christian mission workers and theologians who are accustomed to working among the poor and outcaste people. At the same time, in the name of religious tolerance in the postmodern pluralistic world, Western as well as Indian Christian theologians seem to neglect the need for a mission to the Hindus, whereas Hindus appear to be taking advantage of the freedom and openness of Western countries by bringing increasing numbers of Hindu Gurus to present their religious perspectives and possibly win converts in the West.

Despite the presence of nearly three million Hindus in the United States, and the popularity of Hindu practices such as yoga and meditation, most American churches tend to keep their distance from them, thus making Hindus in the Diaspora one of the most neglected and unevangelized people groups. Christian witness among them is possible, provided that serious efforts are undertaken in developing comprehensive partnerships at the church, individual minister, and family levels. The reality, the need, and the challenge of witnessing to the Hindus in the Diaspora in North America demands a comprehensive partnership, without which most of them will remain untouched by the Christian message.

Constructive Interfaith Encounters in Diaspora

Dr. Wilson Paluri

Diaspora studies have been mostly concerned with the sociopolitical and economic dimensions of the dispersed peoples of the world by developing various theories and typologies using respective disciplinary lenses. But these studies have generally overlooked the religious life of immigrants in foreign lands. Martin Baumann suggests that the factor of religion in Diaspora studies is relegated to second place in favor of ethnicity and nationality.[1] The religious aspects of the Hindu Diaspora, in particular, have received limited attention. In this chapter I will (1) analyze the religious facets of the Hindu diasporic experience and the factors responsible for changing the expressions of Hinduism in Diaspora; (2) redefine Hinduism in the contemporary diasporic context; and (3) explore a response toward interreligious encounters.

Conceptualizing "Hindu Diaspora"

During the 1960s and 70s, sociologists studied the Indian community as one of the groups in a multicultural European society. From the 1990s onward, several writings on the Indian Diaspora, Indian identity, and Indian communities have appeared. Some scholars have used religion as a base for categorizing the Indian Diaspora and terms like "Hindu Diaspora,"[2]

---

1 Baumann, "Sustaining Little Indians," 95.
2 Dessai, *Hindus in Deutschland*; Vertovec, *Hindu Diaspora*.

"Sikh Diaspora,"[3] "Muslim Diaspora,"[4] and other Diasporas. There has also been an attempt to understand Diaspora from the background of regional identities, such as Telugu, Tamil, Malayali, Gujarati, and others.[5]

Reference to the term *diaspora* within a religious context is a recent one. In the field of Study of Religions (Religionswissenschaft), this notion mostly implies a Judeo-Christian setting. The understanding of whether the concept of diaspora could be detached from Judaism and Christianity and employed as a theoretical concept applicable to various religious traditions, was discussed and debated by some scholars in the past.[6] Due to its religious connotations, it is important to isolate the term's theological meanings and emphasize its structural and functional characteristics for it to be freely used in other diasporic contexts.

There are examples of recurring patterns and developments of the preservation and transformation of Jewish tradition during Hellenistic times.[7] It can be deduced that the preservation and perpetuation of one's own religious identity becomes a core issue in the Diaspora. Hindu Diaspora has struggled with the preservation and alteration of its religious identity in its encounter with other religions.

Baumann proposes "Diaspora" as being "made up of a religious, often ethnic group which lives as a minority outside its land of origin. The immigrant minority has a religious orientation different to that of the members of the host society."[8] Apart from the aspects of minority status and religious affiliation, the issue of space and territory becomes paramount for religious communities such as Hindus, in diasporic contexts. Through the establishment of Hindu schools, temples, and religious associations, the Hindu Diaspora has been making its representation strong in foreign lands.

Gabriel Sheffer suggests that diasporic groups can be characterized by a "triadic relationship" between—a collectively self-identified ethnic group

---

3 Agnihotri, *Crisis of Identity: Sikhs in England*; Brack, *Sikhs of Northern California*; Tatla, *Sikh Diaspora*.

4 Werbner, *Imagined Diaspora among Manchester Muslims*; Leonard, *Locating Home*.

5 George and Thomas, Indian Diaspora Series editors for *Malayali Diaspora* (2014), *Tamil Diaspora* (2020), and *Telugu Diaspora* (upcoming).

6 Baumann, "Conceptualizing Diaspora," 19–35; Rothenberg, *Diaspora, Zerstreuung*, 372; Kruger, *Das Biblische Paradigma der Diaspora*, 98–99.

7 Safrai and Stern, *Jewish People in First Century*; Elazar, "Jewish People as Classical Diaspora." Chapter 8.

8 Baumann, "Conceptualizing Diaspora," 22.

in one particular setting, the group's co-ethnics in other parts of the world, and the homeland states or local contexts from where they or their descents came.[9] Most often the real or imagined land of origin is bestowed with qualities like "purity" and "religious authenticity," as in the case of India. The younger generation of the Hindu Diaspora has internalized this imagined identity.

Religious Facets of Diasporic Experience

It is important to recognize that outside influences in the form of other religions and individual religious freedom alter belief systems. Ninian Smart suggests three reasons for the study of religious aspects of diasporic experience. First, the study of diasporas and their modes of adaptation provides insight into general patterns of religious transformation. Second, diasporas may impact the development of religion in the homeland: wealth, education, and exposure to foreign influences through diaspora may impact practices and beliefs. Finally, multiethnicity and religious pluralism have become commonplace.[10]

Scholars like James Clifford,[11] Dale Eickelman, and James Piscatori[12] suggest that the religious "traveling cultures" have also changed the conventional notion of culture and place. Through religious travel, they make an imaginary connection with many sacred centers that have a significant impact, collective identity with those in another place, and ritual practice that is both universal and localized. Benedict Anderson[13] and Pnina Werbner[14] have termed this an "Imagined Diaspora"—an imagined cultural and structural boundary where the community is seen as a transnational homogeneous group. It is an "ethnic identity" that results from social interaction.[15]

---

9 Sheffer, "New Field of Study"; Safran, "Diasporas in Modern Societies," 83–99.
10 Smart, "Importance of Diaspora," 421.
11 Clifford, "Traveling Cultures," 96–116.
12 Eickelman and Piscatori, "Social Theory in Study of Muslim Societies," 3–25.
13 Anderson, *Imagined Communities.*
14 Werbner, *Imagined Diaspora among Manchester Muslims.*
15 Barth, *Ethnic Groups and Boundaries.*

Talking about Hinduism, however, Ninian Smart suggests that intrinsic themes such as caste, *yoga*, *bhakti*, pilgrimage, temple rituals, household rituals, cow veneration, and other religious practices that are woven together into the complicated fabric of Hinduism in India do not travel easily to new environments.[16] Ethics, morality, and what constitutes appropriate ritual activity may be defined differently by believing Hindus in their context, as they negotiate their beliefs and practices in a particular cultural milieu. Identifying what Hindus believe or do in terms of authentic religious practices in various contexts is complex.[17]

Robin Cohen argues that religions do not constitute diasporas themselves, except Judaism and Sikhism, because "they span more than one ethnic group, and normally religions do not seek to return or to recreate a homeland." However, they "provide additional cement to bind a diasporic consciousness."[18] The "Hindu Diaspora," Steven Vertovec suggests, could be considered an exception, since most Hindus tend to sacralize India and have a unique relationship with their spiritual homeland.[19]

Stephen Warner writes that religious identities mean more to individuals who stay away from home in their Diaspora, and they undergo modification as time passes. One of the reasons for this is that "the religious institutions they build, adapt, remodel and adopt become worlds unto themselves, 'congregations,' where new relations among the members of the community are forged."[20] Diasporic identification involves complex permutations; some people continue to regard their land of birth as "home," while others come to identify primarily with their land of settlement.[21] There are "multiple, co-existing identities,"[22] which is true with Hindu Diaspora.

The study of the Hindu Diaspora reveals that Hindus have successfully established a sociocultural, religious, and commercial infrastructure of their own. Raymond Breton states that in a short time, they have managed to have "institutional completeness" for the continuation of their cultural and

---

16 Smart, "Importance of Diaspora," 424.
17 Pappu, "Hindu Ethics," 155–56.
18 Cohen, *Global Diaspora*, 189.
19 Vertovec, *Hindu Diaspora*, 2000.
20 Warner, "Immigration and Religious Communities in the US," 3.
21 Karpat, "The *hijra* from Russia and the Balkans," 131–52.
22 Eickelman and Piscatori, "Social Theory in Muslim Societies," 17.

religious traditions.²³ There are certain factors—challenges of new interfaith context, growth and impact of neo-gurus and Hindu nationalism, and stereotypical presentation of Hinduism in Western academia—that provided an impetus to such religious and cultural modifications in the Diaspora.

Challenges of Interfaith Context— Religious Homogeneity and Plurality

Raymond Williams produced a pioneering work discussing the institutional development, identity formation, and adaptation of various religious traditions of Indian immigrants as they established communities in the Diaspora.²⁴ For American Hindus, their religion allowed them to maintain an individual and group identity, a coherent value system, an organized form of social participation, and strong social bonds. It also permitted them to emphasize and propose one identity marker over another, depending on which one they decide to emphasize.²⁵

The situation of being an "outsider" and a minority "other" often stimulates a mode of religious change through increased self-awareness. Kim Knott suggests that many Hindus in Leeds are realizing that their religion is just one minority faith among others. The awareness of religious pluralism has affected the way they think about themselves and their faith.²⁶ Penny Logan's research on the religion of Gujaratis in Britain points out that "many adults have reported becoming aware of their religion in Britain as a result of belonging to a minority group."²⁷ Terence Thomas believes that the minority status of British Hindus may have "forced them into self-awareness and strategies of protection and preservation of their self-identity."²⁸

The self-awareness and negotiation of acculturation and pluralism provide a new personal and social identity (unity in diversity). The threat of a possible loss generates new interest toward their cultural customs and religious beliefs and practices. Williams states that Hinduism in the United States began as a reconfiguration of the religion, including ecumenical inclusiveness of regional and sectarian variations of Hindu traditions, deities,

---

23 Breton, "Institutional Completeness of Ethnic Communities," 193–205.
24 Williams, *Religions of Immigrants from India and Pakistan*.
25 Williams, 12, 27.
26 Knott, *Hinduism in Leeds*, 46.
27 Logan, "Practicing Hinduism," 124.
28 Thomas, "Hindu Dharma in Dispersion," 187.

symbols, rituals, and the adaptation of higher-caste practices by lower-caste individuals to create an "all Hindu" inclusive tradition.[29]

Interaction with and Assimilation into Other Socioreligious Practices

Most scholars agree that there is a rich body of work on immigrant incorporation, but such research does not shed sufficient light on how continued relations between home and host-country institutions transform religious practices. More importantly, Peggy Levitt stresses how transformations toward globalized everyday practices and relations affect religious practices in both home and host contexts.[30]

Adaptation—i.e., how to adapt to the environment without giving up one's own group identity—is central to Diaspora peoples.[31] For example, in Malaysia basic Hindu ritual procedures have become condensed,[32] in Britain they are refashioned,[33] and in East Africa they have been eclectically performed.[34] In Scotland and the United States, basic rites and rituals are mutually negotiated to create socioreligious bridges between migrants from distinct traditions.[35] Many rituals are modified and popularized to appeal to the younger generation. This includes the conciliation of religious doctrines and practices over time.

Impact of New Gurus and Hindu Nationalism

An assortment of *gurus*, *swamis*, *babas*, and *yoga* teachers visited the Western world in the 1960s and 70s. This created an ambiance or occasion for discussing within family and academia the appeal and conflicts created by new kinds of teachings on religion and religious practices. The approach undertaken by most of the *swamis* was to run spiritual retreats for lay people and take an active part in academic discussions at the centers for religious studies.

This period witnessed, particularly, the arrival of Transcendental Meditation, ISKCON (International Society for Krishna Consciousness)

---

29 Williams, *Religions of Immigrants*, 40–41.
30 Levitt, "Local-level Global Religion," 75.
31 Shaye and Frerichs, *Diasporas in Antiquity*, i.
32 Hutheesing, "Thirate Kalyanam Ceremony," 131–47.
33 Michaelson, "Domestic Hinduism in a Gujarati Trading Caste," 32–49.
34 Bharati, "Ritualistic Tolerance and Ideological Rigour," 317–39.
35 Knott, *Hinduism in Leeds: A Study of Religious Practice*; Nye, *Place for Our Gods*; Lessinger, *From the Ganges to the Hudson*.

or Hare Krishna Movement, Chinmaya Mission (Swami Chinmayananda), Swami Muktananda, Rajneesh Osho to name a few and spokespersons for other spiritual gurus, such as Swami Vivekananda, Sri Aurobindo, Ramana Maharshi, Satya Sai Baba, and Swami Sivananda. These gurus did not seek to engage in any serious interaction with the host religion or religious groups. They considered the ancient spirituality of Hinduism to be an answer to the materialistic and secular West. Purushottama Bilimoria observes that compared to these spiritual gurus, Dayanand Saraswati (founder of Arya Samaj) appeared more open to interreligious interactions.[36] Knott observes that the influence of these *gurus* and *swamis* created an apparent diversity of two forms of religiousness—of the Indian Hindu population and the Western converts.[37]

The nineteenth-century reinterpretation of Hinduism in India and the sending of Arya Samajis to virtually all overseas Indian communities had a lasting effect on the reformulation of religious concepts in the Diaspora.[38] Apart from Arya Samaj, the Sanatan Dharma Maha Sabha was influential with its control over ritual practices and capacity to establish competing Hindu schools in regions where Indians lived. In Trinidad and other places, the Maha Sabha worked toward the coordination of temple activities and the standardization of rituals. It formulated the Hindu creed and catechism, modeled similar to that of Christians. Through *satsangs*, *pujas*, *yajnas*, and weekly temple worship, belief was inculcated among the followers. Marion O'Callaghan notes that "beliefs were also reinforced through contacts with the parent Maha Sabha in India, by visiting swamis and by the importation of Hindu literature from India."[39]

On the religious front, Bochasanwasi Shri Akshar Purushottam Swaminarayan Sanstha (BAPS), a sub-sect of the Swaminarayans, has been playing an important role. It is one of the largest groups spread across the Western world and is a highly centralized organization with operations in different countries. This helped BAPS propel into different countries, while remaining a close-knit community.[40] Initially, *satsang* (corporate worship) began with a small gathering in homes every Sunday, and as the number

---

36 Bilimoria, "Hindu-Christian Dialogue in the Making in Australia," 32–33.
37 Knott, *Hinduism in Leeds*, 235.
38 Vertovec, *Hindu Trinidad: Religion, Ethnicity*, 57–59.
39 O'Callaghan, "Hinduism in the Indian Diaspora in Trinidad," 4–5.
40 Kurien, *Place at the Multicultural Table*, 103.

grew, *hari mandirs* (temples) were constructed making BAPS a global organization. With the construction of *Shikarabaddh Mandir*,[41] *sadhus* were permanently placed in these temples.[42] About the Swaminarayan tradition in Great Britain, Williams states that in the early 1980s members of its second and third generation discussed missionary interpretations of their diasporic existence. For them, "The lost youth of the West—lost in materialism, drugs and violence—need the spiritualism of India best represented by the Swaminarayan religion."[43] Such perspectives and missionary approaches undertaken by neo-gurus and Hindu nationalistic groups have contributed to the progress of Hinduism in the Diaspora.

Academic Monologue—Stereotypic Presentation of Hinduism

In recent years, some Hindu groups have mounted challenges to the Western academic study of Hinduism, condemning it as hegemonic, elitist, and not representative of the understandings and experiences of practicing Hindus. How Hinduism is presented in Western academia is a major concern of Hindu organizations such as the Hindu American Foundation (HAF), Infinity Foundation, and Hindu Forum of Britain, which make efforts to maintain accurate and relevant information on Hinduism.[44] Indian American sociologist Prema Kurien identifies many independent Hindu organizations—such as the American Hindus Against Defamation (AHAD) and the Hindu International Council Against Defamation (HICAD)—which are working toward protecting Hinduism against defamation and misrepresentation.[45] It seems safe to say that the average Westerner is misinformed as to what constitutes the central beliefs and practices of modern Hindus, along with the evolving character of Hinduism in a diasporic context.

The "Textbook Controversy" in California (from 1991 to 2005) is one such example that shows the lack of accurate knowledge of Hinduism among people at large. Two lawsuits were filed against California public schools for negatively portraying Hinduism—i.e., emphasizing the rigidity of the caste

---

41 In 1995, the first *Shikarabaddh Mandir* outside India was built at Neasden, London, by Pramukh Swami, which became an important location for BAPS.
42 Williams, *Introduction to Swaminarayan Hinduism*, 220.
43 Williams, *New Face of Hinduism*, 203.
44 Chappell, "Negotiating Contemporary Hindu Beliefs and Practices," 82.
45 Kurien, *Place at the Multicultural Table*, 1.

system and 170 other factual errors.[46] Such confusion is understandable, as Hinduism is often defined as pantheistic, polytheistic, henotheistic, and even monotheistic.

Since the early 1990s, leaders of the Infinite Foundation have been contesting what they view as the monopoly of Western scholars on knowledge about Hinduism. They have even suggested that Western scholars may have been funded in propagating damaging negative stereotypes about Hinduism.[47] Prema Kurien, however, has found their pro-Hindu propaganda more biased because of their association with *Hindutva* ideology (though Infinity Foundation tries to deny it) and anti-Islamic and anti-Christian campaigns. Their attack is not just leveled against Euro-American scholars but also against Indian American scholars, who have been characterized as agents of the West. The "insider-outsider" distinction they make is "between individuals (including non-Indians) whom they define as Hindu practitioners and those (including scholars from Hindu backgrounds) whom they define as pseudo-Hindus."[48] There is a group of these Hindu intellectuals who scrutinize the writings of Western scholars on Hinduism to project their inadequacies and to generate renewed interest and sciences.

Patterns of Religious Modifications

The process of transplanting Hindu religious practices across *Kala Pani* (black waters) to new regions has generated new identity, institutionalization, and socioreligious modifications in the new places of residence.[49] Since the late nineteenth century, the religious environment in Diaspora, especially Hinduism, has been impacted by the formation of religious centers such as the Vedanta Society by Swami Vivekananda, the Self-Realization Fellowship of Paramahamsa Yogananda, and others. The creation of ISKCON by A. C. Bhaktivedanta Prabhupada in the 1960s strengthened a temple-centered devotional form of Hinduism.[50] From the latter half of the twentieth century, Hinduism began reformulating in the Diaspora as a strong minority religion in a new setting by first-generation Hindus and their descendants.

---

46 Larson, "Hinduism in India and America," 194.
47 Dhand, "Hinduism to Hindus in Western Diaspora," 274.
48 Kurien, *Place at Multicultural Table*, 188–92.
49 George, "Crossing *Kala Pani*."
50 Eck, "Negotiating Hindu Identities in US," 227–29.

Gerald James Larson identifies five categories of Hinduism in the United States: *Secular Hinduism* refers to those who do not want to associate with any religion; *Nonsectarian Hinduism* refers to those who follow an eclectic form of Hinduism; *Bhakti Hinduism* refers to those who are part of a tradition that offers worship to Vishnu or Shiva as a manifestation of Brahman; *Nationalist Neo-Hinduism* refers to those who follow Advaita tradition and maintain the importance of India as their homeland; and finally, *Missionizing Neo-Guruism*, popularized by ISKON and modern gurus, which seeks the conversion of people from different socioreligious and ethnic backgrounds.[51] Most of the Hindus in the Diaspora seem to keep to the universalistic view of Hinduism.

Hindu Rituals and Practices

It is observed that group size and the length of stay in the Diaspora affect the type of religious practices of Hindus. Hindus worshiping as a small group staying for a short period tend to be more inclusive and ecumenical and those with larger groups worshiping for a longer time may shift to a more sectarian or region-specific mode of worship.[52] Those who stay for more time begin to become more structured and build permanent religious organizations. Younger observes that in East Africa, the community center served the first wave of migrants, but the second and third wave of migrants outgrew the community center and built many religious temples.[53]

Though there is no prescribed set of beliefs for all Hindus in the Diaspora, organizations like the *Vishwa Hindu Parishad* (VHP; World Hindu Council) and the Himalayan Academy have listed basic tenets commonly accepted by various Hindu sects.[54] The Nine beliefs of Hindu spirituality are 1) one, all-pervasive, immanent and transcendent Supreme Being; 2) four Vedas and Agamas as divine revelation and foundations of belief; 3) the endless cycles of creation, preservation, and dissolution of the universe; 4) *karma* as the law of cause and effect; 5) the innumerable births of the individual soul; 6) significance of temple worship, rituals, sacraments, and personal devotion to *devas* (gods); 7) importance of *satguru* (enlightened master) for guidance in the spiritual life; 8) the practice of *ahimsa* (noninjury in thought, word, and deed); and 9) all genuine religions as different facets of God's revelation.

---

51 Larson, "Hinduism in India and America," 193–94.
52 Williams, *Religions of Immigrants*, 41–42.
53 Younger, *New Homelands*, 202.
54 See https://www.himalayanacademy.com/readlearn/basics/nine-beliefs.

Some scholars point out that these fundamental beliefs are validated by personal and family *pujas* (worship) of gods and gurus with prayers, meditation, and *japa* (chanting) in their homes; arranging family events to coincide with auspicious dates by consulting astrologists; celebrating popular festivals such as Shivaratri, Holi, Gurupurnima, Satyanarayan Puja, and Navaratri; observing the most important *samskaras* (rites of passage); getting acquainted with scriptures through religious study groups at homes and temples; being part of sectarian groups like Arya Samaj, Chinmayananda West Mission, Ramakrishna Mission that flourished through yoga institutes, ecumenical Hindu organizations, and devotion to gurus and swamis.[55]

However, Chappell observes that many Hindus do not participate in religious rituals as they did in the diasporic context of the 1970 and 1980s. While they reiterate the notion of being a good person, it doesn't necessarily include participating in rituals, doing regular *puja*, or celebrating major holidays. Modern diasporic Hindus also disagree with the practices and beliefs related to vegetarianism, arranged marriages, and superstitions. They assert that vegetarianism is a part of the culture and not a religious practice.[56] Other cultural features, such as marriage patterns, diet, and dress, have mostly weakened.[57]

Structures of Cultural and Religious Preservation

Overwhelmingly, Hinduism is considered a "tradition" and a "way of life" adopted from one's primary social group, which could be the immediate family in the Diaspora. Knowledge of religious practices and moral behavior is derived mainly from the cultural transmission of values from parents.[58] Kim Knott observes that men became responsible for developing the public aspect of worship while women continued to teach their traditions to children through stories and helped maintain domestic practices in the Diaspora.[59]

The establishment of Hindu temples acquired special importance for Diaspora communities to preserve their religion. These temples include a wide variety of deities to accommodate varied sects of diasporic Hinduism.

---

55 Williams, *Religions of Immigrants*, 43–63; Eck, "Negotiating Hindu Identities in the US," 223; Larson, "Hinduism in India and America," 195–96.
56 Chappell, "Negotiating Contemporary Hindu Beliefs," 90–92.
57 Anderson and Frideres, *Ethnicity in Canada*, 105–26.
58 Williams, *Religions of Immigrants*, 47.
59 Knott, "Bound to Change? Religions of South Asians in Britain," 101.

Temples also became a place where culture and tradition are kept alive. The current guru of BAPS states, "Wherever one goes, one should keep four aspects of our culture firmly rooted in our life: our diet, our language, our dress, and our devotion."[60]

Temples became the center of *sabhas* (meetings or assemblies), exhibitions, and festivals cultivating the feeling of home away from home. Hanna Kim notes that temples built by BAPS in the West include an exhibition component in their temples, which becomes a useful guide to learn about the roots of Hinduism and the Swaminarayan Sampradaya. The weekly *sabhas* for children and youth were organized at BAPS temples to instill religious identity. They are taught traditional forms of dance, public speaking, and skits, along with traditional music and languages, to imbibe a better understanding of their religion and culture.[61] Celebrations of megafestivals like *Janmashtami*, *Ekadashi*, and other observances also played a significant role in transporting the children and youth to their original homeland without leaving the new and present homeland.[62]

In his study on the two temples in Pennsylvania, Frank Chappell observes an ecumenical side of Hinduism. The Shiva Lingam, *havan kund* (fireplace for *yajna*), and statues of two Jain *Tirthankaras* within the walls of the same temple is "an eclectic example of the multitude of co-existing traditions within Hinduism."[63] Ninian Smart reiterates that "Diaspora itself contributes to the process of self-definition of an ecumenical spirit and a kind of new orthodoxy."[64] The scriptures such as the *Bhagvad Gita* and *Ramayana* are widely read at homes and religious gatherings, governing the ethical actions of Hindus. How the concept of *dharma* (religious and ethical actions) is conceptualized in the diasporic community may differ according to sect, philosophical inclination, or the vestiges of caste mentality. Practicing Hindus even sort and synthesize teachings from different scriptures and local traditions in order to discover appropriate ethical and moral practices in complex circumstances.[65] Smith observes that various moralities

---

60 Answer to Question #6: Why build mandirs outside India? See https://www.swaminarayan.org/faq/mandir.htm.
61 Kim, "Public Engagement and Personal Desires," 15–17, 21.
62 Williams, *An Introduction to Swaminarayan Hinduism*, 178.
63 Chappell, "Negotiating Contemporary Hindu Beliefs," 85.
64 Smart, "The Importance of Diasporas," 294.
65 Pappu, "Hindu Ethics," 169–73.

are advocated for different life stages and are associated with modes of prescribed behavior correlated with a social structure.[66] Certainly Dalits or Ambedkarites will not emphasize the same theological tenets or conduct the same rituals as that of Brahmins.

Syncretistic and Scientific Outlook

Hindus in the Diaspora perceive themselves as asking questions and reasoning about ritual practices, ideologies, and belief systems, often in response to their children's interrogations. In this sense, they consider themselves to be better informed and more religious than the Hindus in India.[67] Hindus throughout the Diaspora face a common dilemma that entails moving toward a self-conscious rationalization of the distinction between religion and culture. David Pocock gives the example of BAPS, where a tendency has emerged to consider a certain aspect of Gujarati culture as a quasi-religious phenomenon and as a behavioral and ideological facet contributing toward the fulfillment of *dharma*. The subsequent problem for the Sanstha, Pocock discerns, would be "dis-embedding a set of beliefs and practices—a 'religion' from a 'culture' which would then be defined as secular."[68]

The self-consciously distinguishing elements of religion and culture involve both some kind of adaptation to religiously and culturally plural environments or to the intensifying of distinct "ethnic" sentiments. Among the later generations, Knott and Khokher explain, there is a "self-conscious exploration of the religion which was not relevant to the first generation."[69] Vertovec agrees that the phenomenon of a new hybrid culture is found among the younger members of the migrant community, who are exposed to different cultures from an early age.[70]

A common Hindu practitioner in the Diaspora brings out the lack of *conversion imperative* in Hinduism as a vital difference compared to other religions. Hinduism does not require a significant conversion to its tenets or dependency on a particular figure to be considered as "good" or to be "saved," as it is in other religions. The teachings of "good *karma*" override religious affiliations, and essentially become the determinant of a person's

---

66 Smith, *The World's Religions*, 12–81.
67 Williams, *Religions of Immigrants*, 47.
68 Pocock, "Preservation of the Religious Life," 357–62.
69 Knott and Khokher, "Religious and Ethnic Identity among Young Muslim Women," 596.
70 Vertovec, "Three Meanings of 'Diaspora,'" 277.

fate. The idea is that being a "good Hindu" and a "good Christian" is the same. It indicates a common attitude of "positive morality" perceived to be shared by all major religions. Such kind of reasoning allows one to ignore major theological or teleological aspects of world religions and focus on their inherent moral values to inform one's own.[71] Most modern Hindus tap into a pan-religious moral ideology for their behavior, which need not be attached to a particular religious outlook or doctrine.

Toward a Formative Interfaith Encounter

Interfaith encounters lead to a cross-religious comparison of certain beliefs and practices. The Christian-Hindu encounters in the Diaspora assume a comparable degree of rationalization and conceptualization of Hindu religious content by Christian partners. Questions related to scripture and essentialization of belief are sought after, especially by Protestants—the assumption being that all religious traditions have a central creed and authoritative texts. In this way, interfaith encounters have contributed to a reconceptualization of the conceived "Hindu way of life."

In Diaspora, there is an attempt to perceive Hinduism as a rationalized religion. Knott observes that the perception of being a minority religion in a secular and multi-faith society affected the way Hindus think about themselves and their faith. "Some are thinking of Hinduism as many people think about Christianity; something to be remembered during large festivals. Others have retained a more traditional view of Hinduism as a 'way of life.'"[72]

Jackson and Nesbitt claim that "Hinduism, for the children we studied, is becoming a more discrete area of experience, one which can be deliberately avoided or which can be visited for cultural enrichment or fellowship with co-religionists."[73] Van Dijk calls it a process of becoming an organized religion (*Religionisierung*), in which the former "ethnocultural religion" changes to a "systematized religion."[74] The clear examples of such reconceptualization are the formation of "Hindu catechisms" and the "nine beliefs of Hinduism" as cited above.

Groups such as Sanatana Dharma Maha Sabha have been making efforts to consolidate and systematize Hindu rituals and practices modeled

---

71 Chappell, "Negotiating Contemporary Hindu Beliefs," 89.
72 Knott, *Hinduism in Leeds*, 46.
73 Jackson and Nesbitt, *Hindu Children in Britain*, 179.
74 Dijk, "Hinduismus in Suriname und den Niederlanden," 193.

according to Christian practices. The celebration of Hindu festivals such as Diwali, Navratri, Janmashtami, and others has been consciously fed into normal life by groups like Society for the Promotion of Indian Culture (SPIC). Talking about the growth of Hinduism in Trinidad, O'Callaghan observes that it "has proved itself capable of re-working crucial aspects of Hinduism in India to bind Hindus abroad as an ethnic group and to provide a strategy for upward mobility."[75] Hence, it is predictable for Hinduism to be more structured and organized to counter the religious, social, and political pressure laid on its minority status and to respond constructively to the growing influence from the homeland. It began with preserving the values within the family structure, followed by establishing temples, Hindu schools, and organizations promoting Indian culture and religion, traditional art, and music centers.

As a response to interfaith encounters and secular freethinking, the young Hindu Diaspora has rejected the superstitious, ritualistic, and mythological form of Hinduism to give space to a more logical, balanced, ecumenical form. The idea of "universal morality" underlying all religions; a broader understanding of *dharma* as doing good, vegetarianism as nonessential, promoting interfaith and intra-faith ecumenism, drawing ethical and moral values from scriptures such as *Bhagvat Gita* and *Ramayana*—are some of the important traits of Hindu Diaspora.

These religious encounters are a challenge, as well as an opportunity, for constructive dialogue. Talking about the impediments to Hindu-Christian dialogue in the United States, Williams points out that the Hindu temples and organizations are predominantly in the hands of lay leaders who are trained primarily in medicine, science, technology, and business, and they are neither interested nor competent to engage in interreligious dialogue. On the other hand, the religious specialists brought from India are more sophisticated in Indian language and rituals than in English or Western philosophy. Another concern for Hindus to be part of the dialogue process is the inclusion of Muslims as dialogue partners by Christians and Jews, as the history and current state of Hindu-Muslim relations in India tend to distort views in the United States.

The surge of the Bhartiya Janata Party (BJP) as the ruling party in India and the growth of the Vishwa Hindu Parishad in North America introduced

---

75 O'Callaghan, "*Hinduism in the Indian Diaspora in Trinidad,*" 9.

a strident element into the rhetoric of some Hindus against Muslims. This tension is maintained by the annual visits of leaders from India and by constant communication through the media. Williams suggests that Hindu-Christian dialogue and collaborative study must take account of these tensions within the Indian diaspora communities.[76] New Christian immigrants from different countries experience living and negotiating with people of other faiths, and their experience should also be taken into account. For example, Indian Christians have been living with Hindus and Muslims, and their experience could bridge the sociocultural gap in genuine interfaith dialogue.

The Hindu groups that are part of the larger self-assertion that Hinduism has made in recent years are another challenge to interfaith encounters. They perceive Western Indology as facilitating insensitive and inaccurate work on Hinduism. Ramesh Rao suggests that there is a need for cultural sensitivity, limits of free speech in academic settings so as not to hurt others' feelings and the percolation of religious prejudice from the academic to mainstream settings.[77] It is important to listen to and include these voices if the interfaith interactions are to be healthy and progressive.

Despite such hindrances, some academicians have made efforts to reach out to Hindus in the Diaspora. Scholars and teachers whose primary interest has been Hinduism and comparative religion have continued dialogue between Hinduism and Christianity. A. L. Basham, J. T. F. Jordens, and others have made positive comparisons between Hinduism and Christianity. A strong advocate of Hinduism, Eric Sharpe, has welcomed the contribution that Hindus are well-placed to make in a religiously plural society. He also welcomed the challenge of religious ecumenism.[78] The talks and discussions of a most revered scholar in interreligious interaction, D. Bede Griffiths, presented many noble virtues of Hinduism, such as meditation, *yoga*, *sannyasa*, and the input Hindu mysticism can make in current sociological and theological cross-cultural thinking. Griffiths embodied the perfect blending of Eastern and Western spiritualities.

Though there have been such sincere efforts in bridging the chasm between Hinduism and Christianity much more work remains to be done in the area of bringing a more historically informed, theoretically balanced,

---

76 Williams, "Immigrants from India in North America," 23.
77 Rao, "Hindu God, Must Indeed Be Heathen," 398; see also Ramaswamy, "The Diaspora Press," 398.
78 Bilimoria, "Hindu-Christian Dialogue in Australia," 33.

and scholarly-oriented approach to Hinduism into the discussions. There is a greater need to create mutual understandings and common commitments for healthy interfaith encounters. It requires what Joseph Kitagawa called a "realistic equilibrium of a tripartite scheme—namely, piety in religion, morality in political life, and knowledge-rationality in culture."[79] A formative interfaith encounter and collaborative study must move in this direction to reach out to the Hindu Diaspora.

---

79 Kitagawa, *Christian Tradition: Beyond Its European Captivity*, 273.

Pollution and Cleansing from *Kala Pani* Crossings
Sin and Salvation for the Hindu Diaspora
Dr. Sam George

In this chapter, I will explore the traditional Hindu religious sanction against crossing any large body of water, generally known as the statutes of *Kala Pani*. I will begin with the restriction on sea voyage in Hinduism from a cultural perspective, and later I will analyze how migrants were viewed and treated by communal and religious institutions back in their ancestral homelands. Then I will examine the purification rituals and penances associated with the returning migrants and conclude by presenting metaphors of alienation and cleansing through the blood of Jesus Christ to develop a theological understanding of sin and salvation for Hindus in the Diaspora.

Crossing *Kala Pani*: Migration Causing Pollution

Hinduism is a geographically imprisoned religion, meaning that people who adhere to the faith are forbidden to migrate and are held captive to a particular region of the world. Until the past few decades, those who left the two Hindu-majority nations of India and Nepal have remained minuscule as compared to its populace. Those who have gone overseas recently have achieved significant success but are treated ambivalently in their native lands.

The religious and civilizational outlook of these nations is opposed to relocations, and thus people believe they are destined to live their entire lives near their birthplace. Individuals could only travel to places where their feet could carry them. The natural barriers of mountains in the north and oceans in the south confined Hindus to a geographic region for most of recorded history. Those who remain in their birthplaces treat the migrants who have gone abroad as contaminated, defiled, polluted, and unworthy of salvation.[1]

For the Hindus, India is the *Punya Bhumi* (sacred land), the land of spiritual preeminence; and people consider themselves fortunate to be born in the holy land. The place of birth (*Jnama Bhumi*) is considered sacred, and one's destiny is closely linked to it (*Karma Bhumi*). It is bound within the notions of *Dharma Bhumi* (land of duty) and *Moksha Bhumi* (land of salvation). The concepts of *Pitru Bhumi* (fatherland) and *Matru Bhumi* (motherland) call for fidelity from its residents, while the related idea of *Bharatmata* (Mother India) demands loyalty, devotion, and veneration from all who live in India. These ideas are deviously employed to stoke nationalistic sentiments, and some radical Hindu groups have befuddled the idea of Hindu *rashtra* (nation) to tyrannize religious minorities and dissenting voices in India.

Hinduism has clear prohibitions against sea travel, and such religious shackles are strictly enforced in some circles even to this day. As per Hindu scriptures, "making voyages by the sea" is a punishable offense and is known as the *samudara llangana*, or *sagara ullhangana*, which means that any sea travel or leaving one's native land is treated as a sin. The act of crossing seas and oceans is believed to cause the ultimate soul defilement, and those who have perpetrated unpardonable offenses are banished. Brahmins are particularly sanctioned against seafaring, and severe penalties and penance are prescribed for transgressors. The *Manusmriti* (Laws of Manu) and *Dharma Sutras Baudavana* call those who had gone to sea as unworthy of *sraddha* (devotion), annual appeasement of spirits, and various rituals associated with paying homage to ancestors. In the *Ramayana*, after defeating Lanka, Ram was asked by Laxman, "Why go back to *Ayodhaya* since Lanka is so beautiful?" Ram replied, "Mother and motherland are greater than even heaven."

Recently, the religious pontiff of the famed Krishna temple in Udupi ran into controversy for crossing the oceans to minister to devotees in Europe and America.[2] None of the priests serving the inner sanctum of the Balaji

---
1 George, "Crossing *Kala Pani*"; George, *Desi Diaspora*.
2 Gopalakrishnan, "Crossing the Oceans."

Temple in Tirumala can cross any ocean, even though their training school is tutoring priests for temples abroad for lucrative returns. Likewise, Jain monks and nuns cannot travel overseas but are required to walk everywhere barefoot. However, the global Jain Diaspora has forced the religious bodies to slacken their stringent constraints to travel beyond where their feet would carry them.

For the upper-caste Hindus, going beyond India posed the double jeopardy of not being able to perform their daily rituals and of coming into contact with *mlecchas*. The Vedic Sanskrit term *mleccha* means more than mere impurity but denotes any interaction with foreigners, aliens, or barbarians. In ancient times, it was used as a derogatory term to refer to inferior people and stood for non-Aryan aliens. Brahmins are required to worship three times—at sunrise, noon, and sunset—which cannot be carried out when they are airborne since it must be done on earth. They must refrain from any contact with defilements. The twice-born Hindus regard people who have undertaken the transgressive journey as causing excommunicating pollution and require rituals of purification before they can be accepted back into their homes. The concept of *mlecchas* and the sacrilege of beef-eating expanded into untouchability, which had been utilized to exploit the large masses of lower caste and outcast people in India.[3]

Historically, these religiously motivated injunctions and traditions limited any large-scale emigration of Hindus to distant places, but instead, they remained entrapped to the land. It forced individuals to isolate themselves from others and not to build meaningful relations with foreigners. Although people from many parts of the world had come to the Indian subcontinent since ancient times, Hindus remained largely migration-resistant. As a result, others have easily traded with, exploited, and colonized the region. Hindus seldom pursued seafaring vocations, and most maritime activities were limited to the coastal regions of Malabar, Bengal, Coromandel, and Gujarat among non-Hindus or lower-caste Indians. No wonder some allege that shipbuilding or communication technologies did not get developed in India despite a large coastline and the sprawling Indian Ocean, unlike their counterparts like the Chinese, Arabs, or Europeans. The colonial indentured laborers in the nineteenth century mostly came from the lower strata of society, were struggling for sheer survival, and were considered social pariahs in famine-devastated regions.

---

3 Ambedkar, *The Untouchables*.

Of course, there are exceptions of migration from the Indian subcontinent through its northwest corridors and across seas, citing examples from history and even Hindu scriptures. They argue that Hanuman flew over to Lanka, and the *Rig Veda* alludes to the sea voyages of Varuna. Others allege that the South Indian Hindus were not at all dissuaded by the sanction and rejected the ban on sea travel, citing the example of maritime imperial aspirations of the Chola dynasty from the ninth to the thirteenth century.[4] The religio-cultural vestiges of Hinduism seen in Southeast Asia suggest that these outposts have received substantial maritime sustenance from the mother country. Earlier, Emperor Ashoka had sent Buddhist evangelists across Asia while Arabs took Indian pilgrims to Mecca. Much later, the European colonizers took trophies and converts along with cotton and spices from India. The merchants, fishing communities, and descendants of Muslim traders who had intermarried locally were tiny exceptions to the norm for outmigration from the region, while most remained fastened to their native lands.

The geographical and demographical center of Hinduism remains fixed and immovable. Hindu sentiments are parochial, and gods and goddesses are territorial. The migratory displacement disrupts the devotion to local deities, and when a person goes beyond the provincial boundaries of a localized tribal divinity, he or she must find a god of the new place and be devoted to that god. Likewise, Islam is also a rooted religion, because the religious nerve center of the faith is fixed forever on account of its tenets of pilgrimage (*hajj*), a solitary place to pray toward (*qibla*), and untranslatable scripture (*Quran*). Hence, both the religions of Hinduism and Islam may be considered geographically interned on account of their immovable religious center.

In contrast, since the inception of Christianity, its center has always been on the move and it is a faith that was born to travel. Most of the world's migrants are Christians, and many have embraced Christianity in foreign lands. Hence some claim that if you are a Christian you will travel; and if you travel, you will become a Christian! Throughout history, Christianity has continuously diffused across cultural and geographical lines, and many different people in varied places have been Christianity's chief representatives. The Christian faith cannot be bound to a location or domesticated by any people because its nature is to break free of the prisons we enshrine it in. It is constrained

---

4 Panikkar, *A Survey of Indian History*.

to move repeatedly from one place to another because it is a quintessential missionary, translatable, and mobile faith.[5] It is a translatable faith because it is a transportable faith, as its mobility creates transcultural and interlinguistic dialectics that require translation of its tenets and Scriptures to new contexts and margins to become the new center of the faith.

Dilemmas of Return: Go Back or Not?

One of the characteristic traits of diasporic communities is the strange sense of belonging they have to their distant birthplaces and a deep longing to return there someday. They retain a collective memory of their homelands, feel that they are different from their host societies, and tend to idealize their history and achievements. All of this makes their hearts ache to return "home" or to make a positive contribution to the welfare of the people they left behind. Some routinely embark on trips to visit their families, while others hope to return someday after completing their foreign vocations or when they have saved enough for retirement. Some inherit family properties, while others build homes or invest in land and business with hopes of traveling back to their places of origin.

However, many international migrants of Hindu background, fearing rejection, prejudice, and discrimination, chose not to return to their native lands. The trauma of the indenture journey, with its high mortality rate and the anticipated societal backlash of being treated as polluted, kept most from returning. Despite the hardships of indentured work in Fiji, Mauritius, Suriname, and other places, the Indian indentured workers never returned even when their contracts expired and their return passages were paid for. The laborers in Suriname who returned to their ancestral villages were "ostracized for having crossed the 'black waters' and having mixed with other castes and religions."[6] Those who returned with money were looted by their brethren and local Hindu priests. *Kala Pani* features glaringly in Anglophone Caribbean history and literature.[7] The predicament of the indentured women not returning from South Africa led to their conversion to Christianity in a racialized society to gain a better education and social upward mobility.[8]

---

5 George, "Motus Dei (The Move of God)," 95–122.
6 Kumar, *Coolies of the Empire: Indentured Indians*.
7 Mehta, *Diasporic (Dis)location: Indo-Caribbean Women*.
8 Marie, "Across the *Kala Pani*," 89–101.

More recent studies have explored the return and transnational belonging of modern British Gujaratis to expose the double standards of religious institutions in offering religious cleansing in exchange for money.⁹ Some returning migrants to Kerala, Punjab, and Andhra Pradesh have banded together to establish non-resident Indian colonies in their ancestral hometowns in order to deflect any social backlashes and for mutual support. They flaunt their success and accumulated wealth from abroad by building luxurious homes and giving generous gifts to family members and neighbors to offset any social demotion caused by religious violations.

In the stratified Indian society, one's social standing is believed to be an unchangeable lot in life (*dharma*) and determines the ceiling within the socioeconomic ladder. A person's destiny is determined by birth, and mobility of any sort across the strict categories of faith, vocation, and caste is considered unattainable. The caste hierarchies are rigid and migratory displacements condemned people to the lowest rung of the order. Since the motherland is considered divine, migrants are treated as unfaithful defectors or disloyal opportunists. Those who resist the temptation to go overseas see themselves as pure, devoted, and superior by carrying out duty while downgrading what migrants could gain in foreign lands, such as education, exposure, experience, connections, and wealth. The migrants upon return are not allowed to enter their homes, draw water from their wells, or eat with clan members. They are forbidden entry into religious temples or to carry out any *pujas* at home. For instance, upon returning to India after his eloquent oratory about Hinduism on the stage of the World Parliament of Religion in Chicago in 1893, Swami Vivekananda was deemed polluted for going across the Pacific Ocean and was denied entry into many temples.¹⁰

Moreover, the migrants' return to India is more complicated than imagined. Any contact with *mlecchas* results in *pataniya*, loss of caste, and forfeit of their purified Hindu essence. They might have surely broken the dietary rules and come in contact with contaminating elements abroad. Vegetarianism kept Hindu society agrarian and bound to sources of water and fertile land, in contrast to nomadic hunter-gatherers. Most of the religious dietary requirements are nearly impossible to observe over long

---

9   Ramji, "British Indians 'Returning Home,'" 645–62.
10 Vivekananda, *Swami Vivekananda and his Guru: Letters*. After the inaugural session of the Parliament, the event host was shocked when Swami asked for beef to eat. That would make him religiously polluted. See also Doniger, *Hindus: Alternative History*.

sea voyages. The migrant returnees are treated as *bedharam*—those who lost their religion—as they would have eaten unclean foods and been with people of other castes and beliefs.[11] Any socioreligious relegation is terribly consequential in Indian society, even to subsequent generations in the form of their marriage prospects. When M. K. Gandhi went to England to study law, he was treated as an outcaste, and anyone who helped him or saw him off at the dock was fined by his fellow-caste leaders. His mother had him take a solemn oath before a Jain monk to abstain from pollution in a foreign land as a result of caste outrage over breaking the sea travel ban.[12] Furthermore, the contention of migrants that they have preserved religious purity abroad through home worship, building temples, and bringing priests/swamis to foreign lands is aimed at lessening the prejudice against them or to ward off any discrimination they experience upon return. They vehemently oppose the mindset of traditional Hindu religious bodies that crossing seas causes any putrefaction of character and posterity and try to reform its archaic religious tenets.

Kala Pani signified lifelong internment with no prospect of return. For women, the stigma, oppression, hardship, and shame of returning would be more than what they experienced before. They are forced to live in social isolation for having transgressed the most fundamental social codes, and all returnees are treated like menstruating women who have to spend their cycle entirely away from the village. Only after the stipulated days of isolation and a purification ceremony are they allowed to reenter the village. If migrants drink water from the communal well or reenter the village, all impurities would be transmitted, and thus reparation would be too expensive for the entire village.

A Bengali businessman, Dwarkanath Tagore, the grandfather of Indian Nobel laureate Rabindranath Tagore, owned a steam-powered yacht and had maritime trade with Europeans, but faced excommunication by his own family. Mystic poet Rabindranath had traveled extensively over waters in the early twentieth century and helped make India better known in the West, had been highly critical of the religious prohibitions on crossing waters, and had written about his sea travels. He considered the travel ban as a stumbling block that forced India to isolate.[13]

---

11 Carter, *Coolitude: An Anthology*, 164.
12 Gandhi, *Story of My Experiments with Truth*, 36.
13 Mortuza, "Beyond '*Kalapani*'"; Tagore, *Letters from Java*.

Purification Rituals: Absolution of Polluted Souls

All migrant returnees are treated as polluted and are required to undergo sanitizing rituals before reentering their ancestral villages or sacred places. They have to make penance for going beyond their sacred homeland, which involves religious ceremonies and a time of separation from sacred things and interaction with family or clan. Without any remorse, ritual purification, or penance, migrants face isolation upon return and are grouped with prisoners, prostitutes, and exiles. When M. K. Gandhi returned after his legal studies in England, he had to go through expiatory rituals. His brother, who came to receive him at the Bombay port, cleverly took him to Nasik to give him a bath in the sacred river before going to their hometown of Rajkot.[14]

The prescribed penance for migrants who return to India includes,

> They shall eat every fourth meal-time a little food, bathe at the time of the three libations (morning, noon, and evening), passing the day standing and the night sitting. After the lapse of three years they throw off their guilt.[15]

However, the purification rituals and penance for crossing oceans vary widely across India and Nepal, depending on Hindu sects and the authority bestowed on some scriptures by different groups. Others argue that the ban only applies to Brahmins, though some claim that it applies to all three upper castes. A contaminated individual can only be restored to normality and communal acceptance through rituals involving the cleansing agents of water or fire. In 2012 a Namboothiri priest and Vedic scholar in Kerala upon his return from London was barred from entry into any temple for having sinned by crossing the seas, and devotees kept vigil around the temple such that the "unclean" priest did not enter. The local temple authorities asked him to undertake a thorough cleansing, penance, and *punaravrodha* (reinstallation service) before allowing him into the temple. He was asked to purify by reciting Gayatri Mantra 1,008 times, which he refused. Eventually the controversy was resolved by sprinkling *theerthom* (holy water), and he was allowed inside the temple. Other Hindu religious sects are much stricter about allowing priests who have crossed the seas to enter the sanctum sanctorum or hold the highest offices of the order, like the famous temples of Kathmandu, Udupi, or Tirupathi.

---

14 Gandhi, *The Story of My Experiments with Truth*, 78.
15 Baudhayana Sutra, II.1.2.2.

All pilgrimage sites of Hinduism are situated within India and Nepal, and those who settle abroad are permanently cut off from the regenerating waters of the Ganges. The geographical captivity was not just in life, but also after death since the ashes of a dead person after cremation were to be scattered over holy waters because that would determine the person's future rebirths. A major deterrent to migration to faraway places is the fear of dying in foreign lands since the requirement of cremation and Hindu final rites are difficult to be observed in other cultures. Moreover, the requirement of a son having to light the funeral pyre of parents kept generations bound to each other and the young ones from straying too far from their ancestors.

However, the younger generation of liberalized Hindus of contemporary India is quick to abandon the outdated religious superstitions regarding the sea travel ban. They do not adhere to the obligations of ritual purification. Besides, it is harder to enforce such restrictions today, and migration is generally seen as a means of upward mobility. In an age of globalization marked by far-flung and repeated migrations, mobility and access to technologies of communication are key elements of social stratification.[16]

After India's independence in 1947, and more noticeably since its economic liberalization in the early 1990s, the educational and employment opportunities resulted in the exodus of young people to Indian cities, which in turn led to subsequent overseas migration for further studies and jobs in flourishing technology industries. After experiencing life in more egalitarian and liberal Western societies, Hindu migrants defy religiously backward attitudes toward migration, as they lived far away from native villages in relative obscurity beyond the authority of their religious leaders who could not coerce religious sanctions. Moreover, the sociocultural ethos moved in favor of foreign careers, as Indian parents preferred marriage alliances for their children from foreign lands, and many returnees lived comfortably without any religious censure or loss of any social respectability.

Sin and Salvation for Hindus in Diaspora: Alienation and Cleansing

The doctrine of salvation in the West since the Protestant Reformation has prioritized the conceptions drawn from judicial (justification), financial (redemption), punitive (acquittal), and religious (atonement) realms. The biblical notion of salvation ranges from saving from danger, distress, enemies,

---

16 Bauman, *Globalization*, 87.

and death to messianic deliverance and bestowal of spiritual blessings. It traces the effect of the Fall as inherited guilt and the corruption of the human race to develop salvation as a reversal of those effects through the gift of grace through Christ's death and the promise of eternal life.[17]

But soteriology limited to these dominant views is extraneous to other cultural and religious contexts. What God has done through the death and resurrection of Jesus Christ can be perceived using other conceptualizations found in the Bible and novel theological interpretations from diverse global perspectives. Some of them include dimensions such as penance (expiation), freedom (liberation), transactional (forgiveness), restoration (propitiation), legal (justice), health (wholeness or healing), relational (reconciliation), etc. In this final section, for Indian emigrants from a shame-based culture, stratified social hierarchy, and Hindu religious context, I will briefly examine the doctrine of sin as alienation and the salvific value of the concepts of cleansing and adoption. These are in no way better or invalidate other interpretations, but together they provide a more comprehensive grasp of Christian salvation.

The language of pollution and purity is prevalent in all major ancient civilizations and religious spheres, yet its association with sea-crossing is distinctive to Hinduism and resulted in the geographical captivity of its adherents for centuries. Every society maintains a complex set of rules and unspoken regulations about polluting actions, objects, places, and persons, which in turn govern their sociocultural, economic, and political orders. They formulate elaborate religious proscriptions against defiling elements and prescriptions to remedy pollution through rituals and penance. The religious prohibition of contact is based on the principle that the profane should not touch the sacred, and generally pollution is considered contagious while purity is not.

Alienation from family, community and all things familiar is germane to all emigrants, even as they suffer some form of estrangement in their host societies. They feel distant from their immediate neighbors in their adopted homelands, yet closer than ever to their distant ancestral homelands. They are unable to integrate fully into their present surroundings while being entwined with the past with a strange yearning to return to their native places. This quandary forces them to explore afresh their identity, belonging,

---

17 White, "Salvation," in *Evangelical Dictionary of Theology*.

and allegiance. They juxtapose their inherited and adopted cultures and associated religious beliefs in new ways to arrive at something deserving of their ultimate fidelity. Additionally, Hindus in the Diaspora suffer from a sense of being polluted on account of their migration and having failed to live up to their socioreligious obligations.

Alienation is an apt conception to understand the doctrine of sin for Hindus who live away from their sacred land; and, correspondingly, the doctrine of salvation needs to be viewed as coming near to the divine being. In the Apostle Paul's words, "All have sinned and fall short of the glory of God" (Rom 3:23 ESV). In other words, we all have moved away from God, not from a particular geographical locale but from a divine being. In the Athenian discourse, Paul argues the sovereignty of God in human dispersion:

> He made from one man every nation of mankind to live on all the face of the earth, having determined allotted periods and the boundaries of their dwelling place, that they should seek God, and perhaps feel their way toward him and find him. Yet he is actually not far from each one of us. (Acts 17:26–27 ESV)

The incarnation needs to be viewed in kinetic terms, as God coming near to us, rather than in metaphysical terms, such as alienated people can draw near to God. Soteriology has to be conceived in a relational and motile language for the reversal of alienation, estrangement, contamination, and ostracization—using conceptual ideation such as *brought near, proximity, purification, cleansing,* and *intimacy*.[18]

The Old Testament has two realms of purity: ritual and moral. The former is associated with defilement, such as bodily emissions, childbirth, unclean food, contact with dead bodies, etc. (Lev 11–15; Num 19), while the latter is related to sexual transgression, idolatry, and murder (Lev 18:24–30; 20:1–3; Num 35:33–34). Ritual defilement threatened the individual, whereas moral defilement polluted the land and resulted in the Israelites' expulsion. In New Testament texts, the cleansing from sin/defilement is through the death of Christ (Titus 2:14; Heb 9:14, 22; 2 Pet 1:9). John emphatically presented that "the blood of Jesus his Son cleanses us from all sin" and cleanses "us from all unrighteousness" (or defilement) (1 John 1:7, 9). Hebrews 9 and 10 depict salvation in terms of cleansing by contrasting old covenant purity through blood sacrifice and the new covenant sacrificial death of Jesus making

---
18 George, "Motus Dei (The Move of God)."

people holy forever (Heb 10:1–14). The shedding of the blood of a sinless God-incarnate cleanses us anew and establishes a new sense of belonging and identity, because there is no forgiveness "without the shedding of blood" (Heb 9:22 ESV).

Another important lens that can greatly assist us in understanding the migrant predicaments of Indians is the issue of shame. Shame is more complicated and harder to deal with than guilt, since the former is personal and relational while the latter is objective and rational. Shame is generally overlooked in Western theological circles, although there are eight times as many references to shame than to guilt in the Bible.[19]

In this regard, adoption is a powerful theological concept in restoring the status demotion brought about by shaming migratory choices. Our relationship with God is dramatically altered from being children of wrath (Eph 2:3) to becoming beloved sons and daughters of God (John 1:12) and "heirs of God and fellow heirs with Christ" (Rom 8:17 ESV). God pursues those who are estranged, shamed, contaminated, and ostracized to make them as God's very own. Total strangers become beloved members of God's family, and this relational reality infuses a new sense of dignity and identity. Adoption radically reorients the person's core being and belonging, as their shaming pollution is washed away and a new sense of purity is implicated. A theology of adoption[20] will not only help us deepen our filial experience of salvation, which is particularly pertinent for the Indian Diaspora who experiences the nuclearization of households and estrangement from host communities in diasporic settlements but also provide a new community in a foreign land that is not based upon geographical or biological incumbrances as well as feature its innate missionary impulse to relate to all people everywhere.

---

19 George, "Shaming the Shame"; Pattison, *Shame: Theory, Therapy and Theology*.
20 Johnson, *One with Christ: An Evangelical Theology of Salvation*, 151–75; Grudem, *Systematic Theology*, 751–61.

Conclusion

Migration beyond the places of birth is deemed polluting for Hindus, and the migrants who return experience the stigma of excommunication from religious circles in their ancestral homelands. For ages, the ill-repute of ostracization and the fear of loneliness in alien lands have kept them in bondage to their native land and from exploring livelihood options beyond their immediate vicinities. However, the younger generations of Hindus and those in the Diaspora are revolting against this ancient religious sanction, as the native bindings fade away in faraway lands and they search for a more universal God who can deal with their alienation and sense of contamination.

God did not leave us in our predicament of alienation, and the toxic shame of crossing seas to foreign lands has been dealt with once and for all. If crossing oceans cuts off a person, the incarnation of Jesus, the Son of God, paves the way for all to return to God and live in intimate relation with the divine being forever. The living God of the universe pursues all with the unconditional love shown by the sacrificial death and resurrection of Jesus Christ. The shed blood of Jesus opens the door for all people to draw near to God and become children of God. The sacrificial death of Jesus offers to all polluted and alienated people wholeness of life through soul-cleansing, restoration of strained relationships, and adoption into the family of God.

Modi, Hindu *Rashtra*, and India's New Internationalism

Mr. Rahil Patel[1]

We live in a post-secular world, in which, as journalists John Micklethwait and Adrian Wooldridge entitled their 2009 bestseller, *God Is Back*. The truth and impact of a "religious," "cultural," or "spiritual" worldview on world leaders is perhaps under-appreciated in the West.

In this chapter, I will explore the impact of Indian Prime Minister Narendra Modi's Hindu faith on domestic affairs and international relations, specifically regarding his dealings with Russia, Israel, Sri Lanka, and Iran. This illustrates the importance of accrediting religio-cultural perspectives by special reference to India's current Prime Minister Modi. A careful study of his approach to diplomacy, and the shaping of India's international relations, reveals a man and behavior that are deeply shaped by a distinctive view of Hindutva[2] and a privileging of the "spiritual."

Two main questions drive this chapter: 1) What are the characteristics of Narendra Modi's approach to life, faith, and leadership? And how

---

1 This chapter is a shortened version of an essay I co-wrote with Professor Christopher Hancock, director of Oxford House. He is a theologian with expertise in contemporary geopolitics, and who traces his roots to India, where he has taught regularly for the past twenty-five years.
2 Hinduism in India encompasses cultural inclusivity, while Hindutva represents an exclusive ideological extremism. Hindutva originates from ancient *Vedic* traditions and was influenced by twentieth-century European fascism. After India's independence, Hindutva became associated with violent protests and fervent nationalism. Since Modi became India's prime minister in 2014, Hindutva has gained prominence as a mainstream nationalist ideology, advocating for policies and rituals that favor India and oppose Muslims and other minority groups.

determinative are these characteristics for the way he governs India today? 2) To what extent is Modi's diplomacy a departure from, or in keeping with, India's past and recent approaches to international relations? And what light does India's relationship with Russia, Israel, Iran, and Sri Lanka shed on this?

We approach these issues, in turn, mindful that the Bhartiya Janata Party (BJP) government in India today is more than its prime minister. But it is also no less than him; indeed, to some, it would have little political, cultural, and international standing apart from him. To a notable degree, the character, influence, and fortunes of Modi, his cabinet, and the BJP party exist in a dynamic, symbiotic, sometimes strained, relationship. As ever, interpreters of India must be ready to admit the presence and complexity of its political, social, cultural, and religious paradoxes.

Modi's Life, Faith, and Leadership

Narendra Modi is not a religious terrorist or suicide bomber, though the human rights record of his BJP government is far from perfect. He is, to cynical Western secularists and vocal Indian critics, a "religiously differentiated" national leader, whose true motivations are veiled in the opaque symbols of religiosity, his character formed by principles and practices that elude doubters, skeptics, and agnostics.[3] To understand Modi's character, intentions, and threat, we must address the Hindu dream that shapes how he sees and steers India through the choppy seas of national affairs and international diplomacy.

So what is Modi's worldview? And how exactly does this impact the way he speaks, acts, and leads India? The simple answer to the first question is classical *Vedic* Hinduism. As a Hindu revivalist,[4] Modi draws his inspiration from the five-thousand-year-old cradle of Indian civilization. His political and spiritual mentor is neither Mahatma Gandhi nor India's first prime minister, Jawaharlal Nehru, but Kautilya, the fourth-century BC political philosopher and advisor to Emperor Chandragupta Maurya. His pragmatic masterpiece,

---

3 In the run-up to Modi's 2014 electoral success, he campaigned with his "close friend," the celebrated Yoga guru (and billionaire media tycoon) Baba Ramdev. Ramdev's *Vedic* broadcasting channels endorse Modi's popular anti-corruption narrative and pursuit of a pure Hindu nation.

4 Indians take pride in their five-thousand-year-old civilization. The founding fathers of India's modern democracy sought to incorporate India's historical legacy into its future geopolitical ambitions. In *The Indian Conservative*, Rao argues that the "band of brothers" who fought for Indian independence adopted different philosophies. Revivalists connect the aspirations of "New India" directly with *Vedic* India (thereby denouncing three hundred years of British and French colonialism and seven hundred years of Islamic rule).

the *Arthshastra* (Science of Political Economy),[5] is a sophisticated manual for statecraft and a practical how-to on effective leadership. Many, including Mahatma Gandhi, have been inspired by this ancient text,[6] but none is more controversial than Modi and the leaders of the BJP party.

Modi's vision for "New India" is rooted in, and inspired by, a mythic view of "Old India," with its Vedic or Hindutva socio-spiritual culture, rituals, and strict hierarchy of castes, priests, and gods. He seeks to repristinate India socially and politically today. Modi has an unembarrassed Hindu spirituality that is politically astute at the point of personal delivery to his supporters, colleagues, and counterparts worldwide. To some, his life and work are that of a guru with genuine, neo-messianic, spiritual zeal, while to others Modi is a vain, ruthless, self-promoting *fakir* (wandering pilgrim), whose high claims to be without hearth, home, wife, possessions, or earthly ambitions, except to "Make India Great Again" through pure devotion, selfless public service, and asceticism—making a mockery of the very traditions he espouses and making India the laughingstock of a cynical, secular world. As a religiously differentiated world leader at present, wherein lies the character and power of his international profile, diplomatic effectiveness, and personal charisma. Atheists beware, in Modi the "gods are back"![7]

At every turn during his premiership, Modi has invoked Hindu themes and practices to win votes, make a point, woo a rival, or bewitch a foreign head of state. When, in September 2014, he addressed the United Nations (UN) General Assembly for the first time as India's prime minister, he proposed an "International Yoga Day." This was dutifully adopted four months later. When he spoke to the US Congress on June 8, 2016, he again invoked yoga as an Indian distinctive and as a point of cultural contact with America. Eight days later, he joined thirty thousand Indians for a yoga *fest* in New

---

5 *Arthashastra* has 15 books and 150 chapters. It covers topics from political philosophy to public administration, diplomacy, foreign policy, and intelligence gathering. In honor of Kautilya (or Chanakya), the diplomatic enclave in New Delhi is called *Chanakyapuri*. Nehru mentions Chanakya often, but there is some scholarly disagreement about Kautilya's influence today. To some, contemporary Indian policy is consciously rooted in Kautilyan principles (Rashed uz Zaman and Michael Liebig), while for others Modi is too proud, pragmatic, and opportunistic to be behooved to another's thought and practice. India's "non-aligned" policy may reflect Kautilya's astute warning: "Be wary of depending on one group of allies."

6 Central to the work is the creation of a *Chakravartin* (universal monarchy). Once the vision of Mauryan kings, Modi, Pramukh Swami Maharaj (former leader of the Swaminarayan Hindu Movement), Ramdev Baba, Sai Baba, and many others have embraced this as their vocation.

7 Modi's appeal is *supra*-political. Like Gandhi, Modi reflects what political scientist W. H. Morris-Jones called the "saintly idiom" (alongside the "modern" and "traditional") of Indian politics. In other words, Modi seeks and gathers spiritual devotees, as much as electoral votes.

Delhi.[8] Modi has effectively weaponized yoga (and other Hindu customs and rituals) as sharp tools in his hands and deceptively disruptive intercultural media to advance a Hindutva agenda.

There are other ways Modi invokes Hindu culture and spiritualizes political life. He ties a *Nada Chadi* (red and yellow thread), a traditional symbol of close friendship in Hindu culture, on the right wrist of a visiting dignitary. He speaks infrequently, as if to intensify and sanctify his utterances, and when he does speak, he does so in sermonic mantras, as if by divine revelation. He resists censure.[9] Those who criticize him risk condemnation as disloyal politically or deficient spiritually. To the enlightened, *their* truth is personally verifiable and dangerously nonnegotiable.[10] When Modi engages world leaders, he does so with the passion of a prophet and the confidence of a Hindutva Messiah. And the countries he is closest to are those that honor this kind of behavior. Why? Because they see him as he wants to be seen.

Modi's religious profile and quasi-messianic vocation are built on propaganda by the radical Hindutva Rashtriya Swayamsevak Sangh (RSS).[11] Central to the ideology Modi and his followers promote is a revivified *Aatmanirbhar Bharat* (self-reliant [Hindu] nation) built on and guided by India's devout leaders and the sacrificial acts and penitential offerings of her long-suffering people. It was to this core vision that Modi, the guru, appealed to when on the twenty-first day of the COVID-19 lockdown he called for devout citizens to light a *diya* (votive candle) for nine minutes at 9 p.m.[12] Pantheism pervades the political realm in Modi's spiritual *modus operandi*. When announcing an extension to the lockdown, daily wage workers, who were and are suffering the most, were called to *tyag* (sacrifice) and *tapasya*

---

8   Modi's supporters interpreted the UNGA's International Yoga Day as heralding India's superpower status.

9   NB (nota bene): For the first time since 1950, Question Hour in Parliament (the first order of the day) was canceled on September 2, 2020, purportedly because of COVID. Critics continue to express fears that the BJP government may use Parliament merely as a noticeboard for their actions and intentions, not as a forum for healthy cross-examination of government policy.

10 As was once wisely said, "We should never forget there is not a million miles between the 'inner light' and the 'outer darkness'!"

11 Rashtriya Swayamsevak Sangh (RSS) was founded in September 1925. It coordinates several organizations known as Sangh Parivar (family). It is associated with violent endorsement of Vedic ideology and the BJP party. RSS was banned prior to Indian independence and has been three times since. Its pursuit of a pure Hindutva culture and vision for an exclusive Hindu *Rashtra* render it a useful ally to the present government.

12 Some may have seen the request as a gimmick, but millions ardently followed through with key astrologers and Vedic practitioners giving Modi an approving thumbs-up.

(penance).¹³ Their painful suffering would be embraced with the resignation shown during demonetization (November 2016). It is *yagna* (sacrificial fire) against corruption.¹⁴ COVID was thereby reframed by Modi as a spiritual opportunity more than a medical threat or social disaster.

Unlike other world leaders, who speak regularly about the pressing issues of the day, Modi makes carefully managed declarations every few weeks. To increase the suspense and exaggerate his authority or beneficence, "big announcements" are embedded in devotional discourse. When he delivered news of a Rupees 20 Lakh crore economic stimulus package, he was Guru Sathya Sai Baba disgorging the golden egg, the mesmerizing amount repeated for maximum effect, as if giving the money himself. The faithful are captivated. His failures to care for migrants or to act justly for the poor evaporate in transcendental stardust. To some in his party, he should remain socio-politically untouched by untouchable Dalits and lower-caste Hindus, dissidents, and disputants. Modi and RSS allies have resisted this elitist pressure and joined Dalits and lower castes in temple rituals and inaugurations to attract votes and curb and counter Christian proselytism. This much is clear: It is hard to explain Modi's leadership style solely in terms of military might or economics.¹⁵

There is a twist to Modi's spiritual leadership. Unlike Vladimir Putin's Orthodox Russia, or Iran's Islamic theocracy, or Israel's sociopolitical Zionism, or Sri Lanka's resurgent Buddhism, Modi is a leader of the largest democracy in the world and serves at the pleasure of the Indian populace and BJP party. His power and position are by vote, not by right. He does not have a divine mandate, whatever he may claim. He presents himself as a democratic leader and China's greatest regional rival to modern Western democracies that are fearful of the growing influence of China or confused by Modi's spirituality.¹⁶

---

13 For interesting Hindu views of pain and suffering in modern medicine, see Whitman, "Pain and Suffering as Viewed by the Hindu Religion," 607–13.

14 NB. Mumbai-based astrologer Shastri Niranjan Shukla, who predicted a Modi victory in 2019, said Modi was following Vedic texts in invoking a mass *yagna* (sacrificial fire) to dispel COVID.

15 Modi's agenda as prime minister is clearly far more than the expansion of his nation's military (already the third-largest in the world) or its economy (prior to COVID, the fifth-largest). Time will tell how much COVID affects India's economy, politics, social harmony, and self-esteem.

16 At the July 2020 India-EU summit, Modi was quick to condemn China's pressurizing of what he called "a rules-based international order" and to confirm India's "humanity-centric" worldview (akin to the EU's) based on "democracy, pluralism, inclusiveness, rules-based multilateralism, and freedom." New Delhi, he made clear, has not welcomed the EU's seeming acquiescence in China's expansionism, aggression, and human-rights abuse.

The former US Secretary of State, Mike Pompeo, made a deliberate connection with India's democratic identity during the US-India Business Council's Ideas Summit in 2020. The US and India, "the oldest democracy in the world and the largest" have, he said, "shared democratic values," which form the basis of a "new age in [the US-India] relationship." With China now officially distancing itself from Western values and alliances,[17] America is not alone in courting and consciously encouraging a "new (democratic) India," as China's largest (politically more acceptable) neighbor. Modi is meanwhile delighted. Janus-like, he can play the role of a Hindu *sadhu* (to impress devotees and disconcert non-Indians) *and* that of a wealthy, Western plutocrat (to frustrate enemies and aspirant allies). New Indians are not unhappy with this.

In a July 2020 interview, India's Minister of External Affairs, Subrahmanyam Jaishankar, spoke of setting a "new tone" to India's foreign policy. In his book titled *The India Way: Strategies for an Uncertain World* (HarperCollins, 2020), he elaborates:

> It is not the image of what it was in the past. It is more of a decision maker than an abstainer, it is a shaper and unique to us as a power is our diaspora and our culture of yoga and *Ayurveda*.

We hear the voice of Modi here; we also hear Jaishankar (a political rival). But the message from both is clear: New India and the India Way involve a confident, differentiated Hindutva cultural agenda in service to India's aspirant New World economy, its vast military, techno-savvy populace, and increasingly sophisticated infrastructure.[18] We get a further sense of this New India in a July 2020 panel discussion with Professor C. Raja Mohan (Singapore University), where Jaishankar declared, "If we are to grow by leveraging the international situation, then we have to *exploit* the opportunities out there. You can't do that by saying, 'I'm going to stay away from it all, and when I find it useful, I will step up.'"

---

17 The recent Indo-China border tension adds further strain to regional geopolitics. Senior officials (notably, ambassadors Shyam Saran, Gautam Bambawale, and Ashok Kantha) have linked (the) recent border conflict to India-US proximation.

18 Tharoor, *Pax Indica: India and World of 21st Century*. Character and role of "New India" in the "Asian century" is described by India's former foreign secretary, Shashi Tharoor. He maintains, "[I]n the information age, it's not the side with the bigger army, but the one with the better story, that wins." Many would agree that China's dehumanizing (Maoist) anthropology pales in comparison with India's Hindu view of humanity as filled with the dignity, dynamism, and potential of *Atma* (soul), to which Modi's vision and policies ultimately seem to appeal.

Either you're in the game or you're not. This is a reminted national-international take on Kautilya's (*aka* Chanakya) upbeat advice to Hindu leaders *Saam, Daan, Dand, Bhed* (advise/ask, offer/buy, punish, and exploit secrets).[19] If yogic practices are presumed peaceable, think again! The threat is enshrined in Kautilya's ancient, practical wisdom. To engage the New India envisioned by Modi is to confront a self-aware oriental giant, not a card-carrying Western democracy.

Modi's characteristic use of reward and punishment to steer his disputatious cabinet is one of the many ploys he uses to safeguard his position. Modi, it is increasingly recognized, has soft feet of clay. *Indian Express* columnist Tavleen Singh sees "a hint of megalomania" in a leader she admits she once admired. Her book *Messiah Modi?* (HarperCollins, 2020) deconstructs the prime minister's famous suit: Once an icon of his simplicity and frugality, to Singh it has become a threadbare emblem of his political duplicity and an abiding image of his cynical use and abuse of popular Hindu spirituality. Indian democracy, to Modi's critics, has never been so vulnerable to co-option by a totalitarian demagogue and his brownshirt bullies.

Modi's Diplomacy

To set the discussion in context, let's start first with *history*. India was a founding member of the so-called Non-Aligned Movement (NAM).[20] It is now the largest association of independent states (120) who are not formally aligned with or against another perceived superpower. A brainchild of Jawaharlal Nehru and other leaders of newly independent postcolonial nations, it was meant to coordinate activity and safeguard vulnerable national sovereignties in the Cold War era (1947–1991). Non-alignment was invoked by Nehru

---

19 Many Hindu denominations and religious leaders consciously embrace *Saam, Daan, Dand, Bhed* to advance their work. The expression has been profiled again today in a popular, eponymous, Indian soap opera!

20 Built on principles agreed at the Bandung Conference (1955), NAM was formed in Belgrade in 1961. Nehru and the presidents of Ghana (Nkrumah), Indonesia (Sukarno), Egypt (Nasser), and Yugoslavia (Tito) all played a key role in its early years. We should not underestimate the extent to which NAM principles satisfied India's desire for autonomy and self-governance after three hundred years of colonial rule. As Lalvani argues in *The Making of India: The Untold Story of British Enterprise*, the problem was not so much "bad [colonial] governance" as a frustrated nationalist passion for "self-governance"—a point reinforced by India's eagerness to join the newly formed British Commonwealth. Revivalists condemn this as indicative of emotional servility born of colonial abuse.

in 1954 in a speech in Colombo, Sri Lanka.[21] The UN is traditionally seen as the premier agency of international cooperation in the West, and NAM states look inward for diplomatic support and ideological reinforcement. But the world is now changing. We see this already in Modi's handling of the recent Sino-Indian border conflict in the Galwan Valley. Tension with China has given him grounds to revisit the founding principles of NAM and good reason to practice two key principles of Kautilya's practical, political wisdom—namely *Bhed* (Divide: Can China and its dependencies somehow be sundered?) and *Dand* (Punish: Should China be punished—and if so, how?). Modi is quietly confident the US will comply with any adjustment to India's "non-aligned" status that nurtures a closer US-India relationship, and enormous political pressure is increasingly exercised by India's affluent diaspora in US domestic politics. Throw into this mix Modi's Vedic vision and spiritual persona and the diplomatic landscape is set for seismic change.

Next, consider *America's remapping of the Indo-Pacific region*. Though India would be as reluctant as China to admit that US politics impact internal and external affairs, neither country was immune from President Trump's vision for America and America's relationship to the rest of the world. Let's see how these connect, in two specific ways, with the theme of this chapter: (1) Before the Trump presidency, US diplomacy spoke of a geographic region "from Hollywood to Bollywood." Then, in early 2019, Trump spoke of a "free and open Indo-Pacific," with shared values and coordinated policies, as a "beautiful constellation of nations, each its own bright star, satellites to none."[22] This assumes the US can still determine the ground rules for dialogue. Modi's India looks to change a changing world, its values those of New India more than those of the US or Old-World West. (2) Some commentators see more than a projected democratic identity in some of Modi's international relations. There is a clear difference between his engagement with nations the BJP deems "inferior" to India and those deemed worthy of its "superior" attention. His active Vedic spiritual consciousness informs his approach to Russia, Israel, Iran, and Sri Lanka, and is altogether clearer.

---

21 We see this anticipated in a 1946 speech by Nehru: "We propose to keep away from the power politics of groups aligned against one another ... [W]e send our greetings to the people of the US, to whom destiny has given a major role in international affairs ... To that other great nation of the world, the Soviet Union, which also carries a vast responsibility for shaping world events, we send greetings."

22 Leoni, *American Grand Strategy from Obama to Trump*, 214.

India and Other "Spiritual" States

Ancient Hindu greetings help focus the issue addressed in this section: namely, to which states do Modi and the Hindutva BJP offer a diplomatic *nada chhadi* (friendship bracelet) and to which no more than a political *pranaam* (respectful bow)? That is, with whom are leaders of the new Indian *Rashtra* (nation) willing to deal deeply, and with whom will they keep a distance?

1. India and Russia

India has had a long, complex relationship with the former Soviet Union and Marxism. One Ministry of External Affairs official said recently, "Ask any child in India who is India's best friend internationally and they will tell you that it is Russia."[23] The evidence to support this is important. It hopes Russia and India would keep in step against common enemies (at times, China, Pakistan, Afghanistan, and the US).[24] Despite explicit assurances,[25] the 1971 "Indo-Soviet Treaty of Peace, Friendship and Cooperation" never offered the secure mutual, military support of the kind NATO provides to member states. The sheer scale of the Indian military (third largest in the world) suggests that for all Modi speaks the language of peace, he and the BJP are armed for war.

Despite historic differences, harmony now thrives. India has consistently opposed EU and US sanctions on Russia over Ukraine, and Russia supports India's stance on Kashmir. Whereas the USSR once pamphleted India with Marxist propaganda, Goa and Bollywood opened their doors to eager divas and wealthy tourists.[26] Both benefit from this relationship. Russia offers India security

---

23 Commentators recognize the cost to India of its "lost years" after WWII, when the nation had the resources, systems, vision, and personnel to develop strongly, but stalled under a pro-Soviet, "passive-gentle" foreign policy and Nehru's socialist government.

24 India is acutely conscious of the ideological, diplomatic, and economic proximation of Russia and China in the light of US decline and Western hostility. The new Sino-Russian axis is geographically plausible and geopolitically troubling.

25 Article 9 of the Treaty required that each party must refrain from assisting any third party engaged in armed conflict with the other party. If either party was attacked or threatened, immediate consultations would be held to address the threat and ensure peace and security. However, in the same year (1971), the USSR did not deploy forces when India invaded East Pakistan; and India did not support the USSR's invasion of Afghanistan in 1978.

26 Russian love for Bollywood films has a dual nature in post-Independence and present-day New India. While Moscow taxi drivers prefer humming Bollywood songs than speaking English, they are aware, as demonstrated by the endorsement of Modi by Bollywood superstars and the notable silence of their Muslim counterparts, such as Shah Rukh Khan, Saif Ali Khan, and Salman Khan, that behind the glamorous facade lies the grim reality of widespread poverty and political oppression. Films, like religion, can serve as both a source of escapism and a tool for ideological control.

to the north and shares technology for nuclear submarines, while India buys huge amounts of Russian military hardware[27] *and* provides insider intelligence.

Let's return to the specific focus of this chapter: there is a recognizable spiritual chemistry in the character and content of Modi and Putin. Russia's 2014 incursion into Ukraine had as much to do with the ecclesiastical primacy of the Kiev Orthodox Patriarch in historic Mother Russia as with any new geographic, military, or political intention.[28] Likewise, Modi's response to Hindutva/RSS pressure to revoke Article 370 and take back control of more of Kashmir, in Vedic minds ever associated with the era of wealth and prosperity under the ancient Mauryan kings Chandragupta and Ashoka.[29] "New India," like Putin's "New Russia," is inspired by the narrative of an ancient age of glory to which strategic modern alliances (must) subserve.

We understand Modi as much through Russia as India. Both countries deal in large numbers and promote the cohering culture of their historic religious identity. Russia accounts for one-third of the three hundred million Orthodox worldwide, and Russian Orthodoxy is preeminent among the fourteen Orthodox jurisdictions. There has been a substantial revival of Orthodoxy during Putin's presidency.[30] Modi is impressed. Putin talks about a "Russian world" that unites Russian-speaking former Soviet citizens with a strong church and visionary state and finds a direct counterpart in Modi's vision for a revitalized Hindu Rashtra ready to support friends and to unite against common enemies. They use terror to manage friends and let corruption (known and unknown) feather their political and personal nests.[31]

---

27 Though India has diversified its defense partners, Russian supplies account for 70 percent. To some, Russia's *entente* with China's remilitarized regime under Xi Jinping risks an oriental squeeze on India's military might.

28 NB. When Putin celebrated the annexation of Crimea from Ukraine in 2014, he claimed the disputed peninsula was spiritually inseparable from Moscow.

29 This era is usually in mind when writers refer to India's great past.

30 70 precent of Russians self-identify as Orthodox today, in contrast to a mere 30 percent in the Soviet era. Putin has savored the vocation of a spiritual "sugar daddy." His ratings have matched his perceived largesse.

31 Since Modi's rise to power, Patanjali, a company associated with his friend Baba Ramdev, has benefited from approximately $46 million in land discounts in BJP-controlled states, as revealed through a Reuters review of state government documents, interviews with officials, and real estate estimates. Additionally, the company has been granted land free of charge and highlights the influence of money in Modi's Hindutva regime. His anti-corruption campaign, which helped secure votes against the Congress party, is seen by many commentators as increasingly implausible.

2. India and Israel[32]

If there is geographical, military, and spiritual plausibility in Modi's intimate relationship with Putin, his affinity with Israel's long-term prime minister, Benjamin Netanyahu, is more complex but still explicable. History, faith, and culture are again important. An ancient Jewish presence in India, and a shared sense of nation, family, and deal-making, create a dynamic connection between Hindus and Jews.[33] Modi's relationship with and respect for the Jews is in keeping with historic Hindu inclusivity and civility.

In 2017, Modi became the first Indian prime minister to visit Israel. As with Russia, there is a *significant* history in Indo-Israeli relations. Both nations share a recent story of division along cultural and religious lines. An Indian Congress government rejected the partitioning of Palestine in 1947 and opposed Israel's joining the UN in 1949. Hindu nationalists, however, gave support to a Jewish homeland. Hindu Mahasabha[34] leader Vinayak Damodar Savarkar, visionary behind Hindutva philosophy, endorsed the formation of a Jewish state on moral and political grounds and denounced India's opposition to Israel's joining the UN.

Madhav Sadashiv Golwalkar, second *Sarsanghchalak* (chief) of the RSS, admired Jewish nationalism and believed Palestine filled Judaism's quest for identity.[35] A shared sense of land and nationhood still shapes Modi's relationship with Israel. His 2017 visit was pronounced historic in both Jerusalem and New Delhi. Modi committed to construct an Indian cultural center in Tel Aviv, gave a televised talk to expatriate Indians, and offered OCI (Overseas Citizen of India) cards to those completing mandatory (twenty-four to thirty-two months) Israeli National Military Service. Effective "soft diplomacy" and a close personal relationship between the two leaders can be seen in everything from Israel naming a new "Modi Chrysanthemum" to Netanyahu calling on fellow Israelis during the COVID crisis to "adopt the Indian *namaste*." Like many world leaders today, Modi and Netanyahu have clear, pragmatically fluid spiritualities and bolster a weak rating at home by a timed trip and judicious photocall.[36]

---

32 This chapter was written before the 2024 war between Hamas and Israel in the Gaza region.
33 Though a religious minority, Jews have not been targeted as in other parts of the world. Baghdadi Jews first settled in Gujarat in the eighteenth century. Many, like the Sassoon family, have amassed vast wealth.
34 The Mahasabha party was founded in 1915 to protect the rights of the Hindu community, after the British administration in India granted the Muslim community their own electorate.
35 India recognized the State of Israel on September 17, 1950.
36 We should not underestimate Modi's support. An August 2020 poll gave him a 78 percent outstanding/good rating. Increased pressure on the media by the BJP renders much news coverage politically suspect.

3. India and Iran

It is to Modi's political credit that he has managed to consolidate his relationship with Israel at the same time as wooing Iran. We should again perhaps not be surprised. Casting himself in the role of an Indian Ayatollah, pronouncing infallible judgments, claiming and wielding ultimate authority, and all the while demonstrating a deep (though to some, artificial) spirituality that embodies the traditional ideals of devout Hindu followers. While others work, and make mistakes, he rules supreme talking the talk and living the life.

With established Parsi and Zoroastrian communities in India, we might expect strong links between India and Iran.[37] Independent India established diplomatic relations with Iran in 1950, but during the Cold War India looked to the USSR and Iran to the US. Now we find radical Hindu India tendering a hand of friendship to radical Islamic Iran. The implausibility of this is as great as its significance, but the relationship is far from straightforward.

When Modi visited Tehran in May 2016, talks focused on bilateral connectivity, energy, infrastructure, and trade. Iran is a useful and strategic ally. It offers natural resources and ready access to North Africa, Central Asia, Afghanistan, and, crucially, to the "epicenter" of its terrorist threat—Pakistan. But neither country feels obligated to the other. On the eve of Modi's visit to Israel (July 2017), Ayatollah Khamenei urged Muslims in Kashmir to repudiate oppressors and in 2019 Modi spoke out against the revocation of Article 370 and passing of the new Citizens Amendment Act.[38] For its part, India pursues its stake in the Arab world (where many potential Modi voters live)[39] and denounces the US drone strike that killed the commander of the Iranian Quds Force, Qassem Soleimani. The bilateral bonds between

---

37 When Arab invaders attacked Zoroastrian communities in Persia, spiritual migrants fled to India. India is now home to the largest community of Parsi Zoroastrians worldwide. Parsis played a significant role in India's business community, entertainment industry, and military—and continue to do so. Though a religious minority, the status and connections of Parsis (tend to) protect them against oppression by the ruling BJP.

38 Ayatollah Khamenei tweeted during the protests that followed the CAA (2019): "The hearts of Muslims all over the world are grieving over the massacre of Muslims in India. The govt of India should confront extremist Hindus & their parties and stop the massacre of Muslims in order to prevent India's isolation from the world of Islam." Vedic followers of Modi found this censure inspirational.

39 India has a significant history with Iraq. In 1991, India opposed the use of force against Iraq and facilitated the evacuation of 170,000 Indians on the eve of the war. During the second week of the war, India declined to refuel military planes bound for Iraq. In August 2002, Saddam Hussein reaffirmed Iraq's unwavering support for India's stance on Kashmir. The relationship between India and Iraq goes beyond economic interests, as personal, cultural, and fraternal ties have influenced their non-aligned association.

India and Iran involve more than a *pranaam*, as their survival of recent international criticism (and India's reported exclusion from the construction of the Chabahar-Zahedan rail line) would seem to confirm.[40]

Two specific incidents shed light on the unique character of Modi's relationship with Iran. In January 2019, Iran's foreign minister visited New Delhi. While there, his words struck a chord with PM Modi: "The US looks at things from their perspective, not from the perspective of this region. The killing of Qassim Suleimani shows ignorance and arrogance; 430 cities across India saw protests against the killing of Suleimani."

Ever the opportunist, Modi saw that his relations with Iran had new domestic potential. His *pro*-US stance must never undermine his electoral base: he must be, and more importantly, be *seen* to be, the strong spiritual leader of and for *all* India. The fact that the large Shia Muslim community in India[41] supports Modi safeguards his reception by Ayatollah Khamenei and President Rouhani.[42] Second, during his visit to Iran in 2016, Modi gave Ayatollah Khamenei a rare seventh-century copy of the Qur'an attributed to the Prophet Mohammed's son-in-law, Hazrat Ali (b. 601 CE). As Modi knows, symbols speak.[43]

---

40 Much could be said of India's construction of Iran's new Chabahar Port (which will provide access to the oil and gas resources in Iran and Central Asia). India is the third-largest consumer of oil in the world. India's participation in the project was in part to counterbalance China's strong economic ties with Iran and its building of Gwadar Port in Pakistan's neighboring Balochistan Province. To the relief of India's elite business community, anxious about souring US-Iranian relations, delays in India's construction led to its being dropped from the project in July 2020.

41 Confusingly, the Indian Shia community now has its own RSS (*Rashtriya Shia Samaj*). At its regular Tuesday *Bada Mangal* (observed to worship Lord Hanuman), it hosts *Bhandara* (community feasts). The ruling BJP and this RSS are well-aware food like finance buys votes and builds ideological and political coherence.

42 Surprisingly, the Shia community supported the construction of the Ayodhaya Hindu Temple on the site of the demolished Babri Mosque. RSS head Bukkal Nawab was clear: "(The) Shia community will unitedly support the BJP to ensure Modiji becomes PM once again after 2019 elections" claiming that no other party cared for Shia Muslims (18 percent of India's Muslims). Modi's home state of Gujarat has most of India's Ismāʿīlī and Shia *Dawoodi Bohra* population.

43 Note Modi's use of new Hindu names and designations—e.g., Ahmedabad (Islamic) in Gujarat is now Amdavad (Hindu), while British-built Victoria Terminus Station in Mumbai (1878) in 1996 was renamed Chhatrapati Shivaji Terminus after the founder of the Maratha Empire.

4. India and Sri Lanka

To set Modi's approach to Sri Lanka in context: The former Sri Lankan prime minister, Mahinda Rajapaksa, spelled out his foreign policy in his 2005 paper, "Mahinda Chinthanaya."[44] His vision was for a "non-aligned" Sri Lanka that turned "neutrality" into opportunistic economic and diplomatic advantage, both locally and globally. However, in keeping with China's export levels in other South Asian countries (which dwarf India's), Sri Lanka finds itself caught between the economic benefits this brings and the tension it creates with India.[45] But Modi and the Rajapaksa brothers are political realists: India's approach to Sri Lanka is practical, firm, sensitive, and culturally adept.[46] Modi took a call from the Sri Lankan president, who was after a $1.1 billion SWAP loan (in addition to $400 million already owed to SAARC).[47] Modi was reassuring: "[W]e are ready to help under terms that are favorable to Sri Lanka." Time will tell if such *bonhomie* survives.

First, investment, security, and terrorism are not Modi's only interests in Sri Lanka. When Mahinda Rajapaksa visited New Delhi in 2020, Modi made clear his expectation that further steps would be taken toward reconciliation with and integration of the country's Tamil minority.[48] Modi's concern was as much for peace in the region as the promotion of his standing among Tamils in South India. The ethnic and family ties between the north of Sri Lanka and Tamil Nadu are strong.[49] Modi's actions in Sri Lanka have had repercussions at home.

---

44 See https://www.ips.lk/wp-content/uploads/2017/01/Mahindachinthana-2007.pdf.

45 China's involvement in the Hambantota Port project is an example of its debt-trap diplomacy. Sri Lanka borrowed heavily from China to build the port but was unable to repay the debt. As a result, China leased 80 percent of the port for ninety-nine years. This left Sri Lanka heavily indebted to China.

46 By offering project aid that employs local people and increases family incomes, India hopes to match Chinese philanthropy while avoiding the scale and impersonalism associated with Chinese inventions worldwide.

47 SAARC (South Asian Association for Regional Cooperation) is a regional intergovernmental organization and geopolitical union of states in South Asia (Afghanistan, Bangladesh, Bhutan, India, the Maldives, Nepal, Pakistan, and Sri Lanka). As of 2022, SAARC comprises 3.3 percent of the world's area, 22.6 percent of the world's population, and 4.4 percent (US $4.1 trillion) of the global economy. SAARC funds helped Sri Lanka address its crippling foreign exchange crisis. Modi is well aware of the demographic, economic, and strategic significance of SAARC.

48 Sri Lanka's 13th Amendment established Sinhala and Tamil as official languages, with English as a link language. A civil war that left one hundred thousand dead, including forty thousand Tamils, has blighted Sri Lanka's global profile. In 2014, India's Modi pressed for a UNHRC resolution against alleged war crimes, but Sri Lanka survived censure with support from Russia, China, Pakistan, and some African countries. Sri Lanka's sense of indebtedness has gone beyond financial obligation.

49 With its capital of Chennai, Tamil Nadu is the tenth-largest state in size, with the sixth-largest

Second, Sri Lankan Tamils are mostly Hindus, although a significant number of them are Christian. Modi's Hindu revivalist outlook shapes his perspective on these Sri Lankan Tamils. History tells Modi that the Chola Empire (300 BC–1279 AD) saw Indian expansionism reach into Sri Lanka.

Third, Modi sees political and electoral advantage in siding with Sri Lankan Tamils. During his November 2019 visit, he stated, "I am confident that the government of Sri Lanka will carry forward the process of reconciliation, to fulfill the aspirations of the Tamil for equality, justice, peace, and respect. It also includes the implementation of the 13th Amendment."

Self-interest, as much as altruism, drives this agenda. To date, the BJP has succeeded in uniting the Hindu vote, but not so in Tamil Nadu.[50] Success overseas will, Modi clearly hopes, impress domestic Hindu doubters.

Of the four countries studied here, Sri Lanka arguably poses the greatest challenge, its recently expanded Buddhist electoral power base being as interested in promoting its agenda regionally as Modi is the Indian Rashtra.

Conclusion

In Narendra Modi, analysts meet a deliberately differentiated spiritual leader who expects to be taken seriously and who unhesitatingly challenges prevailing cultural and religious norms. In him, we find—and do not find— what we are looking for. As I have argued in this chapter, we only begin to explain his decision-making and behavior at home and abroad if we come to terms with both the style and formal content of his Vedic heart and mind.

That Modi has built effective partnerships with sovereign states that do not share his cultural outlook but do share his "spiritual" priority is a testimony to his political and personal skills. It is a reminder that the world has changed and "religion" in all its cultural shapes, shades, sizes, and varieties once again is a major factor in contemporary geopolitics. Micklethwait and Wooldridge are right: "Shiva—and any number of other Hindu gods—is back."

---

population (est. 77 million) and second-largest state economy (₹24.85 lakh crore, namely $320 billion). The economy of Tamil Nadu grew by 3.7 precent in 2020–2022, despite the COVID-19 pandemic. Reflecting its ethnic identity, Tamil Nadu's chief minister, M. K. Stalin, is the leader of the influential Dravidian political party DMK (*Dravida Munnetra Kazhagam*).

50 Modi's difficulties in Tamil Nadu have been myriad. He struggles to combat its independent, southern spirit and anti-Hindi culture. As elsewhere, critics represent the BJP and RSS as northern and upper caste. At the last election, opposition-party slogans were blunt: "Go back, Modi!"

5

Challenges of Pastoring Hindu Converts

Dr. Martin Alphonse

It was my honor to be called again to a threefold Christian ministry of being a pastor and lecturer or professor in (1) a Bible college or seminary; (2) an advanced evangelistic leadership training institute; and (3) as an itinerant evangelist-at-large. I carried out all three ministries almost simultaneously in the three nations I served—namely, India, Singapore, and the US. In all of these contexts, my concurrent focus has been on reaching Hindus for Christ, beginning with a grassroots-level ministry of church planting among nonliterates in a Hindu village in Tamil Nadu, India, to presenting the gospel to Hindu intelligentsia and technocrats in highly sophisticated and prestigious learning centers like the Indian Institute of Technology. I was also honored to serve actively for a few years by teaming with learned men in the field of evangelism among Hindus in the global Lausanne Working Group on Reaching Hindus.

Based upon these exposures to and involvement in efforts to evangelize Hindus and to nurture them in the Christian faith after they accept Christ, I have learned a few important lessons regarding effective evangelism among Hindus. In this chapter I aim to share some of my insights on the challenges of nurturing and providing pastoral care for Hindu converts to Christianity.

I have encountered a few limitations while writing this scholarly article on the topic. One, while numerous literary sources are available on the methods or models of evangelizing Hindus, not much has been written about nurturing them in the Christian faith. Hence, to the likely disappointment of some readers, I am unable to quote directly from other sources on how to provide pastoral care for Hindu converts. Almost everything I write here is based on my own limited exposure to and involvement in providing the needed care for a few Hindu converts during my tenure of pastoral ministry among them in a few churches in India and Singapore—and in my frequent pastoral visits to neighboring Malaysia—and the US.

Two, since some of the things I share here are culturally delicate and perhaps politically sensitive, all names and locations have been altered to preserve anonymity.

Three, I do not presume to offer specific, concrete ways of caring, but only share my thoughts based on some challenges I have faced in pastoring Hindu converts in my pastoral constituency as well as my acquaintances outside of it. Hence, I would very much appreciate your understanding of the generalizations in some of the materials presented here.

Assisting Them in Their Worldview Change

To a common reader, the term *worldview* may be simply defined as "the way people view the world around them." In technical terms, cultural anthropologist Paul Hiebert defines worldview as the "fundamental cognitive, affective, and evaluative presuppositions a group of people make about the nature of things, and which they use to order their lives."[1] One's worldview has its roots in the given philosophy—or to use a better term, in the "way of life" of the community in which the person was raised and in which the person continues to live. The twofold process by which a person's way of life, or lifestyle, evolves is (1) by enculturation, which is the "gradual acquisition of the characteristics and norms of a culture or group" in which the person lives; and (2) by acculturation, which is "assimilation to a different culture."

Religious conversion always takes place at the core level of change in one's worldview, by which a person decides to renounce the fundamental religious beliefs and practices he or she has been brought up with by the process of enculturation (Hinduism) and embrace a new set of religious beliefs and practices by the process of acculturation (Christianity). It is not that every Hindu who decides to become a Christian abruptly walks away from all of his or her former beliefs of Hinduism and is transformed into a

---

1 Hiebert, *Transforming Worldviews*, 15.

full-fledged Christian overnight. It is quite a long process in most cases of conversion, if not in all cases. A genuine conversion from one religion to another is fundamentally a transformation in one's worldview, which is the most difficult change to cope with. A number of Hindu converts continue to oscillate between their former Hindu worldview and their new Christian worldview.

For example, Hinduism can be perceived broadly at three levels or categories—namely, (a) *Philosophical Hinduism*, which tries to define the nature of Cosmic/Universal Reality, or Truth, in various ways: (1) *Advaita* (that Truth is monistic or non-dualistic), as expounded by Adi Sankara; (2) *Vishist Advaita* (that Truth is a qualified non-dualism), as taught by Madhva; and (3) as *Dvaita* (that Truth is Dualism), as propagated by Ramanuja. In this category of Hinduism, God, or *Brahma*, is considered primarily a Supreme Being, or Existence, not a personal God.

Then (b) *Religious Hinduism*, which believes in the personhood of God as represented by a hierarchy of gods and goddesses, beginning with the *Trimurthy* of *Brahma*, *Vishnu*, and *Shiva* at the helm, scaling down to a pantheon of 330 million *avatars*, or incarnations, of *Vishnu* and *Shiva*. These multitudes of gods and goddesses are worshiped by the respective devotees daily.

And (c) *Popular Hinduism*, which is a blend of belief in the personal gods and goddesses of Religious Hinduism and primitive, animistic beliefs in spirits, ghosts, and demons, and their daily interaction with humans, especially devotees.

As evidenced by a few cases of my acquaintance, when Hindus decide to convert to Christianity, contingent upon which category of Hinduism they had earlier belonged, the converts tend to bring with them some, if not all, of the fundamental presuppositions of Hindu thought—as summarized by the *Introduction to World Religions*: "the cyclical nature of time, an essential connection between microcosmic and macrocosmic levels of reality, (and) a principle of causality."[2] A most common belief among almost all Hindus worldwide is in *Karma Samsara*, the cyclical nature of life by an endless cycle of birth, rebirth, or transmigration. According to this bedrock Hindu doctrine, everything good or bad that happens to a person existentially in this life (which is a reincarnation from a previous life) is a result of the good or bad that person had committed in his or her previous life. It is either a reward or recompense.

---

2 Partridge, *Introduction to World Religions*, 175.

The doctrine of *Karma* plays a dominant contributive role to the presuppositions of the factor of the cyclical nature of time as well as the principle of causality. When things begin to get tough in life—such as a broken marriage or even divorce, prolonged illness, or barrenness of a married daughter—some Hindu converts struggle with the question of whether their *Karma* is still catching up with them. Their questions remind us of the question the disciples asked Jesus concerning a man born blind: "Rabbi, who sinned, this man or his parents, that he was born blind?" (John 9:2 NIV).

In the case of Hindu converts their question of causality is something like: "Is this the result of my *karma* or my family's *karma* in our previous birth?" More often than not, cases like this are common among Hindus who got carried away by popular preachers of the so-called "prosperity gospel" who promised them a problem-free life in Christ. Many Hindus are persuaded by such an attractive misrepresentation of the Gospel and decide to follow Christ. It takes an enormous sum of patience and understanding on the part of the pastor in cases of such casualties, to counsel them in the truth that Christian discipleship is fundamentally a matter of taking up one's cross and following Christ daily (Luke 9:23).

Helping Them Transcend Caste-Consciousness

Caste consciousness among the members of the body of Christ has been the most divisive issue in the churches in India for centuries. The unacceptability of fellow members as equals still dominates the mindset of Christians and speaks loud and clear when it comes to matters of electing church leaders both from among the clergy and the laity. Its impact has not spared the Diaspora Indian churches either. Caste division is foundational to the Hindu social structure.

Yet some missiologists have strongly advocated making use of the positive elements of the Hindu social structure of caste as a productive strategy for an effective ministry of church planting. It was spearheaded by Donald McGavran, a missionary to India who was widely acclaimed as the architect of the Church Growth Movement in the twentieth century. He vigorously promoted the Homogenous Unit Principle (HUP) to plant churches along caste lines or ethnic people groups. His basic argument was that "Men like to become Christian without crossing racial, linguistic, or class barriers."[3]

---
3 McGavran, *Understanding Church Growth*, 223.

So McGavran suggested that we should explore ways and means of planting churches within the social boundaries which people do not want to cross to become Christians.

The HUP for Church Planting and Church Growth became *both* a globally supported *and* a globally opposed principle. McGavran answered his critics by asking them, "In view of this great readiness to change should we think of the propagation of the Gospel as a process of change by which all peoples and cultures are gradually transformed into a new and beautiful Christian culture?"[4] On the one hand, McGavran was right in saying that a number of men and women—indeed, if not all—like to become Christians without crossing racial, caste, linguistic, or class barriers. But on the other hand, when a Hindu convert joins an already caste-divided or a highly caste-conscious church, which way would he or she turn? Now it becomes the singular responsibility of the pastor of the church to work patiently with converts so that they would "gradually (be) transformed into a new and beautiful Christian culture," as McGavran advocated.

The problem with this advocacy is that there are two types of Hindu converts in regard to the caste mindset in the Diaspora churches. First, those Hindus from higher-caste backgrounds have renounced every theological belief of Hinduism relating to its system of divinity and have embraced the God of the Bible as their one and only God of worship. However, a number of them are still heavily conscious of their former caste identity and are very reluctant—if not completely opposed—to mingle freely with the members of the Christian community, especially with those of a lower caste or class. Their caste consciousness is quite evident when they share their story of conversion. They almost invariably begin with an opening line such as "I was born and raised in a Hindu _____ (name of the high caste) community."

Of course, we can give them the benefit of the doubt that they say so in pure innocence by simply "stating a fact." However, I have hardly ever heard a testimony by Hindu converts from a so-called lower caste ever mentioning their caste background in their conversion story. I wonder if they do not mention their former caste identity because they are too embarrassed to mention in public their former painful, degraded caste identity. Instead, almost invariably they begin with an opening line like "I was born and raised in a Hindu family."

---

4 McGavran, 223.

Second, when converts from a so-called lower caste join the church, it becomes very disheartening to them when they find some members quite politely trying to maintain a "social distance" from them. In a few cases, I have sadly watched some of them eventually drop out of that particular church and move on to another one where they might find more comfortable acceptance. Of course, at such times, it is not possible to reprimand the congregation publicly or point a finger of accusation at any one individual or a few persons because those who left didn't specifically mention the reason why they left. Yet the hidden reason is evident to any caring pastor who is culturally aware of the menace of the divisiveness of caste or the dynamics of linguistic parochiality, as the case may be, having played a devastating role in a given church context.

Here again, it takes enormous effort, patience, and understanding on the part of the pastor to counsel both categories of caste-conscious Hindu converts and the caste-conscious members of the church that Christian discipleship is fundamentally a matter of love and unity in the body of Christ and that we need to learn to "celebrate the otherness in the other people," as the global pastor Samuel Kamaleson, used to preach, and as the legendary missionary to Hindu India, E. Stanley Jones used to declare that "everyone who belongs to Christ belongs to everyone who belongs to Christ." The Apostle Paul affirmed this in Galatians 3:28 (NIV), "There is neither Jew nor Gentile, neither slave nor free, nor is there male nor female, for you are all one in Christ Jesus," and in Colossians 3:11 (NIV), "Here there is no Gentile or Jew, circumcised or uncircumcised, barbarian, Scythian, slave or free, but Christ is all, and is in all."

In all this, the pastor's great hope is that one day, as McGavran himself hoped, all peoples and cultures will be gradually transformed into a new and beautiful Christian culture.

Caring for Those Who Are Ostracized

One of the most painful reasons why people want to become Christians without crossing cultural and class barriers, as McGavran observed, is the fear of ostracization from their community. In the "honor and shame culture" of Hinduism, many young people pay a huge price for their decisions to follow Christ, get baptized, and join the membership of a church. They face several forms of ostracization, such as (a) complete expulsion from their home; (b) even if they are allowed to stay at home, they still face exclusion from participation in social events in the family or the families of their relatives. They are treated as *persona non grata*. (c) The worst nightmare of Hindu parents, especially of a higher caste, is the fear that when their children embrace Christianity the prospects of finding a suitable marriage partner for their sons and daughters within their caste would be impossible. (d) And eventually the honor of the entire family would be placed at stake.

As a safeguard against potential ostracization, some Hindu converts have resorted to the following two strategies: First, following the advocacy of McGavran, they plant a homogenous unit church with membership open exclusively to members of the same caste or community. A case in point is a couple I have gotten to know: She is a Hindu convert from a high caste, and her husband is the son of a Western missionary couple to an Asian country. They have founded a church exclusively for a distinct high-caste Hindu community in a city in Europe. They said the church is doing well in outreach ministry among the Diaspora Indians of that distinct caste, and they can take good care of the members of the church, both spiritually and socially. However, Diaspora Indians from other castes in the city are normally not contacted. Their answer was rather vague when I asked if Indians of other castes would be welcome if they showed up for their church worship service and other activities.

Second, some parents who are Hindu converts have compromised their Christian faith by finding Hindu spouses for their Christian sons and daughters, according to Hindu rites. In some cases, the Hindu spouse has been formally, but of course only peripherally, "converted" to Christianity by some form of baptism, and the marriage happens in the church, according to "Christian" rites. Once the wedding ceremony is over, in most cases the Hindu spouse continues to live a Hindu way of life while the Christian partner continues to live a Christian way of life. Sadly, they have fallen into the stream of syncretism. On the one hand, in the church, they spiritually worship the God of the Bible. On the other hand, socially they actively participate in the social customs, such as marriage and cremation events, of their relatives. From a Christian perspective, the theological risk of participation in Hindu social events is that there is hardly any Hindu social custom that is not attached to some strong spiritual elements, especially idolatry.

Under the circumstances, it is one thing to be the pastor of a church in which there are absolutely no converts from other faiths. It is a different ballgame entirely to be able to deal with Hindu converts who still struggle with syncretistic tendencies to some extent. Other Hindu converts willingly face the reality of ostracization and learn to live with it. They have already counted the cost of taking the path of discipleship and going through the socially excruciating pain of ostracization in one form or another as discussed earlier. If they have been completely disowned by their family, the church is now their only family. The pastor, in the spirit of a true shepherd, cares for such wounded sheep and provides the holistic support these persons need spiritually, physically, emotionally, and socially.

Deliverance from Demonic Oppression

Speaking about demonic oppression in the context of pastoring Hindu converts might sound rather strange to many readers who are not familiar with the category of Popular Hinduism. Most popular writers and scholars on Hinduism normally cover various aspects of Hindu thought in its more sophisticated forms, such as the Philosophical Hinduism represented by *Jnana Marg* (Way of Knowledge, including *Yoga*) or the visually appealing forms of Religious Hinduism expressed by religious *Bhakti* (Way of Devotion and Worship) and the existential daily struggles emerging out of *Karma Marg* (Way of Action and Transmigration).

Unfortunately, not much is said about the implications of Hindu phenomenology as embedded in Popular Hinduism. It is "the living everyday religion of Hindus … (which) is made up of the worship of not only their innumerable gods but also of objects like the cow and the serpent, trees and plants, rivers and planets, and tools and grain" … and … "belief in evil spirits."[5] It is the most common form of Hinduism practiced by millions of Hindus in the villages of India and by almost all tribal communities. The majority of Christian missionary work in India is being carried out among the adherents of Popular Hinduism. It is widely prevalent among Hindus around the world, in countries like Sri Lanka, Singapore, Malaysia, Fiji Islands, and South Africa, to name a few.

Of a matter of importance to the discussion here is that quite many Hindu converts from this brand of Hinduism continue to experience demonic oppression even after they have publicly professed their faith in Christ and have been baptized and incorporated into the membership of the church. Still, some Hindu converts are frequently tortured by nightmares "by a serpent which is coiled around my neck and is trying to kill me." Some

---

5 Ayrookuzhiel, *The Sacred in Popular Hinduism*.

are physically attacked by strange kinds of sickness which are medically incurable. Even highly advanced medical technology in the United States is unable to diagnose the health issues in such cases.

In general, the Western mindset quickly assigns such unexplainable phenomena to the domain of psychiatry or psychology and encourages therapeutic counseling. With due respect to scientific opinions, the question is what if what the Hindu converts are going through relates to the domain of "spiritual warfare"? Paul vividly describes this in Ephesians 6:10–17 (NIV), especially verse 12: "For our struggle is not against flesh and blood, but against the rulers, against the authorities, against the powers of this dark world and against the spiritual of evil in the heavenly realms."

It seems that to most Westerners, including Christian leaders, pastors, and professionals in academia, any reference to the reality of demonic oppression in the postmodern era only belongs to the third world, and not to the Western world as such. Such thinkers have forgotten what C. S. Lewis, one of the greatest Christian thinkers of the West, cautioned the church in 1942:

> There are two equal and opposite errors into which our race can fall about the devils. One is to disbelieve in their existence. The other is to believe and to feel an excessive and unhealthy interest in them. They themselves (the devils) are equally pleased by both errors.[6]

Hence, regarding the spiritual warfare in Ephesians 6:10–17, the reality of the painful experience the converts go through is theologically comprehensible. No matter how others around them, including members of the church, may or may not be able to understand the mindboggling narrative of the convert's struggles, as far as the Hindu convert is concerned it is the devil who is waging a war to reclaim their soul by launching weapons of nightmarish dreams and physical illness on them. Unless a pastor is knowledgeable in the area of spiritual warfare, as described in Ephesians 6, it will be extremely difficult for him to be able to comprehend fully the struggles of the Hindu convert in context and cater meaningfully and sympathetically to the needs of such victimized Hindu converts. In his book *The Invisible War*, an American pastor Chip Ingram, who has dealt with members of his church who were under demonic attack, offers valuable insights on how to win over the "invisible" enemy in spiritual warfare by the "invincible" power of Christ.[7]

---

6 Lewis, *Screwtape Letters*, 19.
7 Ingram, *Invisible War*.

Conclusion

The challenge to provide holistic care for Hindu converts in his congregation is enormous for pastors. However, there are particular types of Hindu converts who can be a great source of strength and support to the pastor in times of his struggle to care for the suffering converts. The resourceful converts are mainly among those who have followed the *Bhakti Marg* (Devotion to a Personal God) of Religious Hinduism. They have passionate devotion to Jesus Christ and are soaked in prayer. They are eager to rally around the pastor and help him understand the dynamics of "market" Hinduism, interpret the mindset of a common Hindu, the meaning of various rites and rituals Hindus follow, and the distinction between Hindu culture and Hindu theological beliefs. I have been greatly helped by some of such Hindu converts drawn from the *Bhakti* tradition to cater to the needs of other Hindu converts as described above.

The Home Church among Hindu Households in Diaspora

Dr. Danny Sathyadass

Many Hindu households tend to practice the "one another" passages of the Bible much better than nominal Christian households. It is against this backdrop of close-knit, religious, and successful Hindu families, which generally constitute urban India and the Indian Diaspora, that I attempt to highlight home-church values to possibly help draw urban Hindus to Christ. Phenomenal reports of home-church growth within rural India have been reported,[1] but it does seem more difficult among urbanites.

In providing a brief overview, I will identify seven characteristic features, or values, of home churches, interspersed with insights and precautionary steps; hopefully, this will highlight how the home church might be conducive to Hindu households. I don't claim to offer an exhaustive list, nor do I delve into the details of Hindu culture. These values focus on how they either serve as bridge-builders or how they question the Hindu status quo—or, for that matter, even traditional Christian practices—based upon our experience of home-church planting.

My wife and I adopted the home-church model in 2007, after two years of using conventional church-planting methods in the outskirts of Bangalore. One of the primary motivators to make this change was witnessing the way that small groups of young Christians who worked in call centers, met at odd hours in office cubicles and homes nearby to stay

---
1 Garrison, *Church Planting Movements*, 49.

connected to Christ. Playing a catalytic role and observing the transformation and growth of home churches beyond Bangalore and even the rural sector prompted us to form an apostolic team known as Citylight, which endeavors to spark home-church movements across the world. Subsequently, when we relocated to Dallas, Texas, we began a suburban home church and also trained several leaders to pioneer a network of home churches.

Understanding the Home Church

Whenever the Apostle Paul referred to the church,[2] he referred to an actual gathering, customarily in homes, in a local area. The allusion to the "whole church" in 1 Corinthians 14:23[3] suggests an occasional gathering of multiple home churches from the city, and that the "whole church" was relatively small.[4]

Spontaneity, openness, flexibility, adaptability to changing scenarios, and participation are characteristic features of the house church.[5] The home church, which essentially is a small group, provides a sense of belonging, camaraderie, and fellowship that larger gatherings cannot easily provide.[6] The authors of *Simple Church* state that elaborate multilevel strategies actually hamper growth and productivity.[7] They state, "Many of our churches have become cluttered … so cluttered, that many people are doing church instead of being church."[8] Simplicity is a key feature of the house-church model. Roland Allen stated that "the church reduced to its elements is *a very simple thing*…The organization of *a little church* on the *apostolic model* is *extremely simple*," (italics mine).[9] The home or house church (used interchangeably

---

[2] The concept of a voluntary association of people, gathered for a specific purpose, was not a novel idea that belonged to the church alone. Across the Roman Empire were fraternities that were formed for various purposes, such as sports, mystery cults, and secret societies. Though Paul was a Jew, he didn't adopt the synagogue model, whereby ten men were required for its formation. Neither did he adopt the monastic order, such as the Essene communities that existed throughout the empire. See Banks, *Paul's Idea of Community*, 5–14.

[3] The qualification "whole" would be unnecessary had the Christians met as a single group, which suggests that smaller groups existed in the city. Banks, 35.

[4] Banks, 36.

[5] Snyder, *New Wineskins: Changing the Man-Made Structures of the Church*, 130–31.

[6] The attractional feature of most large churches is either the celebrated preacher/teacher, worship experience, or the programs. Intimate fellowship and a sense of belonging must be created through additional initiatives, which may pose a cultural hurdle for a first-generation Hindu-background believer. A homey atmosphere easily provides the intimacy and fellowship they need.

[7] Rainer and Geiger, *Simple Church*, 8–11.

[8] Rainer and Geiger, 19.

[9] Allen, *Spontaneous Expansion of Church*, 156.

here), is therefore a simple and small gathering of Christ-followers who meet in homes or other suitable locations.

Home-Church Values That Help Hindus Draw Closer to Christ

The following overview of seven home-church values, interspersed with insights and precautions, is an attempt to aid Christians who are working among Hindu households. Though not prioritized, these features help to further understand how home churches function.

1. Holy-Spirit Driven

Throughout the book of Acts we take note that the early church grew in the context of prayer and by the power of God's Spirit (Acts 1:8, 14). Today devotion to Christ seems reduced to merely one day of the week—with an emphasis on organizational structures and professionals to carry out various ecclesiastical duties. This does not have much bearing on Hindus, because Hinduism is, in fact, not considered a religion. Dayanand Bharati asserts, "The most basic point to grasp is that Hinduism is not a religion like other religions but a dharma. … dharma is a comprehensive word which includes spiritual, moral, social, and even secular values."[10]

Therefore, an average Hindu could possibly find the early followers of Christ to be more appealing than today's Christians who lean on tradition. Paul Pennington states that "Traditions and denominations can embody fundamental cultural assumptions that are then imposed on believers in other parts of the world unwittingly or sometimes intentionally."[11] In contrast, Bharati claims, "Worship is the pivot on which the entire spiritual life revolves, particularly for Hindus. They never worship just three hours in a week plus … one house prayer meeting."[12] The puja room in their homes, the display of idols in their places of work, and how they pay obeisance as they pass temples, or when they begin their work, provide a glimpse of their constant devotion. Hindus therefore admire persons who are truly devoted to Christ rather than being obligated to tradition or denominational values.

Some Western agencies today give undue importance to achieving a unified process, which is then articulated, branded, and marketed rather than being dependent on the Spirit and appreciating the diversity of methods.

---

10 Bharati, *Understanding Hinduism*, 21.
11 Pennington, *Christian Barriers to Jesus*, 51.
12 Bharati, 74.

For example, gospel tools seem to be reduced to mere laws, beads, cubes, and colorful diagrams. While the creativity is impressive, it does not attract Hindus, especially in the Diaspora. A Sri Lankan Buddhist-background believer from Dallas questioned how Christ can be marketed as one would attempt to sell a used car. We heard of Hindu students warning one another via WhatsApp when "evangelists" approached their residences. Pennington states, rather, that Hindus are "drawn when they see personal devotion in the life of believers. They long for connection with the divine and they are attracted when someone has truly found this in Jesus."[13] This applies to home-church practitioners too, because they can inadvertently rely on cultural forms, without being sensitive to God's Spirit.

2. Obedience-Based Discipleship

It is easy to miss the emphasis or call to obedience in the Great Commission (Matt 28:19–20). "… and teaching them *to obey* everything I have commanded you." The focus is apprenticeship, or discipleship. It doesn't merely involve instruction but emphasizes the need for an application of the truth. Luther, known for his clarion call *sola scriptura*, lamented in his later years that his followers were not as obedient as the Anabaptists,[14] who demanded a "practice of faith," rather than merely giving assent to a "statement of faith" framed by intellectuals.[15]

Home-church practitioners use various methods to ensure obedience to the Scriptures. One such example is the "Discovery Bible Study" method, which is being used by various mission agencies involved with home-church planting.[16] Neil Mims, currently involved with house-church training, states that this method questions and "seeks to strip away much of the 2,000 years of cultural adaptation and change, that make up 'church' today."[17]

The risk of syncretism and doctrinal deviations within the home church is lower compared to a traditional model of the church because mutual accountability is ingrained within it. Discussions, dialogue, and debates are encouraged, thereby preventing individuals from misleading the whole church/group. This approach also counteracts the Hindu "guru culture," where the guru's/teacher's opinion is taken as God's word. The collaborative

---

13 Pennington, *Christian Barriers to Jesus*, 182.
14 Bender, "Anabaptist Vision," 42.
15 Sathyadass, "Study of the Process of Discipling Listeners," 158.
16 Watson and Watson, *Contagious Disciple Making*.
17 Neill Mims, Personal Interview on Feb 22, 2021.

learning approach of Discovery Bible Study ensures that the authority lies with Scripture rather than in one teacher's interpretation.

3. Empowered Rather Than Controlled

The Apostle Paul did not micromanage or embroil himself with administrative responsibilities and social projects or build extensive hierarchical structures to manage various needs of the church, be they spiritual or physical (Phil 1:15–18). Paul instructed his team members, such as Timothy and Titus, to hand over responsibilities eventually to reliable local believers (2 Tim 2:2). The following example gave us insight as to how we could operate in the future and possibly serve as a guide for others in similar initiatives.

> We were encouraged by the many home churches Srinivas (a Hindu-background believer with some Bible-college training) started through his circle of friends, after we had trained him on aspects of the home church. Eventually, Srinivas started a window-cleaning business through one of our contacts who was eager to train people to serve God bi-vocationally.
>
> As business flourished, Srinivas decided to construct his house with dedicated space allocated for a church building. We feared that the idea of a "church building" would curtail the growth of home churches across the state. Despite our cautionary words, Srinivas chose to go ahead. However, after only a few services, COVID-19 lockdowns were imposed.
>
> Recently I quizzed Srinivas, half expecting to hear a trace of regret. But surprisingly, this initiative exceeded our expectations. I realized my apprehensions were unfounded. Srinivas was indeed wise to have invested his earnings in property when business was good. He could have built a comfortable home in the city, but Srinivas chose to build his house and a multipurpose hall in the village. Apart from worship and training events, the facility was used to tutor schoolchildren, aid women's self-help groups, and offer basic medical care during the pandemic.
>
> Srinivas's house serves as a beacon of hope for the overall development of the village. He had also entrusted the home-church groups in other villages to the young people he had discipled. This was certainly admirable; I had misjudged Srinivas. Our active involvement in this village lasted barely a year, but the work continues to thrive, and it released us to serve as catalysts through other organizations and institutions.

In contrast to Srinivas's initiative, in 1946 a traditional church denomination set up a mission base in the same vicinity. They established a reputed hospital, a school, and a church-planting ministry that incorporated buildings with trained priests as overseers. Though the sacrifice and labour of love are commendable, all responsible positions of authority still lay with the "foreigners" from the neighboring state, even after seventy-five years of active ministry!

Home churches thrive when the onus is on the recipients. They do not need organizational or denominational oversight imposed by outsiders, or knowledge of historical Christianity. Likewise, it is unnecessary to take charge or manage the development of the whole community when reaching out to diverse Hindu groups. It would be better to "shadow-pastor" and influence the one individual or family that God leads us to. The local family or household then becomes the persons of peace, or "ambassadors," to influence their community.[18]

Given the fact that the members of the Hindu Diaspora are generally known to be highly disciplined, hardworking, and enterprising, ministry initiatives should be appropriately empowering from inception. Free food and "handouts" are definitely not the best bridge-builders to reach unbelieving Hindus. If any aid is rendered, it should be offered with sensitivity and humility, ensuring the dignity of the recipient.

4. Service and Love Precede Leadership Structures

Various leadership styles that are found in today's church structure sadly contrast with those of Jesus or Paul. Paul did not even use the word *leader*; however, he used the word *service* or *servant*—i.e., *diakonia*, and its related forms.[19] At times it implied "waiting at the table," but most often it is simply "serving," which covers various responsibilities and people.[20] Paul made special efforts to bring new Christians, without delay, into close relationships with other believers—both on the personal level and the corporate level. Essentially, a loving relationship with God and with one another sustained growth.[21]

Indeed, there were threats and conflicts of various kinds, but Paul's intervention was like that of a coach rather than a commander-in-chief.

---

18 Coleman, Harrington, and Patrick, *Revisiting the Master Plan of Evangelism*, 27.
19 Thayer, Διακονία (Diakonia), 1248.
20 Paul's usage of the term *service/servant* as opposed to *leader* was not to emphasize inferiority, but to highlight the dependent character of the work and the responsibility to the person. See Col 4:7; Eph 6:21; Rom 16:1. Banks, *Paul's Idea of Community*, 131–32.
21 Coleman, *The Master Plan of Discipleship*, 59.

Moreover, his assistance was either temporary or from a distance. Conflicts, doctrinal misconceptions, or even blatant disobedience became opportunities to reaffirm and clarify the gospel. Lois Barrett states, "We come to unity and intimacy, not by working around the conflict, but by going through its center. … Conflict is a sign that we are involved with each other."[22] All of this aided discipleship and developed the maturity of the local body of believers.

Hierarchical church systems do not question or address the prevailing caste systems within the Hindu culture, but rather perpetuate them. Commenting on many Indian churches, S. Kappen stated that the only way to recapture the values of the gospel would be to "dismantle cultic-legal hierarchical apparatus" which caters merely to the elite Indian class of people.[23] M. M. Thomas called for Christocentric fellowships around the Bible and the Lord's Table.[24] The home church is essentially a Christocentric fellowship, where leadership is not vested in a few. It inevitably, therefore, has the potential to break down cultural norms that are based on caste or class.

5. *The "Priesthood of Believers"*

Despite the prevalent religious practices of the day, the Apostle Paul did not use the term *priest*.[25] He did not direct instructions to a special class, whenever he did refer to priestly service.[26] He addressed these to the whole body of believers. The Jewish Apostle Paul rejected formal distinctions between official figures and ordinary members in the community.[27] Responsibility was with "every member to play their particular part in the leadership of the community, rather than being the task of one person or a select group."[28] Robert Coleman rightly points out,

> Somewhere in our rush for services, I am afraid that *we have substituted institutional programs for our own priesthood*. Pomp and ceremony all too often have *stifled creativity and individual* expression. Tradition has taken precedence over the guidelines of Scripture. We must get back to the apostolic norm of ministry and mobilize *the whole body of Christ* for action.[29]

---

22 Barrett, *Building the House Church*, 101.
23 Kappen, "Church as Bearer of New Values," 63.
24 Thomas, "Church in India: Witness to the Cross," 11.
25 Thayer, "Thayer's Greek": 2409, Ἱερεύς (Hiereus) – a priest."
26 Bauer, *A Greek-English Lexicon of the New Testament*, 472, 468.
27 Banks, *Paul's Idea of Community*, 131–33.
28 Banks, 138.
29 Coleman, *The Master Plan of Discipleship*, 82, italics mine.

The house-church model generally reflects the open and participatory nature of the early church. The "priesthood of believers" is not merely a theoretical concept, but a core value in practice. It thus has the potential to destroy age-old customs related to class and caste existing within Hindu culture. How different are conventional churches than the Hindu priestly class or Brahmanical system if worship duties are limited to an elite class clothed in distinctive robes?

Sanchita, a Bengali Hindu-background believer, eager to find churches like the New Testament churches she read about, eventually joined our home-church network, along with her family, and learned to host a church in their home. A few years later they relocated to Kolkata, partly to help Sanchita's ailing parents. Though Sanchita's parents are devout Hindus, they were quite open to the couple and their three young children praying regularly in their home. I attended one of their gatherings. On entering their "sanctuary," I was struck by the sight of idols of Hindu gods and goddesses around the house. After being warmly greeted, we were led into a bedroom. The little kids cozied up with their grandfather on the bed. After a brief prayer and a few songs, Sanchita's husband, Alwin, led everyone with one of Tagore's songs.[30] After the song, Alwin got one of the children to read a psalm that had a similar theme to Tagore's poem. The doting grandparents listened with rapt attention while their grandchild read the Scriptures. After discussing the passage, we all prayed and enjoyed Sanchita's mom's home-cooked Bengali meal.

I was struck by the simple intimacy of this family gathering and the way Christ was being made known among the many gods. Although neither Alwin nor Sanchita had been a student in a Bible college or seminary, or shared in detail the need for contextualizing, Alwin's idea of using Tagore's songs resonated with his in-laws and proved to be a good connecting point. Sanchita's dad passed away a few years later, but she was comforted knowing that he was appreciative of Christ, compared to his earlier resistance. The family subsequently moved into Sanchita's mother's home.

While the house was being renovated, an extended family member had the idols removed from the living room to make it more aesthetically pleasing. Sanchita and Alwin saw this as the hand of God at work. Even though idols are still present, peaceful conversations and prayers continue. Today Sanchita's mother, and an aunt who is visiting, join with the family

---

30 Rabindranath Tagore (1861–1941) composed songs that are still widely sung by Bengalis. He won the 1913 Nobel Prize for literature.

as they follow a 365-day Bible-reading plan. Church is not a one-day event, nor is it an event presided by priests or clergy; but it is a lifestyle of worship and devotion to Christ. Sanchita and Alwin's example inspired other young urban couples to recognize the importance of being the church among their extended family members from other faith backgrounds.

6. Home Churches Are Economical—No Buildings

Up until the third century, there seems to be no record of Christians gathering in a holy place for worship. Constantine is noted for "bringing to the Christian faith, the idea of the holy site, which was based on the model of the pagan shrine," and he began a building program that spread throughout the Roman Empire.[31] Frank Viola and George Barna point out that "Constantine is still living and breathing in our minds."[32]

Roland Allen questioned the way ministry was done in the early and mid 1900s. He stated that "the opening of a new mission station has become primarily a financial operation."[33] He highlighted complications such as arousing the suspicion of local authorities who are opposed to Christianity, which then would prompt Christians to appeal for legal protection, which negates the very purpose of ministry. The ministry emphasis gets diluted because the church tends to get caught up with legal, commercial, and management responsibilities instead of focusing on evangelism and discipleship.[34]

One of the primary reasons for the rising persecution of Christians in India today is the suspicion, among many Hindus, of the "financial operations in mission stations." They allege that these financial operations are the West's subtle attempt to break down Hindu culture. Members of the Hindu Diaspora are therefore even more skeptical and resistant. The recent financial scandals of well-known Indian Christian mission agencies have only heightened this suspicion. Bearing this in mind, wouldn't it be wise to adopt a church-planting strategy that has little or no connection to finance or buildings?

---

31 Viola and Barna, *Pagan Christianity*, 20.
32 Viola and Barna, 39.
33 Allen, *Missionary Methods: St Paul's or Ours?*, 52.
34 Allen, 49–61.

7. Home Churches Are Reproducible

Church planting today ranges from "land, building, paid staff, legal documents, to a minimum number of believers" for a new church plant. These are obstacles to a rapid and economical church plant, states David Garrison.[35] Several practitioners and authors, including Tony and Felicity Dale and Wolfgang Simson, call for a rabbit type of church multiplication. Elephants reproduce two or three offspring in three years, while rabbits, theoretically, can grow to 476 million in two to three years.[36]

Trans World Radio-India (TWR), in partnership with Vishwa Vani, experienced the complexity of trying to sustain their traditional church-planting efforts across multiple language groups, diverse cultures, and varying economic backgrounds across the country. Later, TWR adopted the principles of the home-church model[37] and saw thousands of groups emerge within a short period—and impacting neighboring countries as well. During the 2020 pandemic lockdown, they thrived even more—because of their size and simplicity—while conventional churches were forced to keep their doors locked.[38]

Given the size and diversity of Indians within the country and beyond, a standardized conventional approach in a hostile atmosphere can certainly be daunting, if not impossible. However, the simple and small Christocentric groups can spontaneously multiply, bringing about transformation.

Conclusion

Having enumerated the seven home-church values, we observe that all these essentially involve letting go of control. Hindus will be able to discover these values even as they read through Scripture. They will not need to go through the ordeal of trying to decipher the truth through the lens of Christian tradition. This shows that being small and simple is big; striving to be a servant is the way up; obedience to Scripture and being led by the Spirit are essential requirements to following Christ the King, which is what the kingdom of God is all about.

---

35 Garrison, *Church Planting Movements*.
36 Simson, *The House Church Book*, 58; Dale and Dale, *The Rabbit and the Elephant*, xi–xii.
37 Sathyadass, "Study of the Process of Discipling Listeners."
38 Information on TWR-India's impact beyond India and during the COVID-19 lockdown is based on my conversation with TWR-India.

Understanding Hindu Neighbors

Rev. Ashwin Ramani

In a world that is becoming increasingly diverse, we regularly interact with people of other faiths. The workplaces and neighborhoods of major cities in the Western world are a rich expression of a plurality of religions. This is no accident; God, in his sovereignty, has orchestrated this global movement of people for his redemptive purposes. It has created many significant ministry opportunities to engage with people of different ethnicities and religions in our backyards.

When my wife and I immigrated to Canada in 2009, our understanding of a culturally diverse world was limited. The last decade and a half have been a phenomenal learning time in ministering to various people groups in Calgary, a beautiful mosaic of people of various cultures and worldviews. This is typical of most Canadian cities, as they have seen a great influx of people from all around the world. As a result, we now have the world at our doorsteps.

Having come to faith in Jesus from a Hindu Brahmin family in Tamil Nadu, I have a special burden to reach out to Hindus with the love of Jesus Christ. The reflections in this chapter are based on my experience of being raised in a Hindu home in India and my interactions with Hindus in Canada. While the task of building relationships and sharing our faith with people of a different religion may seem intimidating, in reality this is not any different than how we Christians ought to engage with all our neighbors.

In this chapter, I will address the significance of getting to know our Hindu neighbors as individuals before trying to share our faith in Jesus. After laying a biblical foundation, I will provide a snapshot of a typical Diaspora Hindu family. I will then address the importance of building relational bridges. In the final section, I will highlight some practical considerations in engaging Diaspora Hindus with the gospel, and in the process, I hope to answer Western Christians' key questions on this topic. Though written from a Canadian context, the insights offered are applicable to witnessing to Diaspora Hindus everywhere.

The Great Commandment and the Great Commission

Before we turn to missional strategies and the pragmatics of engaging Hindus in our neighborhood, we need to lay a biblical foundation. When evangelism becomes merely a project, it turns into a dull exercise instead of the vibrant and exciting calling that God intended it to be. An externally focused lifestyle is a natural overflow of a thriving personal relationship with Jesus Christ. There is an interplay between the Great Commandment (Matt 22:37–40) and the Great Commission (Matt 28:19–20). The cardinal ethic is love, since our love for God and our love for our fellow humans are inevitably interconnected. Daniel Akin puts it succinctly, "The Great Commission and the Great Commandments—they always go hand in hand."[1] The Great Commandment requires us to love our neighbors, and there is no greater way to love our neighbors than by leading them to Jesus and discipling them.

We also need to keep in mind that our authentic love for God and people is what will captivate the attention of our Hindu neighbors. I believe that verbal proclamation of the gospel of Jesus is nonnegotiable, but our demonstration of Christian character and godliness brings credibility to our evangelistic efforts. Unfortunately, the notion is common even among the Hindu Diaspora that Christians are bent on converting others to their faith. Such prejudices prevent Hindus from having meaningful faith conversations with Christians. A lifestyle that exhibits the love of Jesus is the best apologetic for the gospel. Once we earn the respect of our Hindu neighbors, it will be far easier to engage in spiritual conversations with them. As John Dickson points out,

---

[1] Akin, "Axioms for Great Commission Resurgence," 350.

> In the end, the only way to dispel the story that Christianity has been imperialistic, arrogant and harmful is to offer a powerful counternarrative in our lives, day by day committing ourselves to Jesus' vision of a kingdom marked by meekness, peace-making and love.[2]

The need of the hour is for evangelism that is rooted in humility. It takes the pressure off of us to convince Hindus through purely rational arguments or outsmart them with our brilliance. I have heard numerous testimonies of Hindus being drawn to Jesus primarily because they observed the beauty of Christlike character in the person witnessing to them.

The Great Commandment calls us to be ambassadors of God's love, and the Great Commission urges us to be ambassadors of God's truth. When the truth is communicated in love it is far easier for Hindus to see the splendor of the gospel. This foundational ethic ought to guide all of our efforts in engaging our Hindu neighbors.

Connecting with Hindu Neighbors

It is important not to stereotype Hindus. Hinduism is not based upon a rigid statement of faith. The religion is marked by vast diversity in its beliefs and practices. Even supposedly contradictory ideas can peacefully coexist under the umbrella of Hinduism.[3] This is because they receive their identity not from their beliefs but inherit it from the culture and traditions of the family. Considering the complexities of the Hindu religion, it is a steep challenge for Christians to understand Hindu doctrines and beliefs. However, it is reassuring to know one does not have to master Hinduism to be an effective witness to Hindus. While theoretical knowledge can be helpful, oftentimes it is our heartfelt interest in the individual that has a deeper bearing on their lives.

I want to showcase some typical characteristics of Diaspora Hindus from my interactions. Most Hindus in the Diaspora context uphold the value of pluralism. They demonstrate a healthy regard for all religious beliefs. It is fascinating to note that many Diaspora Hindus who are professionals with advanced education do not put their spiritual beliefs to a rational test. To an outsider, worshiping idols of many gods and goddesses, the origin of the caste system, and believing the mythological tales associated with Hindu deities

---

2 Dickson, *Best Kept Secret of Christian Mission*, 105.
3 Richard, "Hinduism: A Brief Overview," 3.

may seem too simplistic. In contrast, even highly educated Hindus do not scrutinize or challenge these age-old traditions but accept them implicitly. A large majority of Hindus today fall under this latter category. The stories, traditions, and rituals are unreservedly passed on from one generation to another. Another notable feature of Diaspora Hindus is their ability to assimilate with the host culture and to make needed lifestyle adjustments to become contributing members of society. Though they value their cultural heritage, Hindus do not have any intention of proselytizing others. This sets Hinduism apart from other proselytizing religions, like Islam.

Hindus move to the Western world seeking a better life. When I speak to first-generation immigrants, I often ask them what influenced their decision to immigrate. The most common response is, "I came to Canada to give a better future for my children." Inherent in the Hindu mindset is the desire to do well in life and climb the ladder of success. Hindus in the West are quite ambitious and hardworking people. The drive for success is evidenced by many Diaspora Hindus sending their children to the best schools, engaging them in numerous extracurricular activities, and ensuring that every bit of their free time is spent productively. Most Diaspora Hindu families are diligent at work and professionally successful; many become financially affluent. In this quest for material prosperity, spirituality often takes the backseat. At the same time, it leaves a void in their heart that nothing else can fill, which opens doors for spiritual conversations.

Hindus hold on to the view that you are born into a religion and it is not a matter of one's choice. They have a difficult time wrapping their head around making an individual decision to surrender to Christ's lordship. Hindus may have a deep regard for Jesus; although, in their mind, they assign Jesus as the "god" of Christians.[4] They perceive Christianity as a Western religion. Because of this compartmentalization, Hindus believe that they can learn from Jesus' teachings, but the thought of fully embracing the Christian faith does not cross their mind and is considered akin to becoming Western or joining with the colonial masters of the past.

Hindus have a communal, not an individualistic, attitude about life. The family is viewed as the primary support system to help them navigate through daily life. This is one of the reasons why Diaspora Hindus struggle with social isolation. Many first-generation immigrant Hindus have left their

---

4 Shultz, *Disciple Making among Hindus*, 27.

extended families behind to start a new life. The advancements in technology help them interact with their family through video calls, but the relationships are still long-distance, and they desperately miss their extended family. This is a particularly difficult adjustment for many Hindu families. Also, when they face challenging circumstances, they do not have the counsel of their family members and are forced into an individualistic Western culture. This creates an opportunity for Christ-followers to develop meaningful relationships with Hindus and extend support in times of crisis.

Coming from an honor-shame culture, Hindus pay careful attention to their external image and care about how others perceive them. As a result, they value their status in society and want to be respected. It is not uncommon for them to project an image of perfection in talking about their family or work. It is also one of the reasons why they find it difficult to be vulnerable and share their life struggles. Honest sharing happens only within trusted relationships, where they feel safe.

The Hindus I have come across in Canada also demonstrate an element of curiosity to learn about the Christian faith. I am part of the pastoral staff of a large multiethnic evangelical church in Calgary, Alberta. People from our church regularly invite their Hindu neighbors to our church worship services, and they come primarily out of respect for the ones who extended the invitation. Besides, they indicate a desire to experience a church worship service. While inviting Hindus to a church service is admirable, it is naïve to perceive that by coming to church they will automatically become Christ-followers. But this can create a spark for faith conversations in the context of a relationship.

Lastly, Diaspora Hindus have many misconceptions about the Christian faith, which act as roadblocks in their journey to faith in Jesus. Part of getting to know our Hindu neighbors is about helping them ask questions and clarify their doubts. Common assumptions among Hindus include Christians drink alcohol, eat beef, engage in multiple dating relationships, and get paid to convert others to their religion. Christians must correct some of these misconceptions and false assumptions for the light of the gospel to penetrate our Hindu neighbors' hearts. Without putting all Diaspora Hindus in a box, I have attempted to showcase some common traits that are generally true of this community.

Building Relational Bridges

Having explored some distinct traits of average Hindu neighbors that show there is a void in their life that Jesus alone can fill, I want to address how to build relational bridges with Hindus in Diaspora. Any attempt to engage your Hindu neighbors with the gospel should be preceded by earnest prayer. Evangelism flows out of our ministry of intercession, and God uses this time to prepare our hearts, as well as the hearts of those we engage with the gospel.[5]

Hindu neighbors are friendly but can appear to be reserved on the outside because they are removed from their familiar context. Therefore, Christians have to take the initiative to break the ice and extend friendship. The prospect of getting to know your Hindu neighbors may seem daunting, but in reality, you will find that most Diaspora Hindus reciprocate your efforts to get to know them.

My wife and I have experienced great success in our neighborhood in our efforts to build bridges. We are surrounded by diverse cultures and religions, and as far as we know we are the only Christian family in our block. Our attempt to get to know our neighbors started with inviting them to a birthday party for our oldest son. Our neighbors loved the entire experience. Soon a Hindu neighbor decided it was their turn to host a block party. Suddenly the neighborhood came alive, and relationships were built. It is now common for us to exchange food. The transformation we witnessed in our neighborhood testifies to the yearning within the Diaspora families for a community. Christians often hesitate to share food with Hindus, assuming that they have food restrictions. Not all Hindus are vegetarians, although many of them certainly refrain from eating beef. It is always appropriate to ask clarifying questions to avoid any cultural embarrassment. It may be good to start with desserts and baked goods to alleviate any fears of offending your neighbors with food items that are not permissible.

Showing genuine interest in the person and their family is the way to build relationships with any neighbors, and it applies to Diaspora Hindus as well. When we inquire about their well-being and express kindness in practical ways, we remove some of their misapprehensions. Many Diaspora Hindus try to develop and maintain relationships with fellow Hindus. As a result, most Hindus in Diaspora have never been inside a Christian home. The invisible boundary lines segregate the neighborhoods and people in

---

5 Hoogen and Cook, *Pathway to the Soul*, 25.

the West. Christians ought to be the ones who erase these boundaries and ardently advocate for unity and togetherness. This includes reaching out to the Hindus who live in exclusively rich neighborhoods and are part of the elite socioeconomic class.

These are not insurmountable barriers, and all it takes is conscious, prayerful efforts on our part as Christians. It is when we willingly walk outside of our comfort zone that we see the Lord preparing the way for us. The forgotten spiritual gift of hospitality may very well be our best evangelistic tool in the twenty-first-century world. Hospitality turns our homes into places of ministry. Christine Pohl exhorts Christians with these strong words:

> … those who have benefited from the hospitality of God are expected to offer the grace of hospitality to one another and to those they encounter. That the significance of welcome is so tightly condensed in the central meal of the Christian life, the Eucharist, suggests that welcoming strangers is an expression of the Christian community's deepest identity.[6]

Diaspora Hindus are living away from their home countries, and since many have left their extended families behind, they are craving meaningful friendships. When we invite Hindus into our homes, it takes our relationship to the next level. It provides us with a safe environment to get to know someone, understand their personal beliefs, and allow them the opportunity to ask questions. This will build bridges that will ultimately lead to gospel conversations. Because hospitality is highly regarded in Hindu cultures, Christians should also be prepared to receive hospitality.

Much effort has been put into contextualizing the gospel to Hindus, and we can appreciate these strategic initiatives to help Hindus relate to the Christian faith. However, it is pertinent for us to recognize that Diaspora Hindus are unique. In many cases, they have adopted some Western values while retaining some of the convictions they were raised with. Their children are raised in this third culture, which has blended Hindu beliefs with Western ways of life. Taking all these complexities of cultural fusion into account, contextualizing the gospel for Diaspora Hindus can be daunting.[7]

---

6 Pohl, "Responding to Strangers," 98.
7 Paul, "Impacting the Hindu Diaspora in North America," 131.

The traditional ways of contextualization may not always work with the Diaspora population, and we may need an eclectic approach to be relevant. Generally speaking, Westernized Hindus are far more open to the gospel of Jesus than conservative Hindus. The best way to contextualize the gospel to Hindus is by getting to know them personally and tailoring the gospel message to their specific circumstances. Our sharing of the gospel needs to be flexible, Spirit-led, and unhurried. There is no magical formula that can turn Hindus into disciples of Jesus.

Like Jesus, we need to be sensitive to the felt needs of people and respond with compassion. While individuals may appear to have it all together on the outside, they may still be wrestling with issues, especially Diaspora Hindus of the higher social class. Beneath the veneer of affluence, status, strong family, successful career, and several other positive traits lie deep-rooted issues of hurt, pain, and unfulfilled longings. It is as we get to know them as individuals that we will be able to uncover some of these emotional and physical needs.

We don't have to be professional counselors; all it takes is a listening ear and a sincere heart that demonstrates empathy. One of the best ways to help Hindus in this area is by offering to pray for them and giving them biblical counsel. Interestingly, Hindus value the Bible as a holy book, listen respectfully to what it has to say, and are quite open to receiving blessings from God. This is an opportunity for Christ-followers to help them encounter the risen Christ who is active today. If there is no room for the supernatural in our Christian theological understanding, our evangelistic efforts toward Diaspora Hindus will be greatly undermined.

Practical Considerations

Here are some practical considerations that will serve you well in your engagement with the Hindu Diaspora.

1. Building relationships with our Hindu neighbors and exchanging hospitality needs to be our first goal. Once a relationship of trust has been established, one could invite them to Christian events like a Christmas program at church, an Easter celebration organized by a Bible Study group, or even an Alpha Course. However, church-based programs and events may not be the best starting point, as they often conjure fear. Homes are better suited to minister to Hindus than church buildings.

2. In the North American context, it is common for Christians to introduce their Hindu friends to other Christians from a South Asian background. One should not assume that they are better equipped to share the gospel. By being their neighbor, your Christian witness will always remain of paramount importance. In Paul's message to the Athenians in Acts 17:24–28, he talked about God appointing the precise place where people live. God has not only chosen the place where we live, but he has also handpicked our neighbors! We need to undertake the God-appointed role of being the bearer of the good news to our neighbors.

3. If you invite Hindus to church activities, they may reciprocate by inviting you to some Hindu ritualistic ceremonies conducted commonly in their homes. A well-known dilemma in Christian-Hindu interactions revolves around whether we can partake of food that has been offered to the Hindu idols. Christians should enthusiastically visit Hindu homes and enjoy the warmth of their hospitality. At the same time, we can respectfully decline to participate in any Hindu ritualistic ceremonies without offending their sentiments. In doing so, we are clarifying that we are not pluralists who believe all religions are acceptable pathways to reach God. As far as eating food offered to idols, the Apostle Paul makes clear that partaking of it does not affect our relationship with God (1 Cor 8:7–8). It is a matter of individual discernment.

4. Patience is key when it comes to ministering to Hindus. We need to be in step with the Spirit and surrender our preferred timeline. Changes happen gradually, as Hindus start praying to Jesus as one of the gods before making the profession of faith in Jesus as the exclusive way of salvation. Hindus surrender their lives to Jesus in stages, and it cannot be a rushed experience.[8]

5. We need to move away from one-off gospel presentations to a conversational dialogue about spiritual truths. The brief opportunities to share our faith come by way of passing conversations, so we need to capitalize on them.[9] John Dickson articulates as: "God-talk is brief, casual, passing references

---

8 Paul, "Impacting the Hindu Diaspora in North America," 133.
9 Dickson, *Best Kept Secret of Christian Mission*, 180.

to the faith in everyday conversation. It is not necessarily designed to initiate conversations about Christianity; it is simply part of being a relaxed and natural Christian. It is a refusal to participate in the corporate inferiority complex that plagues many in our churches."[10] God can use those passing conversations to impact a Hindu deeply. It arrests their attention and helps them see the genuineness of our faith.

6. While secularism has begun to infiltrate the Diaspora Hindu culture, there are still some who are genuinely seeking spiritual truths. Some of the most fruitful gospel conversations I have had are with Hindus who are desperately looking for communion with God. A Hindu background believer from our church introduced me to her husband, who was still a devout Hindu. He told me about his spiritual pursuit of truth by way of meditating for hours every day. The quest for true peace and the desire to know God marked his life, leading to intensely rigorous spiritual practices. In the course of our conversation, he fully resonated with my reasoning that God is not hiding from his creation, but rather he delights to reveal himself to all who are sincerely seeking. The picture that I painted of God knocking at the door of his heart waiting for him to open his heart impacted him profoundly. We need to seize these God-orchestrated moments and boldly communicate the truth.

7. Christians in the Western world need to confront the unhealthy prejudices that exist among other Christians regarding immigrants. It appears that many Christians do not realize God's hand in the immigration process and the global movement of people. This has led to some Westerners fearing that immigrants are changing the fabric of the Western world. It has been disheartening to hear Christians calling for people of other faiths to leave the country because they are spreading their false beliefs. Such deep-rooted prejudice minimizes our evangelistic effectiveness and hinders the great work God wants to do in our world.

8. Our lack of knowledge about Hinduism and the nuances of the culture should not keep us from engaging the Diaspora Hindus. The sincerity of our hearts can make up for our knowledge

---
10 Dickson, 182.

deficiencies. Timothy Paul cautions wisely, "One must avoid two pitfalls: analysis paralysis and oversimplification."[11] We can overanalyze our strategies and philosophy of ministry to the point that it distorts our efforts to reach out. On the other hand, we can become irrelevant and insensitive when we entirely disregard the cultural ramifications. What we need is a balanced approach that does due diligence to the task of equipping ourselves without allowing fear to paralyze us from effective ministry.

Conclusion

Christians have the incredible privilege of being good news bearers to the Hindus who live in our neighborhoods and those we interact with at our workplaces. The pathway to engaging Hindus with the gospel is through cultivating relationships. It takes much prayer and time to foster these deep friendships and the process cannot be hastened. Based on our knowledge of Hinduism, we can personalize Jesus to neighbors through the leading of the Holy Spirit. God has promised to be with us as we passionately pursue his mission. What seems impossible, humanly speaking, becomes feasible through his divine power working through us. We experience Jesus's presence in tangible ways as we step out of our comfort zones in the task of introducing our Hindu neighbors to the One we love and helping them to follow in his footsteps.

---
11 Paul, "Impacting Hindu Diaspora in North America," 131.

Christocentric Satsang

Contextualized Worship for Hindus

Mr. Anil Yesudas

A *Satsang* is a fellowship of truth-seekers who are in fellowship with God, the ultimate Truth. In a Christocentric satsang, worship is offered to the Triune God, within the framework of the Bible, in an Indian-Hindu cultural context. The thought of contextualization is not new. It seems that contextualization efforts in the past, however, have died with the personality. Nevertheless, much wisdom has come out of their efforts that can now be built upon. As Roger Hedlund writes,

> One of the most interesting contextual experiments in mission history took place in the early seventeenth century in India. … Roberto de Nobili (1577–1656) … stands as a model of adaptation. … De Nobili is castigated by modern critics for methods designed to appeal exclusively to the Brahmins and other "twice-born" castes. It should be noted however that most converts were from the lower castes who were not excluded by his ingenious approach.[1]

We can look forward to the day when the contextualized approach will become the norm among Indians globally. The Indian Hindu culture is very conducive to practicing biblical faith in the Triune God. A. J. Appasamy, an advocate of indigenous Christian Theology observed,

---

[1] Hedlund, *Christianity Made in India*, 220–21.

While making a plea for an Indian Christian theology, Appasamy said that *Dhyana* and obedience to the will of God are essential for all Christian thinking. Theology can be understood and explained only by those who live close to Christ, guided by the Holy Spirit from within the depths of the soul. Appasamy saw the appropriateness of the three traditional Hindu *pramanas*, and attempted to build his theology of Bhakti on the *pramanas* of *Sruti*, *Yukti* and *Anubhava* while adding *Sabha* (The authority of the Church). He contended that God reveals himself not merely to individuals but to his church, the *Sat Sangh*.[2]

Gathering in a manner that is culturally relevant within the Hindu cultural context has been tried, but somehow it has not taken much root. It has been long overdue that the devotees of Jesus gather in *Satsangs* as a primary format for expressing their biblical faith. Could this be the generation that understands its value and creates enough momentum to educate the Indian devotees of Jesus to take it seriously? Bruce J. Nicholls states,

> The hermeneutical task is not a private or purely individual one, it must be undertaken within the community of believers. Therefore, contextualization must take place within the Church before it can be faithfully interpreted by the world.[3]

Contextualization must be practiced within a community of believers over a period of time for it to be a valuable tool in the communication of the gospel message. We cannot do contextualization as a superficial, momentary drama to entice people. It must become the consistent primary lifestyle of the individual *bhakta* (devotee) and of the *bhakta-mandali* (a circle of devotees). A Satsang allows the participants to continue to know more and more of God, as they sit in an environment of sincere worship to the Triune God.

In the second World Missionary Conference, held again at the Mount of Olives, Jerusalem, over Easter in 1928,[4] Nicol Macnicol though not present at Jerusalem, wrote responses to the discussions, and these were included in the reports printed later. In his view, Hinduism was not wrong; it was not to be rejected. In fact, in many ways, he saw in the Hindu conception a very profound grasp of some of the basic realities of the universe. But it was his strong conviction that Hinduism "needs Christ." What Christianity could

---

2 Appasamy, *Christianity as Bhakti Marga*, xiii.
3 Nichols, "Living Theology for Asian Churches," 134.
4 Ariarajah, *Hindus and Christians*, 32.

bring to Hinduism was an enrichment of its concepts so that Hinduism could in fact fulfill some of its own ideals.[5]

There is a need for a paradigm shift from the idea of a Western church format to a culturally Hindu-Satsang format, which could lead to the formation of a community of Hindu followers of Jesus who remain and express their faith within the biblical frame of reference.

Incarnating into Satsang Lifestyle

The 1910 Commission, arising out of the Edinburgh Missionary Conference, said that a living theology could come only from a living encounter.[6] Followers of Jesus should have a lifelong, genuine interest in people. The encounter should be reciprocal. Often the attitude of Christians toward other religions is "We know the truth; they do not know the truth." So, therefore, "They should shut up and we should speak." That attitude does not reflect a genuine, living encounter. Our living encounter in the community we incarnate will perhaps help them to have an encounter with the living Christ.

Quoting from the statement arising from the Bangkok meeting of the Commission for World Mission and Evangelism, in 1973, David Bosch reminds us that "Culture shapes the human voice that answers the voice of Christ."[7] There is a constant interaction between God and history. It is so important to identify culture as the voice of mankind. There are various people groups, having their own distinct culture. They all interact with God. We hope and pray that these interactions of people groups will progressively move positively toward the Triune God. Those of us who are communicators of the good news should make a note that culture is a medium of communication. If we want to be effective communicators of the Lord Jesus, we must incarnate in the given culture effectively and genuinely.

Bosch says that there can be no doubt that the contextualization project is essentially legitimate, given the situation in which many contextual theologians find themselves. We therefore have to adopt a firm stand against every attempt at a non-contextualized or under-contextualized approach in mission.[8] It seems like Indian evangelical Christians are too preoccupied to make their efforts understandable to the Western world. Could it be

---

5 Ariarajah, 39.
6 Ariarajah, 30.
7 Bosch, *Transforming Mission*, 189.
8 Bosch, 425–26.

because, if the West understands them, they can receive recognition and resources? From their lifestyle, it seems that Indian evangelical Christians subconsciously think that the Western expression of faith is a divinely ordained format. At the very most, they arrive at an expression of faith that is neither fully culturally Hindu nor fully Western.

While there is much value in being culturally relevant, in the minds of the average Indian Christian there is subconscious confusion between Hinduism and *Hindutva*. Prasad Pinto writes,

> It is to be noted that Hinduism is different from the Hindutva movement. The former is India's ancient religion and the latter is a political ideology. … it holds that Hinduism is the religion of *Hindustan* (India) and that India is Hindus' *pitrubhoomi* (fatherland) and *punnyabhoomi* (holy land), by which logic Muslims, Christians and Parsis are not considered Indians, because their *punnyabhumi* is outside Hindustan.[9]

Sadly, the *Hindutva* agenda scares the followers of Jesus away from a beautiful and worthy culture and fertile ground for the expression of faith in the Father, Son, and Holy Spirit. It must be kept in mind that those who contextualize are not necessarily legitimizing the *Hindutva* agenda. In his classic book, *Christ and Culture*, Richard Niebuhr describes "Christ of Culture," "Christ above Culture," "Christ against Culture," and "Christ, the transformer of Culture."[10] In any given culture, whether Western or Eastern, the followers of Jesus can accept and adopt things in culture that are conducive to the Bible, they can adapt things in culture that are neutral to the Bible, and things in culture that are contrary to the Bible they can set aside.

Nicholls believes, "The translation of the gospel into other cultural forms so that it assimilates and absorbs elements that are not contrary to the gospel itself is not syncretism."[11] Sometimes there might be things in the culture that are demonic; for those they can come to their knees, praying against them. It is possible to live a life that is culturally Hindu and theologically conservative, within the biblical frame of reference. We can begin our own spiritual journey in contextualization. God loves all cultures. He is the creator of all cultures.

---

9   Pinto, "Mission in the North American Context" in *Emerging Indian Missiology*, 130–31.
10 Niebuhr, *Christ and Culture*.
11 Nichols, "Living Theology for Asian Churches," 126.

Satsang Format

In the Hindu mind, a guest is treated like God, and God is treated like a guest. The Sanskrit phrase *Atithi Devo Bhava* means "guest is God." The Indian Hindu have reverence for their guests. According to Hindu culture, the guest is shown acceptance through sixteen formalities. The guest is welcomed in, feet washed, given facilities to clean up, given clothes, items for grooming, a seat of honor, snacks, food, drinks, talked to, listened to, offered respect, entertained, given facilities for comfort, space to stay, and rest.

When Hindus show reverence to God, they imagine God coming to their door, and they want to accord all sixteen guest formalities. They want to welcome God into their lives, wash their feet, and bathe their God. They will adorn their God with clothes and ornaments. They will provide a seat of honor and bow before them. They will offer choice food and drinks. They will light lamps and burn incense. They will communicate with their God by listening to Scriptures and offering praises and prayers. They will sing and dance to entertain and show honor to God. At the end of the day, they will sing lullabies and let their God retire for the day. *Sodasopchar Puja* is a Sanskrit term that means "sixteen formalities offered to God as worship."

Stephen Neill, while writing about the understanding of *Bhakti*—i.e. devotion—in the *Saivites* and the *Vaishnavites* circles, mentions the relation of the soul of the devotee to God in the following stages (1) *Shanti*: Calm contemplation of the godhead; (2) *Dasya*: active servitude; (3) *Sakhya*: a feeling of personal friendship; (4) *Vatsalya*: a feeling of filial attachment; and (5) *Madhurya*: a feeling of tender affection between lover and the beloved.[12]

It is good to think of offering *Bhakti* to God, who comes to our door. When we are distressed, we want to go to God. We reach to our door to go out, and we open our door, only to find that God is standing at our door, that God has come to us. In our distress, God does not wait for us to come to him, but he sees our distress and comes to our door. The Hindu heart is overwhelmed with joy and reverence, imagining God coming to their door, and offers *Sodasopchar Puja* to God.

Because we live in a busy world, sometimes it might not be possible to show all sixteen formalities, but there is another shorter Hindu format of worship called Panchopchar Puja, meaning "worship with five formalities." Hindus are pragmatic and we can learn from them that on occasion we can

---

12 Neill, *Bhakti: Hindu and Christian*, 74.

save time and resources. The devotees of the Triune God can also design their format of the Satsang, categorized either under sixteen formalities for a full and elaborate worship, or five formalities for practical purposes. There is nothing necessarily wrong in thinking of God as our guest; however, from a biblical perspective we see that the devotees of Jesus are the guests, and God is our host. We gather around the Lord's Table. God is our host, and we are his guests.

A. J. Appasamy described an Indian form of worship held at the Bishop's Theological College at Tirumaraiyur in the Tinnevelly diocese.[13] It was a monthly devotion, where the devotees entered the chapel after washing their feet. They wore Indian clothes, sang Tamil lyrics, using Indian musical instruments, and went in a procession around the chapel. Once in the chapel, they all sat on the floor. The lessons were chanted. There were times of silence for private confession to God. There was a sermon on the meaning of human existence. Toward the end they all prostrated, and the service was closed with a benediction. Bishop A. J. Appasamy notes that there were mixed reactions; there was considerable criticism, and at the same time there was a great deal of genuine appreciation of the service. The devotees of Jesus in India and the Diaspora need to embrace a format of worship that is Hindu in culture and biblical in theology.

Satsang Content

The devotees of Jesus today can offer worship during Satsang in sixteen formalities, a *Sodasopchar Puja*. For their daily family prayer time they can offer five formalities, a *Panchopchar Puja*. A short time of silent contemplation, as the devotees prepare their minds for the worship of the Triune God, is a good practice. The writer of Ecclesiastes warns and suggests guarding one's steps while going to the house of God (Eccl 5:1). Tangible meaningful symbols can be a reminder of certain biblical truths. Relevant biblical portions can be chanted in Sanskrit. The devotees can engage in prayers of worship and prayers of supplication. Worship songs in Indian melody and languages can be offered. A prominent part of the devotion must be the presentation of the Word of God through biblical storytelling.

---

13 Francis, *Christian Bhakti of A. J. Appasamy*, 94–100. Also, *National Council of Churches Review*, 23–26.

Satsang and Symbols

Communication happens via a combination of verbal and nonverbal methods. The Hindu wants to have *darshan*, which means "to see tangibly." It is alright to have a desire for *darshan*. The devotees of the Triune God long to see Jesus someday, face to face. While there is no need to place any image or idols, instead symbols like the Cross or other meaningful designs/objects that remind of some biblical truth can be used. It is alright to light up lamps and incense, which points to the idea of revelation and prayers. Jerome Sylvester, mentioning the *Khristbhakta* movements, notes that during the festival of *Deepawali*, Jesus, the light of the world, is the central theme. Oil lamps and candles are lit to celebrate it.[14]

Symbols allow us to make use of all five senses. The Lord Jesus endorses symbolic communication by installing the Communion—the Bread and the Cup. When the religious leader handles the utensils containing the Bread and the Juice, one can hear the rattling of plates and cups: the sense of hearing. They see the Bread and the Cup coming toward them: the sense of sight. They pick up the Bread and Cup: the sense of touch. As they bring it toward their mouth, they perceive the aroma: the sense of smell. Finally, they partake of it: the sense of taste. The Lord Jesus is the master communicator who installed the Communion involving all five senses.

H. L. Richard, writing about Narayan Vaman Tilak, mentions that "The influence of the Hindu Bhakti Tradition led Tilak to break out of traditional Christian worship styles into more contextual approaches."[15] Liberty should be given to those who choose, and are comfortable with *tika* (*pottu*), *japmala* (prayer beads), and *gamcha* (a sash over the shoulder). However, it would be legalistic to expect that everyone should and would use it. Wearing an Indian outfit is a good idea, but normal Western clothing generally will not pose a hurdle. However, it is best to avoid suit and tie. Any garment that covers decently should suffice.

Roger Hedlund, while referring to the Hindu-Christian movements in India, writes that various questions may be raised as to what is essential in the gospel and how far one can remain culturally a Hindu and religiously a Christian, but the compromise reached was clearly effective for preserving

---

14 Sylvester, *Khristbhakta Movement*, 79.
15 Richard, *Following Jesus in Hindu Context*, 68.

the strength of the family and for maintaining the faith.[16] Followers of the Lord Jesus must study semiotics and utilize a symbol system to express faith within the biblical frame of reference. Symbols speak louder than words. It is good to be proficient in Indian languages, but it is far more important to learn and utilize the language of a symbol system. Any symbol that points to any biblical truth is valuable for the expression of faith. Jesus spoke against using symbols hypocritically, however, he was not against the use of symbols in and of themselves.

Pravachan—Satsang Presentation

The most important aspect of the content of Satsang is *pravachan*, the presentation of the Word. All presentations must primarily be from the sixty-six books of the Bible. It is alright to quote certain relevant passages and thoughts from Hindu religious and philosophical works, but they should not replace the Bible. In the zeal for context, one cannot supplant the text. In a Satsang, the whole Bible, all sixty-six books, must be valued. There can be multiple ways of presentations from the Bible, which should be designed consciously. It is of utmost importance to cycle through small portions of the four Gospels. This cycling through the four Gospels must never stop, because this allows the uniqueness of Jesus to build up in the minds of the hearers.

The Old Testament is primarily for the Jewish people, and the epistles are primarily written for those who are already followers of Jesus. It is the four Gospels that must be used to communicate to those who are showing interest in the Lord Jesus. When elucidating *pravachan* from the four Gospels as the primary text, it is alright to venture into the Old Testament and the Epistles, but then the speaker should return to the main text—the Gospels. In addition, apart from focusing on the four Gospels, there can also be a weekly summary of one of the sixty-six books of the Bible, with a focus on one portion from the particular book.

Instead of designing lives to meet people one time, incidentally, one must design their lives to meet with them intentionally over a period. Communication does not happen in a vacuum. It happens in the context of lifelong, meaningful relationships. A one-time communication cannot and must not be the primary method employed to communicate all the truth of the Bible. God's truth is like a diamond, it shines through all the different facets. It will take several episodes of communication before anyone can understand and appreciate the person and work of Christ.

---

16 Hedlund, *Quest for Identity*, 69.

I personally believe that Christian communicators are too quick to correct those who are in the beginning stages of understanding the Lord Jesus. The ignorant zeal to push people toward biblical truth can become a major stumbling block. Understanding the person and work of Christ for a brand-new believer is an uphill climb. Trying to expedite the process will cause people to tumble downwards instead. The Word must be patiently communicated over a long period.

The Christ-event needs to be communicated in the Satsang. The Christ-event is the narrative related to the preexistent Lord Jesus: his incarnation and childhood; the beginning of his ministry, his teachings, conversations with friends, family, and opponents; his miracles, parables, prayers, the questions he raises; his suffering, death, resurrection, ascension, enthronement, and second coming. This helps the hearer to have an encounter with the living Christ through the Holy Spirit.

It is through multiple communications, from a range of biblical texts, of the different aspects of the life of Jesus, that the Cross of Jesus would make sense. Once a person understands the biblical perspective, hopefully that will lead to understanding the Cross better. If the person does not reach the Cross, that means the task of communication has not yet been completed. Apart from the Cross of Christ, there is no possibility of salvation. The Cross is central. And it is only through the narration of the life of Jesus, that his death and resurrection can be understood.

Conclusion

It is possible to contextualize the gospel in a manner where we can continue to conserve biblical truth. The Satsang is not a strategy for communication with Hindus; it is a normal, lifelong lifestyle to express our faith in the Triune God in the Indian Hindu cultural context. Perhaps we can understand the Bible and the Lord Jesus better by following him in the Hindu cultural context. As far as communicating the life and work of Christ is concerned, that communication will happen organically as a normal and natural part of our expression of faith. Satsangs must be explicitly biblical, trinitarian, Christ-centered, Cross-centered, and salvation-centered, while being true to the cultural context that God has placed us in.

A paradigm is greater than an individual, and even an organized group cannot change a paradigm by ordinary, artificial means. God, in his supernatural power, can shift paradigms to accomplish his own purposes.

God wants people to seek him during this *Krupa Yug*—this "age of grace"—while he may yet be found. It is God's mission, and he is carrying it out in his own way. The devotees of the Triune God who practice their faith in the Indian-Hindu cultural context will become better communicators of the good news of Jesus. The *Yesu-Bhakthas*, the "devotees of Jesus," come to his feet and seek his plans—especially regarding the things that he is working out in our communities.

If the message of Jesus is communicated by an individual to another individual, there is a likelihood that the individual will come to the Lord Jesus. If the good news is communicated by a family to another family, there is a likelihood that the family will come to the feet of Jesus. If the biblical message is practiced contextually by a community that communicates to another community, then it is likely—at least in theory—that the community will become devotees of Jesus, possibly sparking Christ-ward movements. As God's Word exhorts us, specifically in Hebrews 10:23–25, "let us not neglect to meet together" corporately for Satsang.

9

Dealing with Family after Conversion

Dr. P. T. Subrahmanyan

I was born into a Brahmin family at Veeranakavu, Neyyardam, Kerala, and brought up in the traditional attire and atmosphere of a Malayali Brahmin family (*Madom*). Being part of a priestly family, I was trained in all the temple traditions during my childhood, from the age of eight onward. I was taught *poojas* and *mantras* by my grandfather, Sri Kochu Sankaran Potti, and by my father, Sri Thirumaleswara Brahmananda Teertha. I had the *upanayana* ceremony at the age of twelve and was sent to study the *Vedas* at a *Gurukula* near Cholapuram, Sivagangai, Tamil Nadu. After returning to Kerala, I served as a Hindu priest in about twenty-five different temples.

However, I faced a lot of personal challenges from my joint-family structure, which was caught up in disputes and quarrels concerning lands and properties. During my college studies, a friend introduced me to the New Testament and the gospel of Jesus Christ—and that turned the trajectory of my life. I found the living God and Savior in Jesus Christ and abandoned the worship of lifeless idols. Naturally, this brought bitter opposition from my family and dear ones, and I was excommunicated in 1994.

Nevertheless, life with Jesus was a new beginning in an entirely new world. God called me to the gospel ministry, so I pursued theological education at different seminaries in India. After earning a master's, I conducted research at *Vrije Universiteit*, Amsterdam, Netherlands, and completed a PhD in Philosophy from Mahatma Gandhi University in Kottayam, India. Currently, I serve on the faculty of religion and philosophy at the India Bible College and Seminary in Kumbanad, Kerala, besides serving in different capacities as a trainer in theological institutions and as a witness to Hindus in various parts of India and abroad.

As a majority of Hindus are converted as individuals, dealing with the rest of the family and old friends poses many challenges and is extremely complicated. The individuals who come to the Christian faith usually come without the consent of their parents, siblings, and other relatives. Such individual conversions often create "family shock" and bring the converts into direct conflict with their immediate family, neighbors, society, and culture. As a result, their family members have not *yet* accepted Christ and have serious differences with the converted ones. And even if an entire Hindu nuclear family accepts Christ, they have to deal with their extended family members after their salvation experience. Therefore, dealing with one's close family members after conversion needs much care, patience, prayer, and godly wisdom.

A person's relationship with God, as well as human beings (family and friends), is very important for the balanced aspect of the Christian faith, involving experiences in both the vertical and horizontal dimensions of their spirituality. When Hindus accept Christ, it is a costly decision, as their family may not agree with nor accept their decision to convert and can cause serious tension with their blood relatives. This often leads to conflict, and even to the extent of losing one's father, mother, brothers, sisters, spouse and children (Luke 14:25–27).

One is often expelled from his or her own home, and all support from the family is denied, and all relations are totally or at least partially cut off for the rest of life (which can be for a long time). The converted ones are never invited to the funerals of their close relatives, or any social gatherings like marriages and house dedications. No one informs them of the serious sicknesses of their dear ones, and they experience some form of social ostracism. They go through the difficult trauma of "separation and alienation." In other cases, the family and relatives may keep a relationship with the converted ones but show indifference. *The family is there, and yet not with you.* Only a very few cultured and educated Hindu families are open to conversion and accept their daughter or son who converted to a different religion.

Conversion as an Issue and the Issues of Conversion

The caste Hindus despise Christianity, as they see Christianity as a religion of the *mleccha* (or untouchables)—the foreignness or Westernness of Christianity being a cause of pollution and rejection. The higher castes especially view mingling with other castes and religions as a lowering of their inherent standards. Thus, converting to Christianity is usually perceived as a stigma in family circles. The convert is the one who rejected—or even betrayed—his or her faith, ancestral religion, traditions, family, and the culture into which one is born and brought up; this is never tolerated in Hindu family and society.

For a traditional Hindu, religious conversion causes one to lose ritual purity, culture, and status in the caste hierarchy. Hence it is commonly found that the profession of Christianity by certain individuals of the family often affected the status quo of the entire family. For example, a study I conducted among twenty Brahmin converts[17] found that conversion negatively affected the relationship of the converts with their family members. Sixty-five percent of the converts shared that they were excluded from social gatherings after their conversion and that the extended family members mistreated the immediate family of the convert, which resulted in a lack of acceptance and shaming in family circles. Forty percent agreed that the marriage prospects of family members were adversely impacted due to conversion. Other undesirable consequences include areas such as education (5 percent) and employment (5 percent), while 20 percent of respondents replied that other areas of family members were affected by their conversion. After conversion, the converts suffered shame, ridicule, insult, mockery, defamation, belittling, and demotion of social standing from their family members.

Conversion is viewed as something that brings shame in a traditional Hindu family. In other words, conversion is linked to identity and membership in family and community. Hence, changing one's religion of birth has serious and far-reaching implications for that individual's life and social circles in the Indian context, most evidently seen in family relationships. Conversion is a very sensitive, complex, and controversial issue in India. It is often interpreted as antisocial, anti-cultural, and anti-national, as many Hindus think that converting out of Hinduism is a threat to their ancestral religion, society, and culture.

Moreover, conversion from one religion to another is seen as unnecessary by the dominant Hindu society and is strongly opposed. Hinduism in the past, as well as in the present, has been engaged in religious conversions from within and outside. Hindu converts are seen as anathema by society, and conversion is forbidden by all possible ways and means. The converts face

---
17 Subrahmanyan, "The Conversion from Hinduism to Christianity."

bitter opposition from immediate relatives, like mother, father, grandparents, wife, husband, etc. The opposition to conversion arises from the political and religious spheres.

Thus, on account of their conversions, Hindu converts to Christianity face multiple issues in their lives from both Hinduism and Christianity. These include rejection, starvation, malnutrition, severe opposition, personal uprooting, enormous pain, mental and emotional breakdown, social ostracism, physical violence, harassment, persecution, excommunication from family and home, loss of property or inheritance, identity crisis, frustrations, struggles, isolation, loneliness, etc. Finding a life partner is difficult for Hindu converts, and the reaction from in-laws and extended family of your spouse can be extremely challenging to navigate through.

The ceremony of baptism is often the final separation from the Hindu social and religious community. The converted individual, who is thrown out of the family, cannot expect any support and care from near and dear ones for the rest of his or her life. This brings solitude and deep emotional wounds. Although conversion as an event happens once in life, it creates lifelong issues. Hence the questions for any convert include: To what extent do new followers of Jesus need to change their former ways of life, community memberships, sociocultural patterns, etc.? Should you change your name or take on a Christian name? Should you give up traditional attire for more Western clothing and lifestyle? Eating meat and other prohibited food remains a major challenge for converts.

Understanding Conversion

Conversion is an evaluative term used positively by those in the religion to which one converts and negatively by the religion which one abandons.[18] Usually conversion is viewed as something disturbing the social equilibrium, which has detrimental consequences for the convert, his or her family, community, and society. It is understood differently in different religious, cultural, and social contexts. Nevertheless, biblically speaking, conversion is an authentic spiritual experience, a spiritual event, the new birth from heaven leading to a new-creation experience (rather than merely an outward change of religious affiliation), as the result of the work of the Holy Spirit and the Word of God in a person's heart and soul (John 3:1–21; 1 Pet 2:1–3; 9–10). It is actually repentance (or turning) in a person's life and is a conscious

---

18 Mathew, *Contemporary Religious Conversions*, 4.

act, which brings changes in the old ways of life. Sin-consciousness and the urgency of salvation necessitate conversion. So it is not something happening due to brainwashing, by force, or by fraudulent means or acts, as the common allegations against conversion denote.

The Christian revelation and faith, with its message on the life, teachings, death, and resurrection of Jesus Christ as presented in the Bible (especially the New Testament) can quench the thirst of many truth-seekers of the Hindu religion, as they were able to find life, light, peace, love, joy, and hope in the gospel of Christ. As a result, conversions occur through the conviction and voluntary commitment of the people based on their personal encounter with Jesus Christ. Their hearts and minds are gripped by the living presence and love of Christ, through this salvation experience. Disillusionment and deep dissatisfaction with the Hindu beliefs and practices, such as caste and untouchability, idol worship, and superstitious beliefs and practices also play a role in choosing the new faith. It is usually understood as reorienting life, the change in one's philosophy, faith, worldview, ideology, and religion from one to another. It connotes the born-again experience, inward turning, enlightenment, reform, renewal, and transformation in an individual's life. It is a deeper spiritual experience as well as a very personal choice, which is very decisive for the rest of life.

Hence conversion is understood as a spiritual experience with social and cultural dimensions; the concept of conversion is multifaceted. It is often meant to transition from one's traditional milieu into another social group. By conversion, a person/group adapts to the new modes of worship, art forms, and theological categories that draw little from one's own religious heritage.[19] Therefore the convert gradually gets/gains a new identity with significant alterations and adaptations to the new community of faith. However, there is a tension between the former worldview and the new one. Thus, the converted Christians are called to live in two worlds,[20] as there are variations in social customs, practices, traditions, and ceremonies related to marriage, death, and so on between the former and the latter world views. Often many of the former cultural practices are not welcomed in the Christian fold, as they are "pagan practices."

Conversely, converted Christians may have to follow some of the customs that are commonly practiced by their family/community if they have to live

---

19 D'Mello, "Letting the Converted Speak," 14.
20 Louis, "Conversion and Cultural Alienation," 69.

within their society. Otherwise, they can be excluded/denounced from their community for not following age-old customs. Converted Christians are put into a dilemma by both worlds, causing "cultural alienation" of two types: first, estrangement from one's own community; and second, alienation from oneself. Therefore, many people who have been converted to Christianity often live according to two worldviews and keep plural identities. A typical example of this trend can be seen in many people calling themselves "Christian" in faith but remaining "Hindu" in culture (for example, secret Christians or Hindu Christians).

Keeping Contact with Family

As we have seen, curtailing of family bonds and social belonging happens when Hindus move to the Christian faith. Most converts find it very difficult to preserve relationships with their family members and feel separated from them. Breaking up of one's blood relations and family is thus a traumatic aftermath faced by those who embrace Christ from Hindu families. They often lose their family members' warmth, care, love, and fellowship on account of their new religious experience. In many cases, baptism is the final point of separation in a convert's life.

Due to the various challenges associated with conversion, many missiologists recommend evangelizing people in groups/families in their natural social networks rather than as individuals, since the latter may cause family breakup, social ostracism, and isolation.[21] But how can one bridge this gap? It means being in touch with Hinduism and Hindus, at the same time not being a Hindu. Hence keeping and maintaining a point of contact with one's family and friends is the real challenge after conversion. One should discontinue what is contrary to the Christian faith but should continue relations with one's family and friends.

Here there is a twin challenge of both continuity and discontinuity. The new convert should keep or remain in contact with his/her own family and community as an opportunity for witness, as maintaining the horizontal relationship is basic to one's spirituality. For example, in a study of a group of converts (mentioned above), about 20 percent said conversion to the Christian faith meant ceasing to be a member of one's own community. However, 80 percent of them said that while being a Christian, one can be and should be part of one's own community, family, and society, and should

---

21 Love, "Conversion," 232.

keep relationships. For them, conversion is a change of heart and way of life; it is joining to Christ rather than joining or disjoining a community/church.[22] Thus, keeping contact with one's family is very important in a convert's life. Even if the relationship is broken at present, one should look for ways of reconciliation, without sacrificing one's faith in Christ.

Issues in Christianity

Through conversion, when one becomes a member of the church or the family of God, the same person also loses his or her membership in an ancestral and biological family. Nevertheless, it is for sure that the newfound Christian faith is strong enough to guide and nurture new converts from the Hindu religion. The church and Christian friends can provide fellowship and play a great role in inspiring, developing, and strengthening the new faith of the converts and in many ways be helpful in supporting and helping them grow in their newfound faith. However, in Christianity, too, the new converts face several issues. There are cases when the church becomes a real *koinonia* for new converts, and there are also cases when it does not. Often the existing issues in the church, such as doctrinal disputes, disunity, and denominational pluralism, affect the new converts, as they slowly discover the unworthy elements in institutionalized Christianity and its structures. The unequal treatment in churches and the favoritism based on kith and kin rather than on merit or faith are disturbing factors for many converts. It gradually makes them realize that the church is like any other community, rather than being an ideal community of love, justice, and equality, based on the kingdom model of Jesus.

Some traditional Christians with a superiority complex look down on the new converts as "pagans" or "Gentile Christians," causing emotional torture to the individual converts and demeaning them into a status of "second-class Christians." Some converts said they were continually forced to give up even what is good in their mother religion, particularly some of the Hindu cultural practices like following a vegetarian diet, wearing ornaments, etc., which are not necessarily contrary to Scripture.[23] Further, these cultural aspects can become the indigenized ways or media of expressing the Christian faith and love by the converts to their own community. This can also reduce, to a great extent, the projected differences between the converts, and their families and friends.

---

22 Subrahmanyan, "Conversion from Hinduism to Christianity."
23 Subrahmanyan.

The identity of an individual convert is another crucial issue. Who am I in the church and in my previous community? Where or to whom do I belong? How do I live my Christian calling? Among others are crucial questions for an individual convert related to self-identity. Some converts are confused about their real identity. They seem to be neither Hindu nor Christian and sometimes keep dual identities as both Hindu and Christian or as Hindu-Christian. This is because of the social pressures from our society. Due to these issues of publicly joining with a visible church in society, many Hindus like to remain as secret Christians or devotees of Christ (*Kristu-Bhaktas*) and like to be called "churchless Christians."

Change of name is also a serious issue in the life of a convert. In Indian society, parents are generally the sole authority in naming children (*nāmakaraṇa*), and change of name is alien to the Indian context. Moreover, such practice was considered disrespectful to the parents and traditions. For example, in the case of the famous Hindu convert and theologian, Nehemiah Goreh, the change of *Nilakantha* to *Nehemiah* aroused opposition and estrangement, which caused him deep distress. Many converts also face existential questions, such as issues of shelter/accommodation (Where will I go/live/stay after conversion, especially after excommunication from home?) and other necessities of life, education, and so on, as they lose the basic support of their families.

Conversion means not only a change of religion but also a shift in personal law. The multiple personal laws existing in India can also cause legal issues for converts. Hence, when one Hindu is converted to Christianity, there is also a shift from Hindu personal law to Christian personal law. This can affect many procedures of a convert's family relationship, as this can become a ground for divorce, as well as loss of inheritance and maintenance. An irony of a Hindu who became a Christian is that he/she even has to face the issue of divorce and family breakup, as conversion is a valid legal ground in India for divorce according to Hindu personal law.[24] The life partner can go for a divorce, and there are such cases that happen and family life is disrupted on account of the change of religious faith.

While considering these complex issues associated with conversion, the pastors in the Christian churches should be given special training and orientation in handling the cases of new converts, as this needs tender care,

---

24 Subrahmanyan.

support, love, and much patience with a shepherding heart. The special needs of a new individual convert, whether spiritual, mental, or physical, should be addressed immediately with a sensitive mind and an open heart. Rather than imposing any church's tradition and culture, the pastors should build the individual converts in faith and Scripture, ensuring their spiritual growth in Christ. Above all, the inner world of the convert—and the wounds caused by family breakup and isolation, which need much healing and comfort—should be understood as it is. The convert should be accepted as he or she is. The convert has to be made to feel at home in the atmosphere of the new faith community as a home away from home in order to integrate them well into the Christian community of faith.[25]

Suggestions to Improve Family Relationships

1. One suggestion, which can help in many ways for converts to retain relationships with their family and friends, is to not cut off relationships with those dear ones. Even if the relationship is broken, it can and should be rebuilt and the bond strengthened. Efforts toward reconciliation should be initiated by the converts themselves.

2. One must fulfill his or her moral and social duty and responsibilities toward family and parents. This is honoring one's parents (Eph 6:2) and fulfilling basic commitments toward one's family. This will give credibility to one's long-standing relations with family members, even if no one comes to the Christian faith; this can be a real witness to one's family members and friends.

3. The new life of converts to Christ should be a model and living witness for others to emulate, and steadfast progress should be shown in their character and calling. The inner change should be evident to others in regard to attitude and approach in real-life contexts.

4. The converts should voluntarily forgive their family members for the wrong done to them in relation to their conversion or to incidents prior to that. They should forgive their family members as Christ forgave them.

---

25 Isaiah, "Post-Conversion Pastoral Care," 212.

5. The converts should try to visit their dear ones in times of need and serious situations, such as sickness, accidents, crises in family life, business failures, etc. Personal visits, words of counsel and encouragement, and prayers of confidence and trust in God at these times are important avenues for reconciliation and goodwill. Also try to participate in family events (as much as one can), such as weddings, funerals (*antyesti*), housewarmings, and other social gatherings, to keep your relationships alive and active.

6. Indigenized ways or methods of inculturation are suggested, so as to facilitate cultural integration and transformation rather than alienation and separation of families. For example, to express Christian love and faith, converts can retain their original cultural elements from the Hindu way of life, such as dress sense; language; knowledge of Hindu texts, stories, and mythology; wearing of ornaments; using Indian musical instruments, like veena and thamburu for worship; food patterns; and so on. Dance in Hindu cultures can also be used to communicate Gospel episodes.
This can help in easily relating with their close family and friends by expressing their identification and solidarity with the Hindu cultural milieu while keeping faith in Christ at the core of their hearts.
For example, the famous Bengali convert—Brahmabandhab Upadhyaya—felt that he was culturally a Hindu while being at heart a Christian. This can sometimes mean that one can become a Christian without ceasing to be a Hindu.[26]

7. New converts should be trained in interacting with the unconverted members of their own family and handling the difficulties, questions, and criticisms faced in articulating their faith with the unconverted.[27] They should prayerfully use literature, media, and opportunities for personal sharing and witness with their family and friends.

---

[26] Staffner, *Jesus Christ and the Hindu Community*, 22.
[27] Nameeta, "When Being Christian Means Losing," 440.

Conclusion

Conversion as salvation through Christ denotes a joyful spiritual experience, but it results in many negative experiences due to resistance to the Christian gospel in the Indian social and cultural context and due to the negative *imprints/images* of Christianity in Hindu minds as a foreign/colonial religion. Untold sufferings are part of real conversion, and the individual converts face multiple issues from both "old" and "new" faiths. These are spiritual, intellectual, personal, cultural, and social crises in their lives.

The issue of family breakup is a very crucial one in a convert's life, on account of one's faith in Jesus Christ. Pastoral care and fellowship should be extended to them, and the converts should be encouraged to relate themselves with their families and friends as much as they can. Relevant and praxis-oriented suggestions are given to tackle the issues related to conversion and to be effective witnesses of the gospel concerning one's family and friends.

10

Ministering to Hindu Families

Mr. Srinivasa Moorthy

I was born into a Tamil Hindu family. I became a Christian believer when I was twenty-one years old. Marriage, as an institution, had not inspired me, largely because of the dynamics I had seen between husbands and wives in a variety of contexts—i.e., family, friends, acquaintances, and society. When I was twenty-two, I decided to be celibate for life. But then when I was twenty-nine, God showed me, through Genesis, that "It is not good for man to be alone," so I decided to get married. I reasoned that if God has actually designed marriage, then it must be filled with purpose, meaning, and happiness instead of two people merely going through a set of motions.

I started studying marriage and ended up getting an MA in Family Life Education. My wife is a qualified counselor, and together we have helmed more than one hundred episodes of family life on television, besides conducting marriage seminars. Such is the irony of life—transforming a celibate to become a family man who teaches others how to live a healthy and fruitful family life!

I worked in the Information Technology industry for fifteen years before getting into full-time ministry. I lived in the UK briefly, and I also visited Singapore and Malaysia for work, where I interacted with friends and family. Many of my Hindu friends from school, college, and IT companies have gone abroad to the US, UK, Australia, Singapore, Malaysia, South Africa, UAE, etc., and we have kept in touch through various channels over the years. And my cousins, uncles, and aunts are all abroad and have framed my input for this chapter.

Here I will explore how to minister to Hindu couples in Diaspora settings. To begin, I will present a brief understanding of marriage and family from a Hindu perspective. Then I will present some opportunities and challenges faced by Diaspora Hindu families. And, finally, we will consider how we can minister to them.

The Stages of Hindu Life and Family

According to the Hindu scriptures, there are four stages (*Āśramas*)[1] in human life. These stages are 1) student life (*Brahmachari*), marked by chastity, devotion, and obedience to one's teacher; 2) householder life (*Grihastha*), requiring marriage, the begetting of children, sustaining one's family and helping support priests and holy men, and fulfillment of duties toward gods and ancestors; 3) retired life, or forest dweller (*Vanaprastha*), beginning with the birth of grandchildren and consisting of withdrawal from concern for material things, the pursuit of solitude, and ascetic and yogic practices; and 4) renounced life (*Sannyasi*), which involves renouncing all of one's possessions and wandering from place to place, begging for food—concerned only with union with Brahman (the Absolute).

Traditionally, *moksha* (liberation from rebirth) should be pursued only during the last two stages of a person's life. Of these stages, only Grihastha allows sexual gratification. Today only a few Hindus strictly follow all four *ashrams*. Nonetheless, the idea of enjoying the world in a religious and regulated manner, followed by gradual retirement, remains a powerful ideal. According to the Veda, the Hindu sacred writings, marriage is a union between a masculine and feminine entity, with commitments to pursue *Dharma* (duty), *Artha* (possessions), *Kama* (physical desires), and *Moksha* (liberation) in unison. *Manusmriti* (The Laws of Manu) notes eight different types of marriages, though not all eight are approved. The last four were not advocated and the last one was condemned.

The eight types of marriage are *Brahma* marriage, *Daiva* marriage, *Arsha* marriage, *Prajapatya* marriage, *Gandharva* marriage, *Asura* marriage, *Rakshasa* marriage, and *Paishacha* marriage. Of these, Gandharva marriage refers to love marriage and Brahma marriage refers to an arranged marriage of the best type: i.e., where the bride and groom are of the same Varna, where no extensive gifts are given, and the groom's family seeks out a bride. In Prajapatya marriage, the marriage is completed for the young groom

---
1 See Britannica, "*Ashramas*: Four Stages of Life."

and bride before they reach adulthood, but the marriage is consummated once they reach adulthood. Daiva marriage is where the bride's parents are poor and cannot afford to conduct the marriage ceremony, and a wealthy person selects the groom and conducts the ceremony for the poor. In Arsha marriage, the groom pays a price to get married to a bride. In Asura marriage, the groom is generally not likable or from a lower caste and pays a huge amount of money to marry a bride. Rakshasa marriage occurs by abduction. In Paishacha marriage, the bride is intoxicated or not in a conscious state of mind to get married.[2]

Rituals in Hindu Marriage and Duties in Grihastha

Vivaha (wedding) is the rite of passage and the rituals associated with marriage. While there are many rituals in Hinduism, Vivaha is the most personal ritual an adult Hindu can undertake in his or her life. The detailed rituals and processes of Vivaha vary widely, but the key elements of a Hindu wedding ritual are *Kanyadaan* (father gives away his daughter), *Panigrahana* (holding hands near the fire to signify union), and *Saptapadi* (couple makes seven vows to each other before the fire). The *Vivaha sanskara* is essentially a Vedic *yajna* ritual, with a recitation of Vedic hymns.

The primary witness of a Hindu marriage is the Vedic fire deity *Agni* (the Sacred Fire), in the presence of family and friends. The post-wedding rites of passage include *Grihapravesa*—the welcoming of the bride to her new home by the groom's mother, father, siblings, and other relatives. *Chaturthikarma*, is a rite performed on the fourth day after the wedding, where the first domestic fire is lit, marking the food-related householder life of the new couple.

Grihastha is the most important of the four stages because the other three stages depend upon it for survival and proper functioning (Manusmriti 3.77). There are duties and privileges attached to this stage. Most of the duties are performed jointly by husband and wife. His duties are to keep a fire at home, known as *garhapatya agni* (fire of householder), along with his wife (Ashtadhyayi 4.1.33). He has to discharge his debts to his ancestors, the gods, the seers (*rishis*), his *atithis* (guests) and the *bhutas* (living beings) by performing *pancha maha yajnas* (five great sacrifices) in his daily routine (Satapatha Brahmana 11.5.6.1).

A husband's second-most important duty is to support his family with the family occupation or any other suitable employment (Daksha Smriti

---
2 Doniger, *Laws of Manu*.

2.32). Though he may get ancestral property in the form of land, house, and other economic means of income, he is expected to generate his own income and keep the family earnings growing continuously. He must ensure that all dependents are well-fed before he takes his meals (Atharva Veda 9.6.38, Satapatha Brahmana 2.2.4.2, and Manusmriti 3.115, 118). He must look after the clothing, medicine, education and other essential needs of family members, servants, poor relatives, and other dependents. To perform so many duties, he is also allowed many privileges. He is permitted to purchase luxuries like scents, ornaments, jewelry, and other objects of sensuous pleasures from his surplus income.

An active sexual life is not only permitted but prescribed as one of the *purusharthas* (aspirations) at this stage, within the limits of religious restrictions (Manusmriti 5.150–51; 9.101–102; Padma Purana Srishti Khanda 45.57). He has to fulfill the expectations of his wife, in regard to their sex life, and to see that she leads a happy married life. He has to beget children in order to repay his debt to his ancestors, otherwise, they may not attain *moksha*. The wife has special privileges as *patni* or *grihasvamini*. Even if he dislikes her, she has a right to his support. Vijnaneshwara goes to the extent of saying that even an adulterous wife has a right to the support of her husband (his commentary on *Yajnavalkya Smriti* 1.70–72).

The term *family* is derived from the Latin word *familia*, which denotes a household establishment and refers to a group of individuals living together during important phases of their lifetime and who are bound to each other by biological and/or social and psychological relationship. The group also includes persons engaged in an ongoing socially sanctioned sexual relationship in order to provide for the procreation and upbringing of children. Unlike Western society, which puts impetus on individualism, Indian society is collectivistic in that it promotes interdependence and cooperation, with the family forming the focal point of this social structure.

The Indian joint-family structure includes three or four living generations, including grandparents, parents, uncles, aunts, nieces, and nephews, all living together in the same household, utilizing a common kitchen and often spending from a common purse, contributed to by all. The daughters typically leave the house. While women are expected to accept a position subservient to males and to subordinate their personal preferences to the needs of others, males are expected to accept responsibility for meeting the needs of others. The earning males are expected to support the old; take care of the widows, never-married adults, and disabled; assist family members during periods of unemployment and illness; and provide security to women and children. Psychologically, family members feel an intense emotional interdependence, empathy, closeness, and loyalty to each other.

But the above has been changing, especially because of increased urbanization. Social and cultural changes have altered entire lifestyles, interpersonal relationship patterns, power structures, and familial relationship arrangements in current times. These changes, which include a shift from a joint/extended family to a nuclear family—along with problems of urbanization; changes of role, status, and power with the increased employment of women; migratory movements among the younger generation; and loss of the experience advantage of elderly members in the family—have increased the stress and pressure on such families, leading to an increased vulnerability to emotional problems and disorders.

Families are frequently subject to these pressures. Joint families that stay under the same roof, but with separate kitchens and separate purses and with considerable autonomy and reduced responsibility for extended family members are common nowadays. Others may stay in separate households but cluster around in the same community. Such transitional families, though structurally nuclear, may still function as joint families. Even when relatives cannot actually live in close proximity, they typically maintain strong bonds and attempt to provide each other with economic help and emotional support.[3]

Diaspora Hindu couples who journey outside of their country still feel connected and have an obligation to fulfill their duties back home and provide support to the family and its structure and its culture. This is especially true for first-generation Diaspora couples who have moved abroad, but second- and third-generation couples slowly move out of these collectivistic approaches and adopt an amalgamated culture, based on the country they live in and the culture they pick up from their parents.

Traditionally, parents or elders in the family arrange marriages. Careful consideration is taken to ensure compatibility in various forms. Generally, they already know a prospective person from within their family circle or they come to know one through family connections—plus a brief bio, including photographs, that is exchanged. At this stage, the social condition of the family is thought through in terms of their social status, financial position,

---

3 Sethi and Jain, "Indian Family Systems, Collectivistic Society," 107–16.

reputation, whether they are a joint family or a nuclear family, whether they live in a city/town/village, etc. Once both families are comfortable enough to proceed, most Hindu families will desire to check the horoscopes of prospective partners for compatibility. If horoscope investigations reveal that this young man and woman would not be compatible in marriage, then they drop the prospective proposal. But if the horoscope investigations indicate that this couple should meet one another, they will do so—usually in one of their homes.

This inquiry is primarily for the benefit of the couple, but there are sometimes more selfish interests, such as family prestige, inherited wealth, and so on, which have tarnished the reputation of such a process. Nonetheless, evidence suggests that such marriages endure longer than those in the West, where individual rights are the primary concern. Many marriages are now arranged with the help of advertisements in newspapers, magazines, and matrimonial websites; plus individuals sometimes find their life partner in their workplace or the like. Within the system of arranged marriages, individuals are normally freely allowed to accept or reject specific propositions.

Modern Hindus increasingly prefer to have complete freedom in their choice of a marriage partner. Most first-generation Diaspora Hindu couples still get married through arranged marriages and settle in the new country they have migrated to for study or work. In case of singles living abroad, parents shortlist a set of profiles which their son or daughter can come to see the selected profiles to choose from. When the couple gets married, they relocate to the new place where they want to live as a diaspora family. Traditionally, there is no such thing as divorce in Hinduism, and marriage is for life unless a person takes *sanyas* (ascetism) in a later stage of life when they renounce their worldly life and leave home in pursuit of a higher spiritual life.

Marriage in Hinduism is very ceremonial, with various ceremonies and customs accompanying the process of getting married—i.e., engagement/betrothal, pre-wedding, wedding, and post-wedding rituals and ceremonies. During these processes or stages, misunderstandings often emerge between family members based on how *their* family members were treated or how a member of the other family did (or did not) carry out a particular part of the ceremony against their wishes/expectations. In many instances, the offenses/wounds of the heart remain in the hearts of the bride and/or groom and their parents or siblings, and they have a grudge or grievance against it and bring it up in times of arguments or conflicts.

The groom, in Hindu marriages, is typically older than the bride; the groom is generally in his late twenties and the bride is in her early twenties. But with more women getting into work and having career goals, women are getting married in their late twenties as well. This is among the professional or educated community, whereas among the rural community women still get married at a young age and are considered eligible for marriage once they attain puberty. The marriage system is commonly referred to as *Vivaha* in Hinduism. In the present day and age, there are only two types of marriages spoken about when meeting a Hindu couple; people ask them if theirs was a "love marriage" or an "arranged marriage." At times a blend of both in the form of arranged-love marriages. There are increased incidence of transnational families where one or more family members live in another city or country for extended periods for work or other reasons.

Gender Issues and Rituals among Diaspora Hindu Couples

Gender is a major factor in determining roles and responsibilities in a home. All expectations of husbands and wives are defined in Hinduism—namely, men are to work and provide, while women manage the home and care for the children. However, diasporic settings require both to work, or visas may not permit both to work. Whoever comes as a dependent (mostly the women) has to be managing aspects of the home: involving cooking, cleaning, and hospitality, while the husband goes to work outside the home. In some cases, roles are reversed when husbands are stuck at home waiting for approval to work or looking for employment in a foreign land, while the wife has a secure job. Such role reversal can be a major cause of psychological crisis for the couple, especially for men who become stay-at-home dads.

Hindu life is marked by various ceremonies and rituals which play an important role in different life stages, such as when the wife becomes pregnant, a child is born, a new house is purchased, a child goes to school, etc. Couples have to get guidance from parents/elders in their country of origin on the exact details of how to carry out the rituals, and the rituals have to be conducted with the help of a priest (*purohit*) in the country where they live. In these circumstances, they need help in planning and organizing, and they invite their colleagues, friends, and, in some cases, neighbors, to participate in and to bless the occasion. These are good opportunities for Christians to build relationships with them, get entry into their homes, and understand their beliefs. These occasions can be useful to provide context for conversations in the future, and they can be an avenue to connect to the other guests who come to these ceremonies or celebrations, as well.

A middle-class Hindu couple will generally follow some rituals that have their origins in their faith. One of their key rituals is *puja* (prayer), which involves praying before an idol or a photo of a Hindu god or goddess, based on their caste or sub-caste and place of origin. This could be one among the millions of gods of Hinduism. Only ten or so gods are most popular. A ceremonial bath in the morning is required before engaging in puja.

Some Hindus practice prayers to what they consider the Sun God in the mornings, and those who are spiritually inclined engage in meditation or yoga. Some Hindus follow demi-gods—Hindu individuals who have proclaimed themselves to be gods. Popular among them are Shirdi Sai Baba, Puttaparthi Sai Baba, etc. The not-so-religious Hindus may not engage themselves in everyday puja, but they tend to pray during important festivals, when they have important office interviews, or they face crises at work or in life outside of work. Also, the menstrual cycle of women in most cases denies them the privilege to do puja during those days. On all other days, it's mostly the women who engage in aspects of cleaning the photos/idols and many times a food offering is also placed before the idol/photo of the Hindu god, and generally either spouse eats the offering after a few hours. It's mostly sweets or sugar, which is kept as an offering. Also, throughout the year there are a number of key days and festivals that are associated with Hindu gods, and almost all of them involve preparing a specific type of food for that occasion and offering them to those gods. Among diaspora couples and families, as the time they spend away from their country of origin increases—their adherence to the number of such special days generally tends to decrease as well.[4]

Influence of Media and Managing Family Resources

Movies play an important part in the lives of many Hindu families; they hum the songs during the course of daily life, singing them to express their joy or sadness or different moods of life. For many of them, watching movies-songs-comedies from films of Bollywood and Kollywood are part and parcel of their daily life and used as stress-busters. It's common for them to identify themselves as fans of a particular hero or heroine or comedian, and they anticipate the release of films of their favorite cine stars with great enthusiasm. Also, movies are consumed through platforms like Netflix, Amazon Prime, YouTube, and other internet channels in diasporic settings.

---
4 Hawley, "Hinduism: Household Religious Practice."

In a similar vein, cricket is very popular in India and people tend to follow it even after they leave the country. Conversations happen around the game, and they watch it or play it when possible. Likewise, political opinions are also quite divided, though some people may not be vocal about it and do not open up easily; there are biases—and some people spend a lot of time talking about their political convictions and parties. All three of these subjects are areas to engage with Diaspora couples.

Family resources can consist of money, time, talent, movable/immovable properties, etc. What is very interesting in a Diaspora family is their collectivistic mindset or worldview. Family members back in their home country expect them to support financially immediate family members, such as parents, siblings, in-laws, etc. For example, if their parents do not own a home, then children abroad are expected to build a house for them; and if siblings, especially sisters, are unmarried, payment toward their marriage expenses is expected. The reason is that their family thinks that as they are out of their home country, they will earn a lot and should support the family back home. Many are plagued by feelings of guilt when friends reach out to them and ask for money for their medical, educational, or business needs, and the couples are not able to provide. In some cases, they lose the money they lent. These couples must seek counseling in handling finances in such complex scenarios.

Ministering to Diaspora Hindu Families

Deuteronomy 6 admonishes that we need to talk about our faith while coming in and going out of the home. The responsibility is on the couple to make the Word of God relevant to aspects of life both inside the house and outside by developing personal and family values based on the Word of God. A Christian family should be focused on nurturing personal spiritual formation, discipling one another, being formed in a faith community, and also being on a mission to bring heaven to the lives of people, while also preparing them for heaven. So there are daily schedules, weekly/monthly/annual schedules of church participation, and participation in seminars/conferences to get equipped for family life and life in general.

Due to the collectivistic mindset of people who grow up in Hindu families, the value of individuals and their lives is not directly realized. Most of life is viewed in the context of family or work or religion. So when Hindus are struck with questions related to morality and to the meaning of life, they struggle to have absolute answers. In such scenarios, biblical answers related to the identity of a human being—as being children of the Most High God and of a loving Father who sees us as precious—could be of value to them. Before we engage in discussing such topics, building a relationship with them helps to ensure that we can communicate in a manner in which the other person is not offended.

Many Hindus believe in the fate of a person, especially when they go through bad patches in life, like losing a child, a job, or some failure in life. They rely on finding remedies through puja or rituals to overcome them. In such situations, the redemptive power of Christ can be shared with them, for the gospel brings freedom from curses and bondages. Christian families can pray for them and with them. They can direct them to Bible passages that offer encouragement and comfort and connect them with a good local fellowship where they can witness God's love in action among believers. Being part of such a fellowship can bring healing to their souls and nurture faith to endure the struggles of life in foreign lands.

Showing love and affection as a couple is not something Hindu couples are taught or mentored in; asking for forgiveness or receiving forgiveness, respecting one another, having healthy boundaries, and having a functional family are generally learned by individuals and couples through commonsense and by observing other couples. But Christians can help in these areas by sharing popular Christian books like *Five Love Languages*, *Love and Respect*, *Four Seasons of Marriage*, etc. Helpful resources are also available in blogs, videos, and audio, and can be shared with couples to enrich their marriage.

In general, Hindu culture teaches self-preservation through their belief in Karma—you will reap what you sow. So each individual and family is expected to earn and provide for themselves and their family members. Thus, families tend to help one another in various aspects of finances, like getting children married, higher education costs for children, building a house, etc. Though these may result in misunderstanding, people generally tend to live with these tensions of taking loans and giving loans within their family circles.

On occasions to remember their dead, or for birthdays or anniversaries of family members, they tend to lean toward giving a meal to an orphanage or old age home but generally, there is a lack of attitude or culture to serve or minister to the needy or poor or downtrodden in society. By and large, common Hindu couples do not tend to build a family culture of service, much of it happens within a family context. And especially in the case of diaspora couples who are financially well off and fall in the upper middle class—they focus on gathering together with similar socioeconomic groups—and spend time together on parties, or celebrations.

But the Bible asks people who are strong to help the weak and to share their provisions. Christian couples can be missional and invite Hindu couples into their home for lunch/dinner and have conversations on the aspects mentioned above. Just as Jesus Christ incarnated into our world to rescue us, it would be appropriate for Christian couples to visit Hindu couples and families in their homes and journey with them by building relationships to share the gospel when the opportunity arises.

Conclusion

At a time when Hindu individuals and families in the Diaspora are experiencing loneliness and isolation from their parents, siblings, and friends, they can realize how God can be like a father, mother, or brother to them. For couples, they can see how God has created a unique relationship between them as companions for life with a purpose to live, which includes discipling their children.

In the midst of their lost-ness, they can be told the story of how Jesus rescued lost mankind and restored them to the Father, so no one will ever feel alone. Also, by making God and his words relevant for all of life—physical, emotional, intellectual, spiritual, familial, and social—we can minister to them in all aspects of their lives: their milestones, education of children, recreation, their need of friendship and belonging, etc. Thus discipling them can be a very productive journey that could lead them to Christ and bring God's kingdom to their world.

Ministering to Hindu Students in Western Universities

Dr. Kamesh Sankaran

In this chapter, first I will explore the motivation behind and the challenges facing Christian ministry to Hindu students who come as international students to study at Western educational institutions. Then, building on the general principles of campus ministry, I will focus on specific issues in regard to witnessing to Hindu students and the discipleship of those who begin a new life in Christ. I write this as a former Hindu from India who moved to the United States as a seventeen-year-old international student to pursue my dream of a career in the space industry and found something far greater—an eternal relationship with the living God through the blood of the Lamb.

Motivation

As we look forward to the vision of Revelation 7:9 becoming a reality, we long for all humanity—specifically those currently living as Hindus and who are presently underrepresented in that great multitude—to worship Christ. To that end, ministry to international and domestic Hindu students in Western universities has a special place in Christian witness and making disciples of the global Hindus in the Diaspora.

In addition to its eschatological implications, this task also has enormous significance for Christian missions today. Missiologists suggest that India has the largest number of people groups that are unreached with the gospel.

India, a religiously pluralistic nation, is the birthplace of Buddhism, Jainism, and Sikhism; has one of the largest Muslim populations in the world; and is home to one of the oldest Christian traditions in the world. Nevertheless, Hinduism remains the demographically and culturally dominant religion. Despite over two centuries of the faithful and sacrificial work of Western missionaries in India, only limited inroads have been made in reaching the well-educated elites of Hinduism with the gospel. Due to social structures instituted by Hinduism over millennia, Indians from those unreached upper castes tend to be disproportionately numbered among the elites of the educational system. Yet, in God's sovereign plan, it is precisely the students from this unreached segment of humanity who are now at the doorstep of many active Christian ministries. This ought to move us to act responsibly and strive to be witnesses to the truth and love of Christ to this audience.

It is no accident that expatriate missionary efforts struggle to make disciples of the elites in the Hindu society in India. As was the case during the life of Christ, those with nothing to lose responded much more readily to the gospel than those with the most to lose … *in this world* (as seen in the secrecy of Nicodemus and Joseph of Arimathea, the despondency of the rich young ruler, and the rejection by the Pharisees and the Sadducees). In the Hindu context, the well-educated, upper-caste youth with a promising future have the most to lose socially by professing faith in Christ. They also face the most social pressure from peers, which prevents them from genuinely considering the claims of Christ. Yet the superiority of God's wisdom (1 Cor 1:20–25) is such that they are removed from their socially constraining religious worldview and put in a place to consider something new when they become Diaspora students.

Starting with the International Student Ministry (ISM) of InterVarsity Christian Fellowship in 1952 and the founding of International Students Inc. (ISI) in 1953, many organizations—such as Cru, Navigators, Reformed University Fellowship (RUF), and others—have focused their efforts on this important work.[1] In addition to these parachurch organizations, in-house chaplaincies in various secular and Christian universities have been ministering to Diaspora students on their campuses for decades. The Association of Christians Ministering among Internationals (www.acmi-ism.org) connects and encourages these organizations. Also, with or independent of these formal campus ministries, individual members of the faculty and

---

1 Chinn, "Making Room at Your Table."

staff, as well as churches in the vicinity of the universities, faithfully continue to serve this group of students as instruments and witnesses of Christ.

They have their hands full. According to the Institute of International Education, nearly 269,000 students from India were studying in the United States in 2022–23.[2] The Canadian government reported that 369,000 students from India were studying in that country in 2023.[3] According to the Australian Government Department of Education, about 100,000 students from India were studying there in 2023.[4] According to the United Kingdom's Higher Education Statistics Agency, about 140,000 students from India were studying there in 2022–23.[5] Numerous students depart India every year to other desirable educational destinations in Europe and Asia, where there are thriving Christian ministries. Though there are no official statistics on the religious affiliations of these half a million Indian students, a majority of them have a background in Hinduism.

In addition to the international students who are Hindu, slightly over 50 percent of the almost 4 million people of Indian origin in the United States[6] and 44 percent of the 1.5 million people of Indian origin in the United Kingdom identify as Hindu.[7] Their children, second-generation Hindu immigrants, are largely unreached by traditional Christian ministries but have an opportunity to hear and respond to the gospel during their time on a college campus.

Even as we prepare for the upside-down ordering of the kingdom of God (Matt 5–7), we function in this world in which God works through human hierarchies. Most of these Hindu Diaspora students are elites and have the potential to influence the receptivity of Christianity in many spheres of society. Some of them continue in academia and proceed to influence the subsequent generations of domestic students, while many others proceed to become corporate and political leaders of their adopted homes. At the moment of this writing, the current CEOs of Alphabet Google (Sundar Pichai), Microsoft (Satya Nadella), IBM (Arvind Krisha), Micron (Sanjay Mehrotra), Adobe (Shantanu Narayan), and Deloitte (Punit Renjen), as well

---

2 Institute of International Education, *Open Doors Report 2023*.
3 Canadian Bureau of International Education, Infographics 2023.
4 Australian Government Department of Education.
5 Higher Education Student Statistics: UK.
6 Pew Research Center, "Asian Americans: A Mosaic of Faiths."
7 Office for National Statistics (UK), "Religion and Participation in England and Wales."

as the former CEO of PepsiCo (Indra Nooyi), came as international students to the United States. Even in the American political sphere, governors who were presidential candidates (Bobby Jindal and Nikki Haley) and the current vice president (Kamala Harris) are children of international students from India. Among those who returned to their homelands to positions of prominence, one must note that King Birendra of Nepal was a student at Harvard before beginning his four-decade reign as the monarch of what was then the only Hindu nation in the world.

As tempting as it can be to rue the lost opportunities to bear witness for Christ, we must remain humble about our ability to forecast. Speaking in 1907 of the potential of international students from China in the United States, John R. Mott, Nobel laureate and the founder of the international students' ministry movement, predicted that they "will furnish a vastly disproportionate share of the leaders of the New China."[8] Mott's prediction was, of course, rendered tragically irrelevant by the rise of Communism in China. This should serve as a reminder for us not to give in to grandiose visions of triumphalism as we engage in this ministry. Yet we must not lose hope of what God can do with the Diaspora students.

A related and relevant account is the life of Bakht Singh, the most prominent Indian evangelist of the twentieth century, which ought to encourage us in the ministry to international students. A practicing Sikh, he was deeply influenced by his Christian host family when he was studying at the University of Manitoba. Their witness in truth and love became the catalyst for his entry into a new life in Christ. He revolutionized Christian missions in India.[9]

Therefore, setting our sights not on how we can change the world but on sharing Christ's truth and love with those God brings our way, we must long for these students to become trophies "in Christ's triumphal procession," so that he may use them "to spread the aroma of the knowledge of him everywhere" (2 Cor 2:14). While Christians ought not to ascribe ultimate value to anyone, including the Hindu Diaspora students, based on one's standing in this world, we must also strive to steward all good gifts and opportunities for God's purposes. Our motivation for this ministry is ultimately not because of who these students are or will become in this world, but how God can redeem and re-purpose the good gifts that he gave them for his purposes and glory.

---

8 Chinn, "Making Room at Your Table."
9 Koshy, *Bakht Singh of India*.

Challenges

Those who are engaged in college-student ministry recognize the importance of earning the trust of the students. This requires owning up to unnecessary and unintended offenses that erect a stumbling block to encountering Christ, and patiently addressing the misperceptions of Christ. In addition to those foundational principles, ministering to Hindu students requires attention to some special challenges. Two categories of understanding the audience are essential in this ministry.

First, we must acknowledge how cultural Christianity in Western culture obfuscates the gospel. Regardless of their level of religious practice, Diaspora Hindu students would be taken aback by the debauchery of sexual promiscuity and permissiveness, marital infidelity and brokenness, and substance abuse and addiction in the wider culture, and might create some association between those sociological patterns and the Christian faith. An observant Hindu would consider cultural Christian morality to be inferior and unattractive. Conversely, a nominal Hindu might be drawn to the licenses afforded by Western culture and miss out on God's purposes in creation and redemption. Furthermore, a conflation of nationalism with the kingdom of God and an expression of Christian faith that is co-opted to accommodate political agendas may lead to some Diaspora Hindu students having a tainted understanding that will require some undoing. It may be necessary to own those misrepresentations of Christian living to move forward toward an accurate Christian witness.

The other challenge arises from how Hindu theology shapes the mind and the heart of its adherents. Because of its inherently pluralistic doctrine and its practice being inextricably tied to a specific societal structure, Hinduism reinforces the idea that each culture has its own religion. Therefore, Christianity may be an appropriate religion for a different culture, but not for one with a Hindu background. Accordingly, unlike the pluralism of classical liberalism that allows for one to change beliefs and affiliations, Hindu pluralism constrains one within its impermeable boundaries. A curious Christian conversationalist might question a Hindu student about the assumption behind the constraint: Is it inherent to nature (e.g., a fish must remain in water) or is it a human-imposed constraint? Most secular Hindus may not know or care about Hindu theology, yet they hold on to their Hinduism as a cultural identity and simply declare, "I'm a Hindu, and that's that." Such a person may not be as keen to engage in meaningful exploration to compare and contrast Hindu and Christian theologies.

Another reason why a Hindu student might not be drawn to theological exploration is that Hinduism is intentionally vague in its theology; this is an inherent design feature of Hinduism. In the dominant *Advaita* branch of Hinduism, popularized by Sankara in the eighth century, human nature is not fundamentally different from divine nature and is only separated by a matter of degree. In this exalted view of anthropology, no one needs authoritative teachings about theology. This has the effect of simultaneously elevating one's allegedly innate knowledge and diminishing a sincere evaluation of alternative claims.

Furthermore, Hindu soteriology toward *moksha* (liberation from the *maya* of the physical) has a strong social component. Because each person's path toward *moksha* depends upon everyone else functioning in their assigned roles, Hinduism requires that no one steps out of their Hindu commitments. It is not surprising, therefore, that Hindus—especially those in the upper echelons of the hierarchy—live under strong social pressure not to abandon their post. Hindu society has a built-in resistance to even consider alternative theological ideas. That bond is somewhat loosened when a Hindu is an international student, so Christians should invite them to exercise that freedom to seek the truth and learn about the one who is the Truth.

While much of this discussion has been focused on first-generation students, we must also consider second-generation Hindu students. As children of those who emigrated (often as international students themselves), the second generation faces a slightly different set of challenges and pressures than discussed above. Though multiculturalism has become more normative in Western universities, they may still struggle to establish their cultural identity. They face the challenge of maintaining a religious identity as Hindus as a way of honoring their parents and as their distinctive cultural identity but may recognize the underlying disconnect of practicing a religious faith that requires a supporting social structure that they lack. This may cause the second generation to be even less inclined to an honest exploration of the Christian faith as a reaction to a desperate attempt to hold on to an alternative identity. They may also be "inoculated" against the Christian faith due to their exposure to its distorted and diluted forms.

The general patterns can be helpful, but also harmful when they are indiscriminately applied to every Hindu student. Given the complexity of Hindu theology and the numerous ethnic and linguistic groups in India that practice Hinduism, it is best to hold these ideas loosely and to hold on to God's call tightly. The inability to comprehend the Hindu worldview may cause fear in bearing witness to the truth and love of Christ; however, a simplistic understanding of Hinduism may also lead to false confidence in it. Instead of doubting our call or assuming that we have "figured out" our audience, we must focus on Christ's love and Christ's redemptive purposes for Hindu students.

Witness

Given the challenges to this ministry, authentic relationships that are characterized by humility and sincerity are necessary to build trust to overcome them. Such relationships are characterized by a natural outflow of trust in God's good purposes and exude peace that reduces the anxiety for both parties. Due to the misconceptions of Christianity that a Hindu student may have, it is worth noting from social psychology that a peripheral route is more effective than a central route to earn trust.[10] In other words, instead of directly stating the facts and arguing to correct misunderstandings, a relaxed invitation to observe our life is better for building trust. Because people have God-given radars that alert them to uncomfortable situations, we must rest in the Lord and not impatiently strive for quick results.

Such a ministry can, and should, happen in a variety of arenas. Let's consider some of them.

- *The academic life of the campus:* The demands and difficulties of academic life, and the financial concerns that accompany them, can provide a common ground for encouraging conversations that establish trust with each other and point to our ultimate source of trust in life. Some of the frustrations and obstacles to success could be from interpersonal frictions and the importance of relational aspects of learning; supporting a Diaspora student in such cases may be especially valuable. There may also be some gaps to be bridged; while higher education in many Western societies operates under federal laws about privacy (such as FERPA in the United States), educational systems in other nations (such as India) to advertise the scores of each student and rank them publicly. To one whose value was ascribed based on accomplishment, the Christian alternative—of striving for excellence but not being defined by successes—can be curious and refreshing.

---

10 Petty and Cacioppo, "Communication and Persuasion."

- *Social life inside the campus:* We long to belong. Despite the variations in the specific longings to be satisfied, this truism is relevant in Christian witness because 38 percent of international students in the United States report that they have no close American friends; and the number is even higher among non-European international students.[11] There is an immense value of fellowship with a peer who cares about our accomplishments and failures, but also about our joys and pains. Friendships are the setting to demonstrate Christianity's true claim about a person's inherent value in creation and redemption. Much of the discussion assumes that many of the Hindu students in Western universities are in the upper castes of the religious structure; however, those from the lower rungs or entirely out of the caste system face their own challenges.[12] Understanding the uphill battles that they faced to get where they are and how that might continue to be a challenge moving forward[13] is an important way to live out the command of Philippians 2:3–4.

- *Social life outside the campus:* Though exact statistics are hard to verify, the majority of international students do not enter a Christian home and experience local hospitality.[14] In addition to the immense value of allowing for normal human relationships outside the narrow slice of age and ability on a college campus, they also provide opportunities for Christians from all walks of life to do the work of ministry (Eph 4:12). Those who are not accustomed to working with college-age students might be surprised by this developmental stage of an intense inward focus. Instead of rejecting it or fighting it, they ought to embrace it and work with the intense desire of students to understand themselves. Coming alongside them in this journey opens the doors for them to consider who they are and who they could be in Christ. To the matters of accomplishment and significance raised earlier, conversations with Christians outside of academia can provide a valuable perspective that may not be found on campus. Christians in non-academic life may better demonstrate

---

11 Gareis, "Intercultural Friendship," 309–28.
12 Rai, "Big Tech Is Importing India's Caste Legacy to Silicon Valley."
13 Subramanian, *Caste of Merit: Engineering Education in India*.
14 Chinn, "Making Room at Your Table."

what it looks like to pursue excellence as unto the Lord (Col 3:23), and not as unto an idol. In doing so, they can demonstrate what Chesterton observed: "Joy … is the gigantic secret of the Christian."[15]

Regardless of the arena, a Christian witness to a diasporic Hindu student requires patience to work through misunderstandings and an appreciation for the magnitude of the gap to be bridged. It is fitting that the Bible is filled with agricultural metaphors because this is slow and ongoing work of tilling, sowing, and watering. The profligacy of God in sowing even when most of the seeds would not produce a harvest for the sake of the small fraction of the case where the harvest is plentiful (Matt 13:1–23) and the reminder that it is God who makes things grow (1 Cor 3:6) ought to free us and motivates us to be his witnesses in these arenas. While we must allow the student to wrestle with the claims of Christ and the offense of the Cross, we must humbly strive not to put any other obstacles before a Hindu student. We are to patiently and purposefully address their thirst that can only be quenched by the Living Water and their hunger that can only be satisfied by the Bread of Life.

Discipleship

While salvation is a gift of the Lord, discipleship—including baptism and teaching new believers to obey every command of Christ (Matt 28:19-20)—is costly for both the disciple from a Hindu background and the mentor. The pre-Constantine church had an intensive two-year catechumen process to make disciples out of former adherents of other faiths.[16] We too should not expect any shortcuts or exemptions for us in that work. This requires trust and transparency, with a willingness to ask and receive hard questions of significance. Yet, without a meaningful relationship, the necessary Christian accountability may be either ineffective or come across as abusive.

Perhaps the first and the most significant challenge in the Christian discipleship of a former Hindu may be in the realm of epistemology,[17] for it requires the new believer to move from a culture-based religion to a canon-based religion. Because Hinduism does not have a canon of Scripture and has a high view of human intuition to learn things about the divine on one's own, it would be a steep transition for a new Christian from that worldview

---

15 Chesterton, *Orthodoxy*.
16 Sittser, *Resilient Faith*.
17 Epistemology in this context can be defined, in simple terms, as trying to understand and make sense of the world around us in categories we develop based on the culture we grow up in.

to accept the necessity of the authoritative revelation of God's Word (2 Tim 3:16–17) to learn of the ultimate revelation in the incarnate Word of God (John 1:18).

There may be other issues that may pose confusion and may require unlearning. Not surprisingly, aspects of Christology (e.g., John 1:1–18) and Christian soteriology (John 14:6; Acts 4:12) that are difficult for new believers from any background to receive will be especially challenging for a former Hindu. It may also be necessary to distinguish the physical reality of the incarnation (despite its linguistic redundancy) from the Hindu concept of avatar. Yet, instead of assuming the inability of the new disciple to grasp them, it is best to allow these items to arise organically during regular conversations or Bible studies and interactively address them.

In the matters of Christian living, we must heed the decision of the council in Jerusalem and not put undue burdens in their early stages of discipleship and only focus on crucial matters such as abstention from the idolatry of their former faith and adherence to a Christian view of sexuality (Acts 15:28–29). It is crucial to emphasize their newfound citizenship in the kingdom of God without implying the need to change their cultural affiliation.

A new disciple will require explicit and repeated guidance to consider their present life in light of the larger arc of creation, fall, redemption, and new creation. In contrast to the cyclical view of Hinduism of physical reality as caught in the trap of maya, a new Christian should be trained to embrace the significance of the present physical reality and its implications to move forward to welcome the kingdom of God. In that journey, it is crucial to re-form a new disciple's view of anthropology and embrace one's identity in Christ. In the context of academic life and its tendency to provide an alternative identity based on accomplishment and rank, the new Christian can rejoice and rest in one's dignity, which is independent of status in this world. There will be many other unforeseen challenges in a former Hindu's integration into the church, due to double alienation from both the old and the new communities, in addition to the expected challenges of Christian growth that every believer faces.

Conclusion

The strategies we have discussed in ministering to Diaspora Hindu students are not a substitute for the reality that this is a deeply relational work of serving people who are created in the image of God yet without any glimpse of Christ in their genealogy. They have risked everything by leaving their comfort zone to pursue success and yet have a deep thirst that can only be satisfied by Christ. This work requires genuine love and humility, which cannot be substituted or imitated. In other words, this ministry requires the fundamental Christian virtue of empathy, applied to a special case. Though it is helpful to learn about these general patterns and minefields, it is best to learn the specifics of their life story from the students themselves. Instead of getting lost in the myriad aspects and nuances of Hindu culture, it is essential to focus on the truth of the gospel and Christ, who is the Truth.

The ministry discussed here may be daunting and is subject to unseen spiritual struggles (Eph 6:12). Yet, the mentor and disciple should embark on this journey in faith and can "approach God's throne of grace with confidence, so that we may receive mercy and find grace to help us in our time of need" (Heb 4:16). Like Paul, we can function in faith that God will grant us grace in this ministry so that, in bringing these Hindu students into the body of Christ, "the manifold wisdom of God might be made known to the rulers and authorities in the heavenly places" (Eph 3:6–10). Therefore, we may boldly continue in this work to "present everyone fully mature in Christ" (Col 1:28) and rededicate them to become witnesses for Christ locally and globally (Acts 1:8).

Ministry among the Indian Diaspora in the Philippines

Rev. Mark Sudhir

I have lived in the Philippines for over a decade now, and I am primarily focused on discipling Indians in and through the oldest Indian Diaspora church in this country. The Indian population in the Philippines has grown more remarkably in the last ten years than at any other time in history. The need to reach out to the Indian Diaspora with the gospel throughout the Philippines is not only important but urgent.

History and Religion of the Indian Diaspora in the Philippines

The presence of the Indians in the Philippines can be traced to 1762–64, when Sepoy troops and some laborers from then Madras (now Chennai) came under British colonial rule during the Seven Years' War against Spanish forces in the Philippines.[1] They used to receive very meager payments from their British superiors and were often reduced to living on charity. But when the war came to an end, the British occupation of Manila was lifted. When the British Fleet sailed back to India, some Indians decided to stay back and mostly settled in the Cainta area of Manila.

The merchants of Gujarat and Mumbai traveled regularly to the Philippines, and then fresh migrations began to trickle in. The later waves of migrants originated from Sindh and Punjab when the British occupied these areas. At the end of colonial rule, when the partition of

---
1 Rye, "Indian Community in the Philippines," 707–73.

India took place in 1947, many Sindhi Hindus and Sindhi Sikhs from the Sindh region (now in Pakistan) fled to India and various parts of the world, including the Philippines.

Among the South Asian Diaspora in the Philippines, the majority are Sikhs or Hindus. There are a few Sindhi Muslims and a handful of Sindhi Christians. In 1924, the first gurudwara was built in the Paco district of Manila and was called the Indian Sikh Temple. At present, there are more than twenty gurudwaras throughout the Philippines. The early Indian migrants, both of Sindhi and Hindu backgrounds, were using the Sikh temple and had a united congregation, but the differences in prayers caused the Hindus to build their own temple, where they also placed the Sikh scripture, *Gurugranth Sahib*. Many Sindhis have a hybridized form of religion that mixes select aspects of Hindu and Sikh beliefs. When we visit their houses, it is not uncommon to see pictures of many Hindu gods and goddesses, as well as that of Sikh Gurus. Among the Sindhi community in the Philippines, a different sect of Hinduism, known as the Radha Soami movement, has many followers. It emphasizes vegetarianism and the worshiping of Baba Shiv Dayal Singh. Their teachings are a syncretism of different religions. A few Indians who have resided here for a long period and many who were born here have become Catholic, the dominant faith of the nation. This has largely resulted from religious schooling, the influence of friends, and intermarriage with locals.

The Indians in the Philippines can be broadly divided into five categories of people, depending on their ethnocultural particularity and migratory history. The first is the Sindhis, who came during the time of the British colonies looking for business opportunities, and then after the partition of India and Pakistan. They mainly live in the business districts, are mostly involved in mainstream businesses, and live very conservative lives. Among this community, one can see up to the third and fourth generations who continue in the same trade and sociocultural practices and might not have any interactions with people in India or elsewhere. Most of their interactions are limited to fellow Sindhis in the country or the broader Sindhi diaspora with whom they are connected for business or local Filipino clients with whom they do business. Nearly 80 percent of the Sindhis found in the Philippines live in greater Manila.

The second group is the Punjabis, or Sikhs, a growing population here. They are small traders and are involved in microfinancing businesses. They live on the outskirts of Manila and in the provinces. Their work involves lots of risks. They lend money to clients, selling goods without any collateral and then collect money in daily installments. They put their lives on the line and go to public markets and small shops and vendors no matter rain or shine. Often they become victims—losing clients, or, in extreme cases, losing their lives.

The Information and Technology (IT) workers form the third group of people. India sends out a large number of computer and information technology professionals to many countries all over the world, and some of them have come to the Philippines. India also has a large pool of English-speaking middle class trained in science, finance, and management who are eager to explore employment overseas. The growing demands for technological solutions in banking, expanding Indian motor-vehicle plants, Indian pharmaceutical companies, various sectors of business, and the growing bilateral relations between India and the Philippines, continue to bring a record number of Indians every year to the Philippines. Many American and Canadian companies have built their call centers and back-office operations in the Philippines and have brought back many technicians and software programmers from India.

The fourth group consists of the diplomatic staff of the Indian embassy. They are often deployed for a shorter tenure and continually change. They are official representatives of the government of India and their primary goals are diplomatic relationships between nations, trade, cultural exchange, and geopolitical issues. Some officials are very friendly toward all Indians in the foreign land, while others are not very approachable to those involved in religious activities and a few others are very opposed.

International students from India make up the fifth group. Most of them are medical students from India who are studying in various medical institutions across the country. In the last seven years or so, we have witnessed a huge surge in the number of students from India coming to do their medical studies in the Philippines. The language of instruction being English and similar climatic conditions are other factors; however, the main attraction is the cost of studies, which is affordable as compared to medical schools in the West and the possibility to do medical residency requirements or pursue further studies in the developed nations.

The number of Indians residing in the Philippines in December 1955[2] was only 1351 persons, but now the number has grown close to a million.

---

2 Regala-Angangco, "Indian Community in the Philippines," 10.

It has grown steadily over the last many decades and seen a sudden surge over the last decade or so. Several reasons attract Indian migrants to the Philippines. At present, business and professional higher studies are the primary reasons, but the need for Information and Technology personnel is another reason for the burgeoning Indian population. Few others faced difficult social challenges in India and wanted to move to a better place, but not being able to migrate to their dream countries, they chose to come to the Philippines as a place where they could stay safely and build a good foundation to move to first-world countries subsequently. Its geographical proximity to India, similarity in physical features, growing middle class, friendly people, and culture are other reasons for the growing population of Indians in the Philippines.

In the last decade or so, bilateral relationships between India and the Philippines have been growing stronger progressively. The specific areas that both countries are strengthening is their bilateral relationships, including trade, cultural, economic, and geopolitical. The colonial past and similar socioeconomic standing of the nations have created a perfect synergy and a sense of mutual understanding. According to the Indian Embassy in Manila, the Philippines and India formally established diplomatic relations on November 26, 1949, shortly after both nations gained independence.[3]

In the area of trade and commerce, both these countries signed a trade agreement in 1979. The strong political, security, and defense ties and interactions between both countries have seen an intensification, especially since the initiation of the ASEAN-India Summit, of which India is a founding member. The historical, civilizational linkages, maritime connectivity, and cultural exchanges between Southeast Asia and India have deepened over the last thirty years and provide a strong foundation for such a regional partnership. Export and import between India and the Philippines have grown significantly. As per the Indian Embassy to the Philippines, "The bilateral trade between India and the Philippines stood at US$2.84 billion in 2021–22."[4] Motor vehicles, spare parts and accessories, pharmaceutical products, machinery and mechanical appliances, boilers and reactors, Indian groceries, Indian garments, and articles of iron and steel are the main imported items from India.

---

3 Embassy of India in Manila, "Bilateral, Political and Cultural Relations."
4 Embassy of India in Manila, "Bilateral Trade."

Culturally, the relationships are getting stronger in the Philippines. Indian festivals like Holi and Diwali are celebrated publicly, and many Filipinos are also celebrating along with Indians. Indian fast foods like samosas and sweets are in high demand in the fast-food centers and in Indian groceries. Filipino people are huge consumers of Indian groceries and foods. Many overseas Filipino workers who have worked in the Middle East or India have developed a taste for Indian foods and include them in their diets. Due to the increase in marriages between Indians and Filipinos, there is greater acceptance of each other. The people of both nationalities get along very well and have developed a mutually appreciative and beneficial relationship.

Ministry Opportunities and Challenges

The growing Indian population in the Philippines offers many ministry opportunities. Almost 98 percent of Indians in the Philippines are Hindus, Sikhs, Muslims, and followers of other religions. In the last two decades, we have observed that Indians are taking root across every region of the Philippines. Almost 90 percent of the Indians are from Punjab, who come here to start micro-financing businesses. Since it is a risky business, they most often lose their income and do not get back what they have invested. They become easily discouraged and are beset with lots of financial problems. They are constantly in need of assistance and reliable guidance to navigate through the many challenges of immigrant life. We reach them through counseling and direct them to a less risky business or to work in local companies.

One of the major issues that we see among Indians is marital problems. When the Indians come here for business, there is no provision for permanent residence visas, and work visas do not permit them to be self-employed. To secure a permanent residency visa, people have to deposit a huge sum of money, which is not possible for most Indians who want to start small-scale businesses. This leads them to marry Filipina women for the sake of a visa. Though already married in India, they get married again in the Philippines, a sham marriage on paper only, to solve their visa predicaments. This creates a huge problem for their family in India. We counsel them not to get married again but to explore other available categories to get visas for their families in India.

Alcoholism is another serious threat to the Indian Diaspora in the Philippines. Due to their persistent business and marital problems, many end up becoming alcoholics. They need help—specifically counseling to overcome their troubles. Their ruthless competition in business practices and survival struggles result in grave enmity among themselves. Some of them hire kidnappers to hold business rivals for ransom and some of them even get killed. The news of the killings of many innocent Indian businessmen is featured in newspapers and television regularly. Some of this can be addressed by helping to build cooperation and diversification in business activities. The deep-seated feeling of missing their native land, culture, and people is clearly evident among them, which is also an opportunity for ministry. As they cannot be friendly with fellow businesspeople, due to competition, when we reach them as non-businesspeople from an Indian cultural background, they find it easier to make friends and they are open to sharing about their life issues. Being away from their homeland, Indians in the Philippines face less societal or family pressure to adhere to communal expectations and are more open to exploring other faiths. Many have shown remarkable openness to hear about Jesus or come to a church and decide to become followers of Jesus.

Alongside the many ministry opportunities mentioned above, there are a few unique challenges to ministry among the Indians in the Philippines that we have experienced in our ministry. Some of them are: First, *Adding One More God*—Culturally, Hindus, and Indians in general, would like to be blessed in their health, family, and business, whatever the source may be. When they come to the Philippines, they are exposed to Catholic culture and are influenced by their Filipina wife or local customers. They do not see or feel it a problem to add Jesus as a God among many gods. When we bring the gospel to them and challenge them to draw a line to confess Jesus as the only God and Savior, they find it very difficult unless the Holy Spirit works in them.

Second, *The Next Generation Problem*—The young children of Indian families, who are born and brought up here, are Hindus or Sikhs culturally, but in their local schools and colleges they are introduced to Catholicism. Due to the pressure exerted by their parents, they go to the temple and Gurudwaras and do the rituals but do not understand anything the priests are chanting or reading from their scriptures. Many young children become confused and disillusioned with religious rituals and eventually become non-religious. Some children become trapped under both traditions. They do not want to hurt the feelings of their parents and are afraid that if they reject their parents' beliefs, misfortune may come upon them in the future.

Third, *Finding Indian Christian Spouses*—One of the many reasons some families do not encourage their children to get baptized and become Christ-followers is that they fear that when their children grow up and are ready to get married, no Indian family may be willing to give their children to them in marriage. Though some parents come to Christ, they do not allow their children to be baptized, even if their children want to be. Some young people are hesitant to commit their lives fully to Jesus because they also think it will be difficult for them to find a spouse from an Indian family.

Fourth, *Indigenous Ministers*—Indians find it more comfortable and are challenged to accept the gospel to follow Jesus when they see a fellow Indian from their own culture, language, and background following Jesus. Indians are spread around every corner of the Philippines, and we need more Indian Christian witnesses in every region of the country. Though we have mobilized many Filipino churches to reach out to Indians (many are praying and have adopted Indians as their mission focus), that is not as effective as a fellow Indian Christian reaching out to them. If more Indian Christians would minister to Indians in diasporic settings all around the world, it would be easier for Indians to follow Christ.

Ministry Strategies and Goals

Here are six proven ministry strategies that have been fruitful in ministry to the Indians in the Philippines. First, *Counseling*—Many Indians in the Philippines easily become victims of visa regulations, business challenges, family problems, and other issues related to living in a foreign country. Many are looking for sound and reliable help and direction for their lives. We have found that culturally appropriate counseling using the Word of God is very effective in dealing with discouragement, depression, and marital problems of Indian diasporic living. They feel that there is no one to listen to their problems, and the people of the host nation do not fully understand their dilemma. When they see our genuine concern for them and our willingness to walk with them, that greatly reinforces their trust in us. When people experience the power of answered prayers in Jesus' name or encounter miracles, they are drawn to Jesus. Many start reading the Bible and are drawn to the life of Jesus and the teachings of the New Testament. As the Bible reminds us, without right counsel, people perish (Prov 15:22; 11:14).

Second, *Hospitality*—When we open our homes to immigrants by extending genuine friendship and fellowship, along with occasional meals, it opens up great opportunities for conversations and gospel sharing. The contemporary busyness of life and demanding workloads leave them longing for authentic heart-to-heart interactions. The loneliness of living in a foreign land without any close friends or family is generally hard for anyone, especially new immigrants who do not speak the local language and are unable to interact with locals. When we make ourselves available to listen to their life situations and offer honest friendship, we are able to earn their trust. Moreover, they are very appreciative of home-cooked Indian food, and fellowship in the home setting goes a long way in building a strong relationship. This biblical practice of hospitality is key to opening the heart's door of immigrants in foreign lands.

Third, *Legal Assistance—Seva* (service) has a great deal of influence on Indian culture. When we offer help in the midst of their problems, that becomes a powerful tool in reaching out to the Diaspora Indians in the Philippines. Practically, this would entail leading them to the right offices and officers when they are being cheated by the agents for their visas or when they are in family problems reaching out to them and helping them to restore peace in the family. We were able to provide practical and timely help to many families, and we believe this has created goodwill in the community for our church. Subsequently, these benefactors refer their family and friends to us when they require assistance. Being networked with helpful people and lawyers in city churches and local government offices is vital in this regard.

Fourth, *Music and Cultural Activities*—Indians are very musically and culturally oriented. We have seen many attracted to the gospel through music. The Indian Diaspora here are interested in playing Indian musical instruments and singing songs of their homeland. In the past, when we were able to arrange musical and cultural programs, huge crowds attended and many of them became a part of the church. We also started an outreach program using cricket matches. Arranging these types of cultural, musical, and sports programs has proved to be an effective strategy for reaching Indians in the Philippines.

Fifth, *Actively Engage with the Indian Chamber of Commerce*—Many Indian businesses, Indian embassy staff, and Filipino political leaders are closely linked with the Indian Chamber of Commerce in the Philippines. A few years ago, we got involved with them and it has opened many new doors for ministry for us. We wrote devotional articles in their business magazine, as well as participated in their programs organized by the Indian embassy regularly. This is very strategic to get connected with Indians widely.

Finally, *Spiritual Activities*—Many members of our church became strong followers of Jesus by experiencing miraculous spiritual breakthroughs and deliverances. Healings from sicknesses, deliverance from demonic possession, liberation from addictions and other influences, and experiencing dramatic change in their behavior are some of the spiritual activities that have been found to be fruitful strategies to draw people to Jesus Christ.

In view of the above ministry opportunities and proven ministry strategies among Indians in the Philippines, we have set an ambitious goal to reach every Indian with the message of Jesus Christ through outreach activities and virtual platforms. With God's grace and help, we hope to achieve them through the following fourfold plans: a) to continue to mobilize Filipino churches and theological seminaries to adopt Indians as a strategic mission field to reach them here so that we can influence India with the gospel through Indian families in the Philippines; b) Strengthen our active relationship with the Indian Chamber of Commerce, and the Indian Embassy: in order to connect with other Indians; c) Continue to reach out and challenge Indian churches here as well as in India to raise ministers to reach the Indian Diaspora in the Philippines; d) Connect Indian churches in the Philippines with Indian Diaspora worldwide to facilitate learning, interaction, and meaningful exchange of ministries, as well as to find life partners for Christian young men and women.

Conclusion

God has begun a ministry among the Indian Diaspora in the Philippines. God has allowed many Indians to come here for his greater purpose to become his followers. With the strengthening of bilateral ties between the Philippines and India, more Indians are going to come here. This is a great opportunity for ministry and God is about to bring about a harvest of souls. They in turn can become our ministry partners in India through their immediate friends, family, and relatives.

Many of our church members have experienced miraculous transformations in their lives. By witnessing this, their families and relatives are encouraged to visit churches back in India. It is a little tough and challenging but it is not impossible for them to come to Christ. Revival is ringing around us. This is a time for all of us to respond to God's movement of bringing Indian Hindus, Sikhs, and people of other faiths to Christ. The Indian and Filipino church has an equal responsibility to carry out this mission.

Malaysia's Tamil Women

Agents of Change or Guardians of Tradition?

Mrs. Anita Lazarus

> *Don't you get it? Can't you see? As we change our minds,*
> *we will change the world.*
> *And until we do, we will remain where we are.*
> —Marianne Williamson, in *A Woman of Worth*

Marianne Williamson differentiates between two kinds of women: those who are agents of change, and those who prefer to remain guardians of tradition. This chapter looks at women and family issues specifically among the Tamil Diaspora in Malaysia, as a way to consider areas of Christian service to them. It identifies efforts made in the past as a learning point for those seeking to serve this group of women. I focus on Malaysia's Tamil community for two personal reasons. For nearly fifteen years before coming to Malaysia, my husband and I worked with disadvantaged Tamil children in India and built lasting relationships with several of them. More recently, a beautiful adopted granddaughter of Tamil origin refreshed our interest in this group.

This material has been gathered from a random sample group of Tamil women from Melaka, Kuala Lumpur, Selangor, Penang, and Ipoh—through personal interviews over the phone and Zoom (owing to COVID-19 restrictions). Secondary sources contributed to the background and setting. Most examples, though current, link back to the experience of either one or two previous generations. A review of the box-office hit movie *Kabali* (2016) adds a popular perspective to issues of women, youth, and caste in this community.

A common language and ethnicity link the Tamil Diaspora globally. Yet in Malaysia, there are two distinct subgroups of Tamils. The Indian Tamils, descended from poor, uneducated plantation laborers who migrated from India between 1840 and 1938, remain on the fringes of Malaysian society today. The second group was originally educated professionals who migrated from Jaffna at the turn of the twentieth century to help the British administration in Malaysia. They contributed to the development and carved out an influential space for themselves.[1]

Women from the first group have been marginalized and still seek acceptance and dignity, while those from Jaffna had the opportunity to become changemakers. Others who tried to find new identities struggled with the issue of belonging. The tension this created could have been destructive, but Selvi's story (which appears later) is an example of Christ's power to transform such tension into freedom, hope, and joy. Each story presents unique pointers for Christian witnesses.

A Malaysian Minority

Let's focus first on the Indian Tamil community. Indian Tamils constitute just 6.8 percent of Malaysia's total population, and of these 6.3 percent are Tamil-speaking Hindus.[2] The majority of Indian Tamils are the descendants of indentured laborers brought to work on plantations, road, and rail construction projects. With no way back to India, their status changed from migrant workers to reluctant immigrants.

Plantation life destroyed the family structures of this group. Indentured women were illiterate, and many became widows, sex workers, or outcasts. An imbalanced gender ratio of just eighteen women to every one thousand men in the early days led to multiple partners, prostitution, crime, and violence. After independence, the Malaysian government left the community to itself, initially invalidating marriage by Hindu rites, as well as denying citizenship to those without proper papers.[3] Restricted to their workplaces, this group was excluded from the socioeconomic initiatives that helped other communities

---

1 Raman, *Malaysian Indian Dilemma*, 18–20.
2 Malaysia Demographic Profile, 2020.
3 Belle, *Indians in Malaysia*, 120.

develop. Over time, they fell between the cracks, with responsibility shirked by plantation owners, the British and Malaysian governments, and their fellow Tamils from Jaffna. Their rights were also betrayed by their political party. They were left in a tragic, orphaned state, "illiterate, backward, inert, leaderless, a source of shame to the other Indian groups."[4]

The continual marginalization of Tamil culture, language, and religion (Hinduism) had a deeply negative impact on the development of the men, women, and youth of this group. Handicapped by a lack of assimilation, employment, education, and economic opportunity, many Indian Tamil men used alcohol and drugs as an outlet for their frustration. They got involved in antisocial gangs, pimping, and violence. While Hindu custom gives the husband the status of a type of "god" (swami), to be honored at all costs (immortalized by the ideal couple, Rama and Sita, in the epic Ramayana), it occasionally misuses denied gender rights to justify violence as discipline. Any protest against unfair treatment was interpreted as a rejection of the culture and even the religion itself.[5]

Research findings among Hindu immigrants in the US have established a direct link between lack of social assimilation and domestic violence.[6] The domestic violence was the most common complaint among the Indian Tamils in Malaysia too.[7] Unlike the Chinese and Malays, Hindu Tamils lack support and welfare from within their own community. At the same time, Malaysia's legal system makes violence punishable only if linked to a penal offense or the use of a weapon. While the country's official Crime Index for 2020 records a drop in crime, domestic violence is excluded from these figures.[8]

The breakdown of family structures and community had drastic repercussions for Tamil women. Though the government aimed for gender equality, statistics show a persistent gap between men and women in the three key areas of sociopolitical participation, economic opportunity and participation, and health and survival. Among women of plantation origin, these gaps were accompanied by a lack of education and skills.

---

4 Tate, *Malaysian History, Problems and Future*.
5 Che Soh, "Perspectives on Wife Battering in Malaysia."
6 Pallatino, "Factors Contributing to Domestic Violence."
7 Women's Aid Organization (WAO) Malaysia cites incidences of Domestic Violence annually. See https://wao.org.my/wp-content/uploads/2021/02/Annual-Statistics-2019.pdf.
8 Che Soh, "Cultural and Legal Perspectives."

Their lives reflected the malaise of their community. Of the 400 women who committed suicide in Malaysia between 1970 and 1990, 293 were from the Indian Tamil community alone.[9] This betrayed a profound lack of hope for the future and a malaise which folk beliefs, superstitions, and rituals are unable to remedy. Inequality, exclusion, violence, and lack of support lowered self-esteem as well as the ability to function emotionally and psychologically. Though made in God's image, these women saw every area of their dignity and respect broken, leaving them vulnerable to predators. Their situation cried out for change through social transformation.

Growing up outside a secure family structure and stuck with inadequate education in the plantations, young people lacked key life skills. The switch from rubber to palm oil cultivation in the mid-1950s pushed young Tamils to migrate to urban areas, though without the educational and entrepreneurial skills to survive in that environment. It is worth emphasizing the repercussions on the community: men became high-risk, urban misfits engaged in gang fights, alcoholism, and antisocial behavior, while women turned to prostitution. The first political rally for Hindu rights was staged by HINDRAF (Hindu Rights Action Force) in 2007. My husband and I arrived in Malaysia in February 2008 and observed HINDRAF's impact through two successive elections. The government of sixty-one years fell in 2018, by which time HINDRAF's influence had waned. The new government's promise of a "new" Malaysia ran aground as it continued to ignore the need for more equal, multiracial representation.[10]

Kabali

The Tamil movie *Kabali* (2016) refocused popular attention on issues HINDRAF had raised—such as inequality and social injustice among the Tamils, especially its youth and women. The solutions it offered created quite a stir among the community it depicted.

Kabali, an Indian Tamil from Malaysia, challenges government neglect while presenting positive family and gender templates for socially "at risk" youth gangs, so as to wipe out their legacy of shame. A reformed gangster, Kabali, educates the youth, rehabilitates addicts, and develops young Tamils as future leaders—not of a gang, but of a wholesome, casteless society.

---

9   Raman, *The Malaysian Indian Dilemma*, 159–60.
10 Kaur, "HINDRAF and the Malaysian Indian Minority," 9–11.

Kabali presents an aspiration for gender equality and harmonious family relationships, in sharp contrast to the present reality. In carrying groceries for his wife, the patriarchal expectation of a wife owing service to her husband is reversed. His respect for her opinions overturns the image of a voiceless indentured woman. Meanwhile, Kabali's gun-toting daughter is a woman able to hold her own in the world of gang warfare.

Tamil Women Changemakers

The women from the Jaffna group, though part of the wider Tamil Diaspora, traced a startlingly different journey in Malaysia. The Tamil community on the plains of Ceylon took advantage of American and British missionary schools to gain an English education. This and conversion to Christianity opened up opportunities. In the late nineteenth and early twentieth centuries, many migrated to take up clerical spaces on plantations in the British colony of Malaya. They were either middlemen between British administrators and plantation laborers, or teachers in mission-run English schools.[11] The women from this group used their influence to build educational structures in Malaysia and worked for justice and equality for women. Thus, they had an opportunity to become agents of change in their adopted homeland.

Rasammah Bhupalan is a trailblazer in this regard.[12] Three influences made her a lifelong freedom fighter. A stint at the age of sixteen with the women's brigade of Bose's Indian National Army gave her the experience of setting aside differences to unite and fight for a common cause. She progressed from the struggle for Indian freedom to freedom for Malaysia's women after its independence. Her passion for women's rights came from a Christian worldview of service, unity, respect, and justice for all. It was shaped by a mother fiercely committed to Christian values and a doting father who was an outstanding teacher. Both belonged to the first generation of the elite Jaffna Tamil Diaspora.[13]

Rasammah cofounded the National Council of Women's Organisations (a non-political, non-religious, and non-communal group), through which she advanced the cause of equality and justice for Malaysian women at the regional, national and international levels. As chair of its Law and Human Rights Commission, she promoted laws to protect women against

---

11 Wilford, *Cage of Freedom*, 132–33.
12 Rasammah Bhupalan, personal interview. February 6, 2021.
13 Gopinath, *Footsteps in the Sands of Time*, 11–14.

exploitation and abuse within marriage. Through the YWCA's vocational training center, she enabled unskilled women to earn a living. Her active role in the National Anti-Drugs Association tackled the widespread addiction that undergirded crime.[14]

Supported by excellent Malayali teachers, most of whom were trained in Kerala, India, she built up preexisting Methodist schools to provide a stable English-based alternative to Malaysia's frequently changing policy on education and language.[15] The Christian fellowships in these schools continued to expose students to the gospel and thus changed their lives. She also united teachers under the Malayan Teachers National Congress in order to secure equal pay for equal work for women teachers.

Together with Ramani Gurusamy and others, Rasammah focused on gender issues among professionals, until a Women's Ministry was finally established in 2001. Two other Tamil names to note here are Ivy Josiah and Ambiga Srinivasan. Josiah, another Jaffna Tamil, pioneered the Women's Aid Organization to bring the issue of domestic violence to the fore, while Srinivasan an Indian Tamil lawyer, championed the cause of gender equality in the courts. Later, Srinivasan linked up with HINDRAF to support the cause of Hindu rights.

After fifty years of women's activism, Rasammah remarked in 2013:

> We have come a long way. But how do we gauge the empowerment of women when we have only touched upper- and middle-income women? What about the lower-income group? What have we brought to them?

Rasammah's question poses a relevant challenge for the women of the Tamil community, the government, and the church.[16]

The Clamor of Many Gods

The following narrative is an interesting profile of Selvi (name changed to protect her identity), a Tamil woman who successfully freed herself from the traditions she inherited, to live her own life. In this way, she inadvertently became an agent of change herself. Her story showcases the complexity of the process of meeting Christ, who is the ultimate change-maker. In reality, it is

---

14 Gopinath, "Introduction."
15 George, Personal interview with the director of curriculum development, February 10, 2021.
16 Soon, "50 Years of Women's Activism."

something only the Holy Spirit can achieve. With all sensitivity and humility, we can at most support others through the process of change.

Selvi was born and raised in Malaysia. She and her husband are qualified professionals working in the areas of their choice. Both were Hindus, and both had mothers (one from Jaffna and the other from India) who were fiercely protective of their religion and rituals as markers of identity. The tradition was enforced through an expectation of obedience and a fear of reprisals by family, friends, and family gods, and other pressures.

Three things stand out in Selvi's journey of transformation: the need for truth, the need to be loved, and the loving community support she received when making her change-over. As an adult searching for answers, Selvi started to seek God but found the crowd of gods clamoring for attention and obedience unconvincing. Exposure to other religions through friends and overseas study awakened her to new possibilities. The process took fourteen years before she accepted Christ at a musical function. It was the work of the Holy Spirit.

Eventually, the gospel pointed her to the truth that God loved her. She said: "'I love you' is something no other god says! When I surrendered to Jesus, there was deep peace! I knew he really loved me. It was so clear!"[17]

Strict adherence to unexplained but rigidly enforced religious rituals held her in the grip of the past, a grip she needed to break free from to be herself. This is how she describes it:

> I was in my early twenties when Mum brought me to the temple, dressed as a bride.
>
> It was her solution for what she believed was a negative influence in my life, which would hinder opportunities for marriage. The ceremony was strange, for my first groom was to be a banana tree. After the ceremony, the tree was cut down and technically, I became a widow free to marry again!
>
> The red of the sindhur (the sign of a married lady) looked like blood—almost like they had cut his neck and he was bleeding! This picture is written deep in my memory.

At this point, Selvi firmly rejected "hand-me-down" rituals. The third factor that helped Selvi leave her family's spiritual background was the connection to a loving, caring Christian community in Malaysia. As she read the Bible with them, she met a God who does not prize ritual or self-effort,

---

17 Selvi, Personal interview, February 13, 2021.

but who values her as she is. Being a music lover, she thoroughly enjoyed worship, as the songs touched a deep chord in her. Finally, she was baptized. Later, her local church helped nurture and guide her teenage children into faith, thus ensuring a change that spanned generations.

It has been interesting to witness some of the initiatives that try to free Tamil women from the past. When women who are influential agents of change in one Tamil subgroup influence those trapped in the traditions of another subgroup, the community as a whole is built up. Here are a few examples of this process:

Indranee Liew[18] (daughter of a Jaffna Tamil father and a Chinese mother) and her husband, Lai Fong Hwa (a consultant psychiatrist for children and adolescents at Island Hospital, Penang), have set up an organization to tackle crucial areas like the quality of early learning, adolescent development, and women's leadership. Though open to all, they reach out to the Indian Tamils who most need help in these areas. Care in early learning helps develop brain capacity and function in children, which will impact their future and, through them, that of their community. Women are encouraged to shed a victim mentality and develop skills and confidence to manage their families appropriately.

Bella Navaratnam is another amazing Jaffna Tamil woman, whose life demonstrates the need for a "tabernacle," as Jesus did. In her younger days, she lived with the Tamils on the estates, sharing their accommodation and lifestyle.[19] Now in her eighties, she continues to work with the church to teach women and children life skills as well as Christ's love for them, to ensure a different quality of life.

The Tamil settlement in Buntong in Ipoh showcases a unique initiative by Indian Tamils (mostly those who migrated to get married) to reach out to their own community. In this "mini-India," the roads are named after Indian cities, such as "Jalan Madras." Non-Indians are prohibited from buying or selling property here. The outreach from a local Tamil Settlement Methodist Church is interesting. Mary Paripuranam[20] (a first-generation immigrant from Tirunelveli, who married the pastor and is an advisor to Tamil Women under the Tamil Conference of Methodist Churches, consisting of fifty-four churches, and coordinates spiritual life issues between ethnic churches)

---

18 Personal interview, February 9, 2021.
19 Personal interview, March 9, 2021.
20 Personal interview, March 17, 2021.

says it involves strengthening and motivating the faith of women within the church to join the social concerns and evangelism teams, in order to serve the downtrodden Indian Tamil women of their community. As church members walk alongside the less fortunate women of their community, they become God's agents of change for those with broken lives and families.

Women and their children are brought to a center, where they are introduced to literacy and given nourishing meals. The process demonstrates that God's loving care is complex and challenging. The women have to be taught the most basic life skills like parenting, managing money, hygiene, etc.—skills which are usually picked up in a stable family environment. The women are slow to learn. They simply spend whatever money they receive, then quickly settle back into old patterns of dependency. Huge efforts by the church often meet with limited response. Some may commit but hesitate to come to church regularly, preferring to stay home and watch movies.

Sustaining change is difficult. A lot of love and encouragement is needed to break old mindsets. Here obedience to the Holy Spirit can never be emphasized enough. As Mary Paripuranam observes, "Our group of older ladies must not be forgotten. They are the ones who, when young, walked from home to home due to lack of transport, and continued to connect and pray, so that we could see fruit today." The lesson is clear: consistent commitment and prayer in difficult times secure change in the years to come.

Many churches have stepped up to meet the need of developing Indian Tamil women psychologically, spiritually, and in terms of life skills. The Mar Thoma Syrian Church in Klang Valley is one such example. Initiated in colonial times by Malayali professionals (not missionaries), its focus was to build and sustain its own community's spiritual needs. During their seventy-fifth anniversary celebration, Bishop Mar Timotheos dared the Women's Wing to not just "pray and give, but also to go out and do."

Hanu Easau, a first-generation Malayali who moved to Malaysia after her marriage, identified two projects for the church to work on: one with abused women—especially among the Indian Tamils, and another with underprivileged women, most of whom were also from this group. Her experience has been that Tamil women who have been abused or involved in prostitution may have underlying spiritual issues that can only be resolved through an encounter with Jesus' power and authority.[21]

---

21 Personal interview, February 4, 2021.

In this context, it's worth mentioning two interdenominational initiatives that reach out to disadvantaged Indian Tamil women, children, and families: Malaysian Care, founded in 1979, and Pusat Bantuan Sentul, founded in 1985. Both of them work to bridge the social and development gap for this community.

In conclusion, let me say that this chapter presents but a small sampling of the issues and responses of the women of the Tamil Diaspora in Malaysia. Despite many ministry initiatives to help the women of this community, much still remains to be done. One hidden but often neglected influencer is prayer for the Holy Spirit to birth what is prayed for, in keeping with God's intention. Malaysia's development paradox conceals great mission avenues. Many Malaysians of Indian descent who are educated abroad (mostly in India) now seek to migrate owing to unequal rights and opportunities at home. There's space for activism with regard to this. Despite government and NGO efforts to bring change, women continue to lag in every area of development. Existing or new initiatives can be explored to make the women of this community self-reliant.

The main focus of these efforts, however, is material betterment, which leaves the soul untouched. Perhaps it is now time to prayerfully consider the wisdom of missionary initiatives of the past that have become involved in development needs (medical in some countries, and mostly educational in Malaysia), so as to offer more of a spiritual connection to the gospel in the future. Food is needed for both body and soul to bring lasting change. If a commercial movie can address social issues creatively, why not the church?

Virtually Possible

Digital Outreaches to Hindus

Mrs. Chandra and Mr. Naveen[1]

Vijay sneaked out of his house deep in the night, quietly so as not to wake his wife and child. Heart pounding, he trudged two kilometers to the railroad tracks, lay down, and waited for the inevitable. Bills had piled up ever since the childbirth in which his wife had nearly died, and he couldn't pay.

But he had life insurance and thought that was his only hope for his family to pay off the bills after he was gone! He was ready to sacrifice himself!

Weeping profusely in the dark, he suddenly saw a light, brighter than the sun. It took the shape of a man in shining clothes, who then said, "Don't do this. Go back home to your family. Everything will be all right."

Vijay quickly ran home. He knew exactly what to do. Two years ago, when his wife nearly died giving birth, he had found a Christian website, where he had written in, begging for prayer to save his wife and baby. He had connected with a caring person whose prayers to Jesus had saved them.

Now Vijay found the same website, wrote in again, and said, "Jesus saved my life. I want to know more about Jesus." That email came to me (Chandra).

Every day, millions of people like Vijay, who are facing personal crises and struggling with spiritual needs, go online to search for the answers.

---

[1] For security reasons, all names referenced in this chapter have been changed.

Why online? Because they certainly don't have a single Christian friend, and cultural restrictions would prevent them from walking into a church building, even if they knew where one was. So we must be there for them! Through the internet, we can offer them a safe place to discover the message of Jesus, guide them to faith, help them grow spiritually, and—where possible—connect them with a local church.

In this chapter, we will closely examine the classic form of internet ministry used to find and connect seekers[2] with online Christian mentors[3] who are ready to engage with them, particularly focusing on the Indian Diaspora. Then we will introduce an emerging missional "digital strategy" and how related partnerships can accelerate your local ministries. Finally, we will explore some digital tools that can assist and equip you to be "always ready" (1 Pet 3:15) for face-to-face ministry.

But first, let's ask an important question: Is the internet (as a medium of ministry) in the Bible? I once asked the founder of an online ministry if he felt there was a verse that captured the essence of internet ministry. He pointed me to Colossians 1:16: "For by him [Christ] all things were created, things in heaven and on earth, visible and invisible, whether thrones or powers or rulers or authorities; all things were created through him and for him." I have asked Christian audiences where they see "internet" in this verse. Most agree we have the Lord's mandate to use this communication power of the internet to bring him glory and spread his Good News.

Online Faith Journeys—Seeker

In the case of Vijay, at a time of crisis he was able to connect to an online ministry website by keying in "prayer." Others have searched for "God" or "Jesus," out of curiosity, or a word describing their current struggle, such as "loneliness," "abuse," and so on. Vijay landed on a website that promised someone would pray for his need in the name of Jesus, so after glancing through the gospel presentation, he sought urgent prayer for his wife and newborn child.

---

2 Ministries use a variety of terms for the website visitor, such as "contact" (too many uses) and "mentee" (uncommon and awkward). We have chosen "seeker" even though not all are seriously seeking to know Christ, simply because they have come to a Christian website and opened themselves to an opportunity for a spiritual conversation, at the very least.

3 Some ministries use the term "online missionary," which is not suitable for presenting oneself to the online seeker; more seem to prefer "mentor," which we have used throughout this chapter.

"I felt such love and peace when I read your prayer" has been a common reply by many whom the Lord touched through the typed-out prayers. Jesus granted Vijay's request, but as is common among people of other religions, he probably understood little of the initial "message of salvation," which required reading before one could request prayer or interaction from a mentor.

Not everyone who visits a Christian website is a sincere seeker of truth or of spiritual help of any kind. In my fifteen years with an online ministry, the majority of emails in my inbox were blank—no comment, even if a "spiritual decision," such as receiving Christ, had been indicated by a checked box. Without a comment to give more information, I would write a personal friendly greeting, referencing the website visited, hoping to draw the silent seeker into a meaningful spiritual conversation. I always reflected that behind each email was a living human being whom God loved. Could I give them one new truth about Jesus in an attractive way that would leave them curious to know more, even if we never "met" again?

There were a few upset writers too! One young man wrote in his first email, "I hate Christians! I hate the Bible! I hate Jesus!" I told him I love his people, and he wrote back apologetically, explaining that his Christian girlfriend had hurt him deeply. I was able to calm his feelings and help him reason things out. Our conversation ended with him visiting a church near where he lived and then telling me he liked it.

An angry man wrote, accusing us of deceiving people and forcing conversions. I asked him to explain why he said that, since he simply visited a website out of his own choice, and he had nothing to say.

So, whether a mentor gets blank emails, angry ones, or sincere ones, each deserves prayerful, respectful treatment. Two years after Vijay's first crisis, at his second crisis point, he was able to go back to the same website by remembering its name and checking his email history. His email asking to know more about Jesus was "randomly" assigned to me.

Online Faith Journeys—Mentor

At this point, we need to back up and describe my path to becoming an online mentor. I was personally recruited by someone who was already doing it. Sometimes whole churches contact an online ministry, wishing to partner, and supply a generous number of mentors who are treated as a special group. Such partnerships are initiated by the online ministry as they seek to bring in large numbers of laborers for the harvest. To become a mentor myself,

I filled out a simple online application form complete with references. Once in, I was put through an online training. Online ministries each have their own unique training, which is usually a combination of how to use the mentor software system, organizational policies, and spiritual training. Ministries want to take ordinary Christians and equip them to be effective in sharing their faith in the digital world. It is very important to be willing to learn and receive guidance from a senior leader who checks the mentor's outgoing emails.

A mentor software system receives details of new contacts via the completed online forms from a website. It then automatically matches this request with a mentor who has the right language skills and gender (if required). Later, when the seeker replies to the mentor's email, the mentor software will assign this reply to the original mentor. This ensures that an ongoing conversation and relationship can develop. The software also assists the mentor with an indexed list of common questions and answers and email templates that can act as a useful starting point in preparing a reply. Mentors responding in languages other than English are often expected to be bilingual.

Since my interest was in South Asia, I signed up to take emails only from South Asian countries. This is where Indian Diaspora believers should take note. It is not only possible but logistically and financially painless to bring Jesus to your home country, without a passport, vaccinations, or flight bookings! With built-in cultural knowledge and language abilities, plus a heart that leans heavily toward "back home," Diaspora Indians should be on the frontlines of internet ministry to share the Good News with their country of origin.

On the other hand, most online ministries, eager for laborers, accept willing believers from anywhere without expecting any cultural knowledge beyond their borders, sometimes resulting in poor communication or religious insensitivity. One example: A young girl from India wrote in asking for advice about her lover, which to an American mentor implies a sexual relationship. The mentor wrote back that "God could forgive this sin." Imagine that girl's confusion to be told that loving someone was a sin! Diaspora Indians with their cultural knowledge could have avoided this mistake.

Realizing the value of internet ministry, I began to recruit more laborers by speaking in Indian churches around the US and other countries. I became a leader of a volunteer community, eventually overseeing more than two hundred mentors, mostly of Indian origin. Although they came with high motivation and cultural knowledge, they were not immune to sharing the gospel, using Christian jargon, sending lengthy emails, arguing, and other common blunders. About this time, my experiences in online and in-person ministry among Indians in the US and other countries led me to develop an evangelism seminar and short lessons specifically tailored to internet ministry. However, most online ministries have continued to place a low priority on cultural background or training for their volunteer mentors.

Internet ministry is safe. The software hides the full name and email of both mentor and seeker, thus keeping them anonymous to each other. Some ministries encourage the mentor to use a pen name. From the beginning, I chose the pen name Asha, which means "hope" in Hindi, because of its meaning, and because a pen name allows my nationality not to be a distraction. Anonymity also makes it easier to discuss more private matters of the heart. This is particularly important for those living in areas where exploring other religious options overtly may be taboo.

Other life questions and struggles may be difficult to ask in person and the "anonymous intimacy" of the internet seems the only place to go for help. Over the years, I have helped many single and married people toying with affairs, addicted to pornography, struggling with depression, or contemplating suicide. With the Indian reluctance to seek professional counseling, it is no wonder people feel as if they have no friends to turn to. Internet mentors are there as Christ's ambassadors, offering hope and healing to those who desperately need this amazing medium.

One morning I looked in my special online ministry inbox for new emails and saw Vijay's request to know more about Jesus. I asked Vijay to tell me how Jesus had saved his life. Over a series of emails, I heard his remarkable story and discipled him by sending him Bible stories and lessons. His early spiritual growth could occur in the protected environment of internet correspondence. We have explored the seeker's typical journey from the point of need to connect with a mentor via a website. A Christian mentor should be motivated by the Great Commission to disciple people through an online ministry.

Online Faith Journeys—The Ministry

Back in 1992, a Christian executive sat in a high-level meeting of a now-giant Silicon Valley company, in the role of the company's first director of operations. The meeting was to discuss the potential of the World Wide Web to change the way the world operates. During that meeting, this visionary thinker had his first ideas about utilizing the internet for gospel proclamation. Later, he founded the first—and now one of the largest—online ministry organizations.

Early leaders in the internet-ministry field began by building interactive websites with gospel content and a response mechanism for website visitors to indicate spiritual interest, decisions, and desire to be contacted by a Christian mentor. Typically, the gospel presentations on these websites consisted of text to read, later supplemented by video to watch. The gospel message is almost always Western-centric and atonement-based. Herbert Hoefer writes of the difficulties our neighbors have in relating to the atonement while being much more attracted to Christ by other key points of the biblical message.[4]

While today there is greater variety and sophistication in the gospel webpages, there is still too much Christian jargon, advanced theology, and Western-based cultural assumptions that do not relate to or attract curious Indians or needy souls searching for answers. Online websites feature a four-point, atonement-based gospel outline, while its content and photos remain the same in all translations. Other websites are themed around life crises and stories of struggle and hope. The testimonies and photos depict the people of India, even on English-language websites. However, with the overwhelming labor pool being Western-based Christians, it is very difficult to find cultural specialists. This gap can be easily filled by ethnic diaspora Christian leaders.

Online Ministry Process

Let's step back a minute and look at the total online ministry process. This involves four areas: online advertising, website-content writing, online mentoring, and handover to a local church. Online mentors are only the visible tip of the iceberg out of a group of people with a diverse array of roles and skills that come out of the above four areas. These skills include online marketing, content writing and editing, computer graphics design, fundraising, website and software development, and, of course, spiritual mentoring.

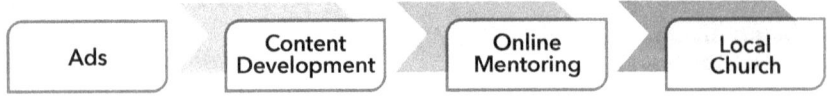

---

4 Hoefer, "Gospel Proclamation," 325–45.

Ads: Simply creating a website or social media page is unlikely to bring many visitors. It takes a carefully planned marketing campaign with appropriate and culturally sensitive advertising to draw a receptive audience. Online ads form an important first contact experience and present a connecting message to guide new visitors to online pages and media. They typically offer a message of hope or discovery that appeals to topics that seekers are interested in. Internet users expect graphics or videos, so these marketing skills are important. Perhaps Vijay selected the most attractive ad out of several that came up when he searched for "prayer." The web page content must match what the ad promised, so the visitor's expectations are met. Online ministries must not deceive, nor are they "selling" anything, so the content of the ads and pages must reflect this (1 Thess 2:3–5).

Content Development: A promoted website, social media page, or web videos provide "touchpoints" that offer opportunities either to explore the gospel directly or to share felt needs that visitors can relate to, which can subsequently lead to a conversation about Christ. Visitors are offered an opportunity to request prayer or to ask a question by filling out a form. Some sites, even at this early stage, make a challenge to pray a prayer of commitment to Christ as part of their response. However, it would be naïve to assume "checking the box" means to someone raised in another religion what the Christian ministry thinks it means. Our Hindu friends can easily agree with the statement "I accept Jesus," meaning "I accept Jesus as one of the gods" and have no idea that we attach great significance beyond that. Before making any assumption that s/he has understood our message of salvation in Christ alone when checking that box, we can at least take it as an open door for further spiritual conversation.

When creating online ads or website content or writing mentor emails, it can be tempting to adopt a *preaching posture* focused on the spiritual truths we are so eager to impart. A preachy message will likely scatter most of our online audience. Our online visitors are really seeking someone who will *humbly* understand their worldview and life needs, so we must adopt a *listening-ear posture* in all our messages, from ads to emails.

Online Mentoring: We have already described the mentoring process. A mentor just writes encouraging letters, which is a very biblical thing to do! We simply *read*, *pray*, and *reply*. Some teams use live text chat as an alternative to email for mentors comfortable with this. One advantage of email evangelism is that we have time to research and prepare an answer. It drives us back to the Scriptures and grows our faith and confidence in how best to respond to each question, as well as equipping us for face-to-face encounters.

Local Church: Online ministries equip mentors with tools to assist someone to grow step by step in their online faith journey, support mentors in this discipleship process, and help them measure their progress. At some point, mentors will wish to offer the seeker or new believer an opportunity to connect with a local church or home group. For some people, no local church can be found, or it may be unsafe for them to attempt to visit a church publicly. In this case, a mentor might become their "church." Some ministries run online gatherings to support and encourage new believers who might otherwise remain isolated.

What happened to Vijay? He gobbled up all the Bible studies I sent him. He watched the *JESUS* film in his language and affirmed that the Jesus he saw in the movie was the shining person who appeared on the railroad track! He told his family what Jesus had done for him and persevered through some rejection. And he asked how he could attend a church. Vijay lives in a small town in a region where only 0.5 percent of the people are Christians. Though I had traveled to India before, I knew no one anywhere near where he lived. We prayed that God would bring a Jesus-follower across his path. Once again, God answered a seemingly impossible request, and he eventually connected with a tiny group of believers who were meeting in a home for worship. My husband and I had a memorable visit with Vijay, his family, and believers in his town.

Helping people transition to a local church is arguably one of the most important components of an effective online ministry. However, this is one of the most difficult challenges and a historical weakness. During our research for this chapter, we were delighted to discover that some online teams are now seeking to better address this crucial need. Although this is a global missional challenge, finding a local group of Jesus-worshipers is clearly of particular importance for new believers from other religious backgrounds living in all parts of the world. In some countries, finding a nearby church can be as easy as visiting Google Maps. Not in our case! The online mentor may know only the seeker's country, or at most the state and city, but not their exact address. Even with that information, there are many hurdles that make it nearly impossible for a mentor across the globe to help a seeker find a church in an unchurched area. This difficulty is also illustrated by Vijay's experience. While I was initially elated to see him join the small house church, the dynamic professional couple leading it soon moved away, and the group fell apart. Vijay remains an isolated believer in a town of 130,000, with no known church. I am now searching for an online gathering of Jesus-followers in his language.

Churches can have very different internal cultures. This goes beyond denomination, language, and culture within the broad sweep of "Indian" and "Indian Diaspora." Some congregations are warm and accepting of inquirers from other faiths, while others make visitors feel unwelcome. Churches within India and throughout the Diaspora have their distinctive theological and cultural issues to grapple with. The meaning and extent of separatism versus an incarnational mentality is not just a seminary classroom debate. An inquirer or new believer who enters a church wearing a *bindi* (forehead marking) may be asked to leave. A mentor or Western-based ministry group may be unaware of such issues, which are very real to the new believer on the ground.[5] So our final challenge, then, is not just to find the new believers a local church, but to find them a genuinely welcoming church. If that proves impossible, an online fellowship may be the only other option.

Facebook and Google ads allow us to select by broad geographical region (countries, states, cities), or more precisely (say 30 km from a given point in a map). We can also select our audience by language, interests, demographics (age, gender, education, and job title), technology (device or operating system), platform (Search, Twitter, Facebook, or Instagram), behavior (responses to online ads), or online friendships. As an example, we could run a campaign to reach young Indian Diaspora men working in Fiji by selecting Language: Hindi; Gender: Male; Age: 18–29; Country: Fiji; Interests: Cricket. Our landing page (the web page where an ad click navigates to) might show an image of young Indian men playing cricket on a beach, with a bridge message about working far from home. Now, suppose the same ministry team wished to use the same page to include other regions, say California and Hawaii. All we would need to do is make a small change to our ads to include these new locations.

Digital Strategy and Tools

It is important to note a subtle change in vocabulary can expand the concept. As already inferred, the website-response model of internet ministry was the first and now classic model of online ministries. Other aspects are

---
5 Pennington, *Christian Barriers to Jesus*.

now growing, as reflected in the term *digital strategies*. These other aspects include Media to Movements; attracting seekers on social-media platforms like YouTube, Facebook, Instagram, and others to use digital media tools in personal evangelism. Let us now turn briefly to these exciting developments in digital strategies.

Media to Movements is an emerging digital strategy that combines two methods. Unlike online mentoring, it is typically run by a small team focused on planting new churches or home groups in a specific region, so the handover to face-to-face contact happens much earlier. They employ geographically targeted social media advertising to find a "person of peace" who may be open to participating in or hosting a Bible study. A local church planter using this method typically uses the disciple-making movements strategy that was pioneered in India and has proven to work well with India's diverse religious cultures. Space does not permit us to develop this strategy here, but we refer the reader to the following resources for further information.[6]

The Mobile Ministry Forum is a network supporting Christians globally with mobile applications to assist in reaching the unreached. They have collated a large list of mobile apps to equip you to always be ready with a relevant message in popular media in the individual's heart language.

Apps that serve Indian people and in Indian languages:

- **God Tools app**—a suite of gospel and discipleship tools
- **The *JESUS* film app**—All JESUS film and related media (in over 1,800 languages)
- **5Fish app**—Scripture, teaching, songs, and much more in thousands of languages
- **God's Gift app**—140 gospel sites covering 50 languages, offering mentor interactions

---

6 Watson and Watson, *Contagious Disciple Making*. Online examples of Media Ministries include www.VisualStory.org/mtmsurvey and www.MediaToMovements.org.

Mobile Phone Ministry Tools:

 https://mobileministryforum.org

MobileMinistryForum.org/apps-for-outreach-spiritual-life

 MobileMinistryForum.org/media-creation-apps

Resources for learning Social Media Ministry skills:

https://digitalacademy.cru.org

 www.MobileMinistryForum.org/social-media-for-missions-an-introductory-guide

https://mediatomovements.com/articles/building-social-media-strategy

Conclusion

From "Roman roads" to the printing press to radio, television, and satellite broadcasting, throughout history God has used available technology to fill the earth "with the knowledge of the glory of the Lord" (Hab 2:14). The internet today offers multiple communication innovations (email, text chat, audio and video calls), each bringing people closer to each other, with the ability to more immediately and personally present the gospel and disciple those who respond—even between distant lands.

As of January 2024, 752 million (penetration rate of 52.4 percent) of India's 1.4 billion population are internet users, increasing by 19 million since January 2023.[7] And there are 1.12 billion cellular mobile connections active in India in early 2024 (78 percent of the population). Low-cost phones and cellular plans allow even the village farmers or rickshaw drivers to afford cellular connectivity. Most of the Indian Diaspora rely on the internet and smart phones to keep in touch with family back home. Digital strategies absolutely must be central to our Great Commission efforts from now on!

Many of those who we interviewed for this chapter suggested that the word *virtual* conveys a sense of unreality to some people, and thus is beginning to be dropped from ministry terminology. These leaders stressed that digital ministry is very real; we are dealing with real people, whether we see them or not, and their real feelings, struggles, and hopes. An appeal we heard over and over is that more laborers are needed. Volunteer online mentors who can respond to seekers in many South Asian languages working from the convenience of their devices form a large bloc of the needed labor force. But a new kind of digital missionary is also needed: one with professional or technical skills to create the ads, raise the funds, write the content, build the software, challenge the partner churches, train the mentors, and do it all with the cultural awareness necessary to communicate Jesus effectively in the context of South Asian peoples. Indian digital missionaries, step up!

---

7 Kemp, "Digital 2024: India."

Ministry among Hindus in the Caribbean

Dr. Krishna Ramsundar

Indians have been part of the Caribbean landscape since their arrival on these sun-kissed shores as indentured laborers on the sugarcane plantations after the end of slavery. While the Slavery Abolition Act of 1833 handed slaves their freedom in most of the British Empire, it also took away the source of labor their owners had depended on for the success of their trade. This created a very urgent need for a cheap and effective source of labor to do the back-breaking work in the Caribbean heat.

> The flight of creole laborers threatened to destroy plantations on several islands. Migrations from one island to another met only part of the need. Most migrants sought jobs in construction, while the better-educated looked for work as policemen, teachers, and nurses. Few wanted full-time work on the cane estates. Thus, Caribbean planters and British officials resorted to various schemes of large-scale immigration to supply additional workers.[1]

The British looked mainly to India to provide replacements for the slaves.[2] From 1838 to 1924 this "new wave of immigration" of half a million Indians were brought to the Caribbean settling mainly in Guyana,

---

[1] Rogozinski, *Brief History of the Caribbean*, 190.
[2] Williams, *From Columbus to Castro*, 349.

Trinidad and Tobago, and Jamaica.³ In cramped spaces aboard ships, but with wide-open minds for the future, they brought with them their culture, traditions, some plants, and, of course, their religious traditions. In these new lands, they planted valuable seeds of their identity, contributing to the great diversity that has now blossomed in each Caribbean country.

In this part of the world, Diaspora Indians range from groups in Suriname, whose main language is still Hindi, to those in the islands of the West Indies (the Caribbean), where, especially the younger generations, have become more "West than Indian." Assimilation into their new Caribbean context and culture meant that while visibly identified as Indian, there is also a shift from some of their Indian customs and culture. The most evident of these is the disappearance of the caste system:

> Once Indians were on the ship together, they became *jahajis* (shipmates) and caste became less important. They started to develop a unity under the Indentureship system. Although Indentureship provided a sense of freedom from the caste system, many Hindus practiced the caste system during their indentureship period as was evident in parental arrangement of their children's marriages within the same caste. However, while caste identification tended to be preserved among Indian indentured laborers who came initially, it became inconsequential in social interactions except in the case of the few Brahmins who were required to perform religious ceremonies.⁴

After traumatic voyages which included sickness and death to get to the Caribbean and many years of struggle to adapt to the brutal and unforeseen conditions of their new homeland, Indo-Caribbeans now tend to identify more as citizens of their island/country than with their roots in India. It is important to note at the outset that the Caribbean is not just a melting pot of different local and Diaspora communities, but it has become its own *pelau* or *arroz con gandules* of peoples. The Calypsonian Arrow has said that the people of the Caribbean are:

> One race (de Caribbean man)
>
> From de same place (de Caribbean man)
>
> Dat make de same trip (de Caribbean man)

---

3 "Between 1838 and 1917, no fewer than 238,000 Indians we introduced into British Guiana, 145,000 into Trinidad, 21,500 into Jamaica, 39,000 into Guadeloupe, 34,000 into Surinam." Williams, *From Columbus to Castro*, 348.

4 Naidu, "Retention and Transculturation of Hinduism in the Caribbean."

On de same ship (de Caribbean man)

So we must push one common intention

Is for a better life in de region.

For we woman, and we children

Dat must be de ambition of de Caribbean man,

De Caribbean man, de Caribbean man.[5]

It is that identity that formed part of my upbringing in Trinidad and Tobago, where "every creed and race finds an equal place."[6] I grew up in a Hindu family surrounded by the flora and fauna of the Northern Range of Trinidad, with an equally beautiful diversity of people. Even as a child in primary school, I was very aware of the presence of a variety of religions and even the subgroups of some of those (especially among the Christian churches). In my village, I had friends who were Hindus, Muslims, Catholics, Anglicans, Jehovah's Witnesses, etc. I was raised with a healthy sense of the existence of God. I was taught to live a good life with others and nature in order to satisfy and please God because this would have repercussions in the afterlife.

My Conversion from Hinduism

At the age of about six, I had a dream about heaven which impacted my life tremendously. I dreamt it was the end of the world and God was calling all the good people to their reward to live in heaven. However, the only person from our family who was actually good enough to go to heaven was my mother. As she ascended into heaven, she was allowed to take any items she wanted from our home. I quite vividly remember her signaling for our newly acquired television, radio, and furniture to be lifted up into heaven with her. That was a dream with the imagination of a little boy who had been processing the talk and thoughts of religion that I heard around me, but I also believe that it was the way in which God had begun to reveal himself to me, place his hand and call upon my life, and make me aware of his existence. This would lead me to the place where I would have to make a decision to either submit myself to his call or reject Christianity altogether.

When I was a teenager, my sisters who had begun attending church were baptized and became members of the New Testament Church of God. They began inviting me to attend special events and Worship Services. Finally, at

---

5 Arrow, "De Caribbean Man."
6 Castagne, "Forged from the Love of Liberty" (National Anthem of Trinidad and Tobago).

a National Youth Convention, after the sermon was preached and an altar call was made, I was approached by an uncle who asked if I wanted to accept Christ as my Savior. He accompanied me to the altar, and I decided to become a follower of Christ. Forty-something years later, I have not turned back, and have even stepped into full-time ministry, and mission work.

Caribbean Identity and Reaching Hindus of the Region

The Caribbean community, as has been earlier stated, tends to view itself as a homogenous unit. Although there is a small indigenous/native population, a sector that was brought as slaves, some others as indentured laborers, and yet others who are in the Caribbean for different reasons, there is the unifying ideology of the "Caribbean man." It is to that identity which churches tend to appeal in the aims of Christian witness. Evangelism is done based on the attempt to reach the unchurched instead of those of a specific religious background. Those unchurched tend to be nominal Christians, those belonging to sects, Muslims, Hindus, "Shango Baptists," etc. And so, when crusades are conducted, or outreach events are done, the aim is normally to reach the lost in general and not a specific group in particular.

Given the fact that each country has its own mandates of religious freedom, it would be difficult, and maybe even counterproductive, to target specific religious groups. In recent years with the rise of political Hinduism, known as the Hindutva movement or Hindu fundamentalism,[7] there has been an outcry by leaders of one of the main Hindu groups against the proselytization of Hindus in places like Trinidad. However, while in the Caribbean there is freedom to protect religious groups from being preyed upon, there is also religious freedom, which allows the proclamation of belief systems.

> Religion has played a significant role in shaping the culture and societal norms of the Caribbean. Without religion, Caribbean culture, as we know it, would not be the same. Indeed, the Caribbean is probably one of the most religious regions in the world. So, whatever your religious inclination, you can feel at home in the Caribbean.[8]

It is that freedom that must be seized upon in order to continue to reach Hindus here.

---

7 Teja and Wagenveld, *A World of Gods*, 183.
8 Wilson, "Caribbean Is One of Most Religious Places."

Building Relationships

I believe my own conversion sheds light on reaching Hindus (and any other faith tradition) in the Caribbean. It is done by building bridges of relationships to cross the divide of creed and faith. Evangelism in the Caribbean is most effective when it is done based on a relationship of trust—first in God who seeks to save those who are lost (Luke 19:10) and then in the testimony of those whose lives have been changed and now walk in freedom (Matt 5:16). I was not forced into Christianity. I was loved patiently and compassionately into the kingdom.

One of my earliest recollections of being a witness to Hindus (and anyone else we found on the streets while we visited students at our Sunday school) was to try to show them how much they were lost and in need of salvation. Unfortunately, many of those encounters ended in arguments with no one really wanting to hear about the truth as we presented it. I can vividly remember many Saturday afternoons being spent in heated theological arguments with everyone from atheists to satanists in scorching temperatures, which left us hotter under the collar than it did to rescue the lost and perishing.

What this taught me at a very young age is that the responsibility of a Christian witness is to give a response for his/her faith (apologetics) instead of arguing with others about what the Bible says. Using the Bible as a proof text has no real validity for people of other religions who doubt that it is the Word of God. If they already reject the Bible—why would they be convinced by Scripture quotations?

In evangelism, on the other hand, we had great success in inviting those with whom we could establish a relationship and whose needs we were able to help meet in a tangible way—and especially those who were searching for a way out of a difficult situation—and who were willing to put their trust in the Jesus whom we had personally experienced as Savior, healer, miracle worker, etc.

Just prior to leaving Trinidad to study at Lee University in Cleveland, Tennessee, I was asked by an uncle to help plant a church in an area that was primarily Hindu, in the central part of the island among the sugarcane plantations. One Saturday afternoon, as we visited a nearby village, inviting children and youth to our Sunday school, we met a young girl who listened intently as we invited her family to church and Sunday school. During that conversation, we noticed that she was in need of medical attention. She had her arm wrapped in bandages which had become quite dirty, to the point that her wound could become infected. We were told that they had been unable to take her to the clinic to get the bandages changed and to get a follow-up examination because of a lack of financial resources.

Immediately, I asked if it would be OK to take her to the clinic to get the medical help she needed. After getting her mother's permission, we drove them to a nearby town, waited for her to get the medical attention she needed, and I paid for the medicine she needed before taking her family back home. The next morning, that young lady and her brother were ready and waiting for the church bus to go to Sunday school. After I left Trinidad and returned at the end of my first semester of classes the church had grown quite rapidly, and that young lady had become very eager to share her faith and was bringing other members of her family to Christ.

It is that bearing witness by works of kindness and sharing of personal testimony that reaches people and is effective in the evangelism of Hindus in the Caribbean. Those who are lost are reached by building bridges and creating relationships: not by being combative, contrary, and trying to destroy their belief system. A Christian witness to Hindus in the Caribbean is effective when people, not their religion, become the focus of attention.

The power and reality of God, who reaches out in a relationship and uses divine authority to intervene in human life in a demonstration of compassion and care to make a tangible difference in human suffering, cannot be denied. The image and significance of the twelve stones Joshua had the people take out of the river Jordan after crossing into the Promised Land, and the use of those stones to create a monument of remembrance which would also serve as a testimony of God's deliverance, continues to be a very practical way of announcing divine intervention. The narrative of Joshua 4:14–24 forms the basis of outreach to people who are not yet Christ-followers—i.e., there is an experience or event in the life of a person or community and that is used as a means of proclamation of the gospel.

In John 9, the healing of the blind man serves as the perfect example of people's response to divine intervention. Those who had known of the beggar's plight and suffering from birth recognized that this was a true miracle: one which pointed them to Christ.

I have listened to countless stories of church planters around the world who have shared with others what God has done in their lives, and their testimonies have become the foundation for new churches in villages and cities. I have seen that it is a very powerful tool for evangelism in India where God is using even the very humble, poor, and illiterate to start churches. In one testimony I heard in Patna, a lady who was healed of a tumor began telling others about her healing and what Christ did in her life. She is now a church planter who supervises over thirty churches and has baptized hundreds in the last few years.

Among Hindus in the Caribbean too, the response is no different. Divine intervention opens doors of opportunity to present the gospel. If the miracles of Jesus were meant to point people to the Father who sent him, then modern-day miracles are also meant to point people to the way of the Cross. The most effective mass evangelism events in Caribbean communities are those "crusades" where healing, deliverance, and miraculous works are evidence of the power of God, who seeks a personal relationship through salvation with each individual.

The Importance of the 4/14 Window in Reaching Hindus in the Caribbean

In October 2013, I was one of the delegates from Latin America attending the 4-14 Window Global Summit in Bangkok, Thailand. The theme was "Rooted and Released: Empowering the Body of Christ to Embrace Children and Youth as Partners in Mission." This summit underlined the importance of reaching children, who, in turn, become powerful disciples and witnesses.

> Not only is this 4-14 Window the time when young children are more likely to embrace Christianity, it is also the timeframe during which they will form first impressions and emotional connections with the church that can potentially last throughout their entire life and shape the way they think of the church. This is important to remember as well because sometimes a child might not accept Christ between the ages of 4 and 14, and they might walk away from the church entirely for a while. But one of the factors that is key when it comes to determining whether or not they will one day return, is the quality of their first impressions when they were younger. Churches should never underestimate the importance and impact that kindness and solid teaching can have in a child's life. It is these things the children could remember when they are older, and they just might be what brings them back.[9]

---
9 Promise Church, "What Is 4/14 Window?"

The 4/14 Window research and practice have solidified in my mind the conviction that children's ministry, which has been very effective in the Caribbean, needs to be continued with even greater emphasis. Hindus, along with followers of all other religions, readily send their children to Sunday School, Vacation Bible School, Sabbath School, Kids' Crusades, etc. instead of having them stay at home because the instruction they receive is fun, exciting, and includes many of their friends from the neighborhood, village, or town. This type of religious activity in evangelism has become an expected summer activity in a part of the world where summer camps and similar events for kids are not prevalent.

It is important to understand that evangelizing those children is an effective tool in the evangelism of the parents also, because "Children within the 4-14 Window are also bridges to their families, and a thriving children's program in a church expresses growth, life, and overall health in the church that will attract families in the community who are looking for a church to call home."[10]

The importance of reaching the entire family in Hinduism is key. It might appear that the children are being reached separately, but ministry is being done involving the entire family. Ministry to Hindus in the Caribbean cannot ignore the fact that "Hindu culture is family-oriented. … People live together as families and extended families, and even when they are scattered for educational or employment reasons there is a sense of being connected to one's roots."[11]

As a young person growing up in one of the most ethnically and religiously diverse countries of the Caribbean, where all faith traditions are afforded equal rights, and religious instruction is part of the school curriculum (especially in secondary schools), it was easy for me to grow in my newfound faith after becoming a believer as a young teenager through the ministry of the Inter School/InterVarsity Christian Fellowship Club (IS/IVCF). Their motto, "To know Christ and to make Him known," became part of my spiritual formation as an adolescent and continues to be part of the formation of many others through the effective ministry of this organization, which is recognized by the Government of Trinidad and Tobago and has a presence in nearly 150 schools on the Island.[12]

---

10 Map Global, "What Is 4/14 Window?"
11 Teja and Wagenveld, *A World of Gods*, 194.
12 IS/IVCF, "To Know Christ and to Make Him Known."

When I was a student at Queen's Royal College, the IS/IVCF Club sponsored various events, including prayer meetings, Bible studies, movie-days, and we even sponsored a week-long crusade with a well-known evangelist. That ability to learn with other youth (classmates) and learn how to share our faith was very instrumental in my faith. Today some of those we ministered to serve as ministers themselves. One such testimony is of a student who was Hindu but is now a Christian and goes on regular mission trips to Africa as part of his ministry.

The freedom of religion found in the Caribbean is a blessing. Churches and ministry organizations can use the open doors to school campuses to empower student groups to reach youth at this very important stage of their development and emotional growth—a time when they are very likely to embrace the gospel. This opportunity should not be missed; every effort should be made to reach these students with the gospel. They, in turn, will be great witnesses to their friends, families, colleagues, etc.

Reaching Hindus via India

One ministry strategy which has been successful in Indian communities of the Caribbean over the last few years has been the use of Christian missionaries from India. While Diaspora Indians in the Caribbean have adopted and embraced their Caribbean identity, many still speak some Hindi, Bhojpuri, Urdu, Tamil, etc. Ministry in those languages, especially from missionaries and ministries from India, offers a familiar connection and appeal. In the past, we have accompanied teams from the United States that went to do evangelism and children's ministry in Trinidad. On one trip, one of the team members was a former classmate from college who was from Kerala and spoke Hindi. He became quite effective in bridging the divide with the older folks because he communicated with them in their heart language of Hindi. Another member of the team was also from India but didn't speak much Hindi. He was very popular with the teens, who readily identified with him, which made his ministry among them even more effective.

The popularity of Bollywood actors/actresses and performers who regularly visit the Caribbean to perform in front of packed-out Indian audiences demonstrates the tug of culture from Mother India. Over the last two decades, the use of sarees, kurtas, salwars, etc. for weddings, funerals, local and national celebrations have become more prevalent. We're seeing a resurgence of Indian identity, which had been absorbed into people's

Caribbean identity. The descendants of those who had so bravely crossed the *kala pani*, who sense some form of "pollution of their soul," for crossing the oceans, are now seeking "soul cleansing."[13]

Ministry to Hindus in the Caribbean would do well to use this "back to India" affinity to design evangelistic outreach that takes this into consideration. The ability to hear the gospel in the language of our forefathers, and to sing songs of worship in Hindi, Bhojpuri, etc. is very appealing, especially to the older generations who can still speak those languages. Additionally, the ability to show Christianity not as a Western religion, but as something which the East offers is very powerful. To show, for example, the ministry of Saint Thomas in establishing churches in India is an important and very appealing way to reach those who might still remember their parents and grandparents telling stories about India.

Conclusion

Effective ministry to Hindus in the Caribbean must continue in the example set by Jesus and the apostles. It was in that type of ministry that the Apostle Paul was involved when he reminisced about his ministry in Corinth:

> When I came to you, I did not come with eloquence or human wisdom as I proclaimed to you the testimony about God. For I resolved to know nothing while I was with you except Jesus Christ and him crucified. I came to you in weakness with great fear and trembling. My message and my preaching were not with wise and persuasive words, but with a demonstration of the Spirit's power, so that your faith might not rest on human wisdom, but on God's power. (1 Cor 2:1–5 NIV)

When my brother was a young child, he became gravely ill. My mother did everything possible to help him get better. She took him to the hospital, medical practitioners, and then to the Hindu pundit and other religious people. However, all her attempts seemed in vain. He was not getting any better. Instead, he seemed to be getting worse. During a conversation with her sister-in-law, my mother was told about the Christian church, where she had heard that the minister would pray to the Christian God and people would get healed. She was encouraged to take my brother to see if the minister would pray for him.

---

13 See Sam George's interview with Steve S. Chang for the Sola Network.

In her desperation, she said she was going to take her son to the church and was even willing to change her faith if that meant her son would be healed. After visiting the church and having the minister pray for my brother, he recovered miraculously. At that moment, the minister did not require conversion, but my mother kept that miracle in her mind, and I can remember many conversations when she spoke to others about the power of God to help them in their situations. Some years after my brother's healing, my mother came to faith, and she has become a prayer warrior and evangelist among her family, witnessing to the power of God to minister in their lives and to their families, and to make them his children through a personal relationship, beginning with salvation.

16

Sense, Sensibility, and Sensitivity

The Case of Evangelism to Hindus in South Africa
Rev. Louie Naidoo

There are a number of challenges that Christians face globally in sharing the gospel message of Jesus Christ, or evangelizing, as given in the Great Commission (Matt 28:19–20). This is largely due to the pluralistic worldview or anti-Christian sentiment that pervades modern-day discourse around the issues of religion, traditional belief and culture, and religious practices. This challenge is more acutely experienced by Christians in the evangelization of non-Christian Indians in the Diaspora.

This chapter seeks to provide some insight into the challenges encountered by Christians (Indian or non-Indian) in the city of Durban, South Africa, to evangelize non-Christian Indians in the Diaspora. And is motivated by a recent case where the utterances of young Indian evangelists in Durban made local and international headlines.[1] In unpacking this case, we will first seek to provide a broad overview of the sociopolitical and religious landscape of South Africa prior to its nonracial democracy. Secondly, we will examine the cultural and religious renaissance which took place in South Africa after 1997. Thirdly, I will address how these two major events have altered the religious and political narrative in post-apartheid South Africa. Lastly and most importantly, I seek to provide some personal, practical, and biblical reflections on how we can effectively evangelize diasporic Indians both locally and even globally.

---
1 Nxumalo, "Outcry over Durban Pastor's Views."

A brief delving into the case of the young evangelist is necessary at this introductory point to offer the necessary backdrop and impetus for the remainder of the chapter. The said evangelist, whose parents were converts to Christianity, made statements from the pulpit concerning the faith and practice of his parents while they were Hindus as compared to now that they were Christian. While these statements were made within a local church setting, the sermon was aired via the church's Facebook page (video now deleted).

This caused quite a stir among both Christians and non-Christians, with the matter being reported by some Hindu individuals and organizations to the South African Human Rights Council so that legal action could be taken against the evangelist.[2] Many viewed his utterances as being overzealous, insensitive, or downright confrontational. The following media headlines captured the sentiment of the Hindu collective calling it "hate speech,"[3] "crimen injuria,"[4] and "denigrating and insulting."[5] As a result, many churches and Christian leaders had to embark on damage control by issuing statements to correct public perception and to foster social cohesion.

To fully appreciate the revival and renaissance of Hindu fervor and zeal among the Indian Diaspora in South Africa, one has to view this against the backdrop of the political emancipation that took place here in 1994. After years of subjugation and oppression under an apartheid system of government, a new democratic government was ushered in with the election of Nelson Mandela as president. This new democratic government sought to enfranchise and empower all South Africans on multiple levels. A country that was considered a Christian nation soon gave way to becoming a secular democratic state that championed human rights, freedom of religion, free press, etc. This change in the political landscape meant that religion also became a contested space. Prior to 1994, the government espoused and favored Christianity as the dominant religion and all other religions were measured through that lens.

With freedom of religion being enshrined in South Africa's Bill of Rights, religions like Hinduism, Islam, Buddhism, etc. which were seen to be on the fringe prior to 1994, started mobilizing and organizing themselves. They began to capitalize on this newfound political and legislative freedom

---

2 Nxumalo, "Outcry over Durban Pastor's Views."
3 Ndaliso, "Hindu Bodies Sue Durban Church."
4 Ndaliso, "Hindu Body Opens Case of Crimen Injuria."
5 Ndaliso, "Hindu Organisation Launches Equality Court."

and started gaining momentum and becoming more visible and vocal. Even though these religions represent a very small percentage of the South African population, they were given prominence at major national and local gatherings through interfaith dialogue and interfaith prayer. South Africa was seen as emerging as a truly democratic society and was affectionately referred to as the "rainbow nation."[6] Celebrating unity in diversity became the mantra of South Africa during these early years, post-1994.

The complexion of religious dominance changed and took on a more complicated nature. Other religious beliefs, traditions and practices were for the first time given space and coverage within the public domain. The stigma of belonging to a faith or religion other than Christianity dissipated and was no longer frowned upon. People were encouraged to explore and engage with people of different faiths. The greater publicity and visibility that previously marginalized religions started enjoying, meant that mainstream religious practice and observation were altered.

The foregoing must be appreciated against the historical arrival of Indians in South Africa primarily as indentured laborers in 1860 to service South Africa's expansive sugarcane farming industry. For a period of over fifty years (1860–1911), some "152,184 indentured immigrants arrived from India … as well as considerable 'passenger' Indians"[7] who settled mainly in what was then known as the colony of Natal. These laborers were housed on the farmsteads where many worked and occupied specially demarcated settlements in and around Durban. It must be noted that this was not a homogeneous group of Indian settlers. There were only two unifying factors among those who found themselves in a foreign land—their common identity as people of Indian origin and secondly, their expectation of a better life for themselves and their children.

The Indian Diaspora in South Africa is now home to the largest Indian community outside of India. From a small contingent of 340[8] who landed in Durban, Natal,[9] aboard the SS *Truro* in November 1860, the numbers have now swelled to over 1.56 million Indians,[10] comprising over 2.5 percent of the

---

6 This statement made by Archbishop Desmond Tutu from the Union Buildings in Cape Town in 1994 was widely reported.
7 Brain, *Christian Indians in Natal 1860-1911*, 4.
8 Nair and Naidoo, *Celebrate Indian Christians*, 8.
9 Brain, *Christian Indians in Natal*.
10 George, *Desi Diaspora*, 211.

population of South Africa.¹¹ The number of Christians who arrived on that first ship numbered 95, while the total number of Christians who arrived in the colony over the next fifty years was 2,150.¹² Indian Christians now comprise over 24 percent of the Indian population in South Africa,¹³ which contributes to the diversity that reflects the Indian Diaspora and the South African nation.

The diversity of the Indian Diaspora is acutely reflected in the Greater Durban area, which has the highest concentration of Indians in South Africa. As such, religious festivals like Deepavali or Diwali (festival of lights), and the Holi Festival, started becoming regular features for celebration and enjoyment and now continue to shape the religious outlook of Durban as well as other cities in South Africa where there is a sizeable concentration of the Indian Diaspora. Other major events that add to this dynamic include the Salt March (commemorating Gandhi's march in India in 1930), the Festival of Chariots (an annual celebration held by the International Society of Krishna Consciousness), etc.

These public events tend to contribute generally to Indian identity and culture but more particularly to mainstream Hindu practice and tradition. Besides fostering a sense of collective identity for Hindus, these festivals and celebrations have done much to attract sympathizers and supporters from the non-Indian sectors of the South African population. Moreover, there has been a groundswell of support and acceptance of Hindu ideology and practice from nominal Christians.

Sense, Sensibility, and Sensitivity: How Should Christians Respond?

In this final section, I will deal with some personal, practical, and biblical reflections on how Christians should respond in sharing the gospel with Indians from the Diaspora in South Africa and abroad. The case under consideration—of the young evangelist—his public pronouncements and his subsequent prosecution and sanction¹⁴ is a very sobering wake-up call for any committed Christian, seeking to proclaim the saving gospel of Jesus Christ either publicly or privately.

---

11 Kumar, "Tamils in South Africa," 11.
12 Nair and Naidoo, *Celebrate Indian Christians*, 9.
13 Kumar, "Tamils in South Africa," 12.
14 The Post, "Religious Tolerance Is a Two-Way Street."

This calls for sense, sensibility, and sensitivity. All three factors need to be harnessed for us to effectively share the gospel. While we cannot shy away from the mandate given to us as Christians to evangelize, this needs to be done with a great deal of commonsense. For the Christian, this means we need to exercise godly wisdom. Godly wisdom implies taking into account the command from Scripture and the compulsion of the Spirit working in equal measure as we attempt to share the gospel message. Further, we need to be sensitive to the beliefs, customs, traditions, and practices of Hindu Indians within our context. We need to appreciate their worldview and be acutely aware of their sensitivities to the issues of religion, religious discourse, and proselytizing.[15] The Hindu's personal encounter with Christians, or even just their anecdotal recollections may become a barrier to effective witness. Our failure to act sensibly closes the door to evangelizing Hindus and gives Christianity, Christians, and ultimately Christ a bad name.[16]

The Apostle Paul exemplified this sense, sensibility, and sensitivity triad so well in his ministry. Consider his address in the Areopagus in Athens in Acts 17 where he speaks to the issue of the "unknown God."[17] This is in stark contrast to the prophet Elijah on Mount Carmel where he taunted and ridiculed the prophets of Baal.[18] The Apostle Paul makes this wonderful statement that he became all things to all people in order he might win some, while at the same time acknowledging the power and efficacy of the gospel to save.[19]

Ours is not to point out what non-Christian Indians are doing wrong or what they are missing. Neither is it to criticize what they believe or critique what they don't believe. Ours is to demonstrate who Jesus Christ is and what faith in Christ means to us—to be the "salt and light."[20] Yes, we must be ready to give an answer for the hope we have in Christ.[21] But this is not to be done at any expense. Our responsibility is to present the hope we have in this life and in the life hereafter, and not to debate our counterparts' faith tradition. This further implies that we act sensibly and do not degrade or demean fellow Indians who are not of the Christian faith.

---

15 Ojong, "Indianness and Christianity," 431–44.
16 *The Post*, "Religious Tolerance."
17 Acts 17:23.
18 1 Kings 18.
19 1 Corinthians 9:22; Romans 1:16.
20 Matthew 5:14–16.
21 1 Peter 3:15.

While many esteem Christians highly and see them as devout followers of Jesus Christ, there are just as many who dislike Christians intensely. One of the reasons for this is the aggressive manner that many Christians adopt when "sharing the gospel." Militant or vocal Hindu leaders accuse Christians of deceptive or vigorous proselytizing—"a conversion at all costs" attitude. Rather than adopting a Christ-centered or gospel-centered approach to soul-winning, many zealous Christians fall foul of adopting a Machiavellian *modus operandi*—the end justifies the means approach. I find in the South African context that with the heightened awareness and understanding of their faith and traditions, Hindus are not afraid to disparage such practices. This has contributed immensely to the wave of anti-Christian sentiment and militancy among Hindus.

Another reason for the greater resistance is that many perceive Indian Christians as people who have embraced a Western religion thereby imbibing a Western lifestyle and language. To a large extent, this is very evident among Indian Christians in South Africa. Many will have nothing to do with Indian culture, dress, or language. Many Christians see this as inherently Hindu and tend to steer far away from it. So much so that these ideological and religious barriers have driven a large wedge between family members and relatives. One might say these nuances have contributed to a continent shift even among many immediate or extended family members and even whole communities.

A further factor that is a barrier to evangelism is the image that people have of churches in general, and pastors in particular. Many churches and pastors have worked tirelessly to maintain a good and godly Christian witness among the non-Christian community. At the same time, there are many churches and pastors who have contributed to a negative view of Christians and Christianity. These factors emanate from the blatant disregard some churches have for communities where they are located. These include the following: the excessive use of public address systems, loud or repetitive music, meetings that start either very early in the morning or go on till late hours of the night (sometimes even all night, with music and sound accompaniment), parking infringements, building infringements, disregarding or not even attending to neighbors' complaints, and reacting to community complaints in an unchristian manner. One cannot separate the church's attitude and reaction from that of the pastor. It is the pastor's lifestyle, witness, temperament, etc. which carries over to his congregation and which contributes to the church's image.

Further, the image portrayed by, and the reputations of some pastors are highly questionable. This is one of the biggest stumbling blocks to effective Christian witness. The non-Christian community looks to the church and pastors as people of integrity, people with high moral values, and decorum. Unfortunately, this image is severely tarnished by many pastors whose private and public lives are incongruent with the precepts of Scripture or inconsistent with their pastoral calling.

This being said, it still behooves the Indian Christian community in Durban and South Africa to maintain an effective witness of the gospel. So, considering the sociopolitical implications, the diversity among the Indian Diaspora and the barriers cited earlier, the Indian church needs to adopt a level of pragmatism in reaching and bringing others to faith in Jesus Christ. This calls for sense, sensibility, and sensitivity.

There needs to be a paradigm shift in our understanding of what constitutes Christian witness, or evangelism. As Christians, we need to be open and teachable. We have to be open and teachable about our Christian faith as well as the faith, beliefs, and practices of other religions in our communities or our sphere of engagement. There is a need for greater dialogue with and appreciation for the "other." We need to remove the element of suspicion and rather adopt a position of openness, to listen, and to engage with Hindus with respect and dignity. There is no need to view those of the Hindu faith as a threat but rather as those who also are fellow human beings in need of a Savior.

There are many different approaches to sharing the gospel that can be adopted, assimilated, and advanced to effectively reach the non-Christian for Jesus Christ. One such approach that is strongly advocated is friendship or relational evangelism[22]—forming and maintaining a relationship with Hindu friends and family. This approach is needed when one considers the complicated, diverse social and religious tapestry that makes up the people of Durban. We need to demonstrate an appreciation for the Indian culture, heritage, and language. The fostering and forging of these relationships become a gateway to sharing the gospel in real life. This approach replaces artificial religious Christian rhetoric for real-life, Christ-like authenticity.

---

22 Kuhatschek, *Evangelism*.

Conclusion

In this chapter, I cited and discussed a case study of how an insensitive and ill-timed comment by a Christian pastor on a public platform incurred the ire and outrage of the Hindu community in Durban, South Africa. While this led to the pastor being taken to court, being asked to offer a public apology, and committing to community service, this case made the headlines for all the wrong reasons and made the task of fulfilling the Great Commission among Hindus in Durban all the more difficult.

Further, I offered a panoramic overview of the sociopolitical and religious landscape of South Africa prior to its first democratic elections in 1994 and the changes that followed. This led to the cultural and religious renaissance in the country, especially among Hindus after 1997. Finally, this chapter provided some personal, practical, and biblical reflections on how we can effectively evangelize Indians in Diaspora. While we remain committed to fulfilling the mandate of the Great Commission as Christians, we need to be sensible, and sensitive, and act with sensibility to win our Hindu friends with love for Jesus Christ.

Conclusion

Christian Witness in Pluralistic Contexts

Dr. Sam George

This volume explored a broad spectrum of locations and contexts of global Hindus and Christian ministry to and among them by providing snapshots by an amazing group of Christian scholar-practitioners worldwide. Hinduism is expansive in its beliefs and practices, and its manifestations in different parts of the world have their distinctive history, adding another layer of diversity and complexity. What is presented in these sixteen chapters herein is not conclusive or the final word on this matter but a select set of case studies of missiological reflections from distinctive vantage points of various authors. We firmly believe that there is no single approach that works for all Hindus everywhere, as one particular ministry approach for one group of Hindus in a diasporic context may not be as applicable and fruitful in another. Nonetheless, these sweeping scenarios and several combinations of them, as well as others you know in your context, and most importantly the Holy Spirit, will enlighten and inspire the readers to engage Hindus in your community, neighborhoods, and nations.

The spread of Hindus to many regions of the world is a relatively recent phenomenon. The notion of diaspora within Hinduism remains relatively nascent compared to other religions like Judaism and Christianity. Nevertheless, in the first two decades of the twenty-first century, the Indian Diaspora—the largest share of whom in terms of their religious background remains Hindus—have grown so impressively that one may claim that the

Sun never sets on the Indian Diaspora, akin to what was said of the British Empire over a century ago. Hindus in the diaspora remain loosely connected religiously to their ancestries in India, Nepal, or with others elsewhere. There is no doubt that emigrants from the Indian subcontinent have carried their inherited faiths with them and were quick to transplant their beliefs and practices in the new soils of their chosen settlements, most noticeably in the West, where there is religious freedom.

In this concluding chapter, I briefly deliberate on the concept of Christian witness and provide a theology of mission for the Hindus in the diaspora. We strongly encourage you to glean many insights from the chapters of this book, while also extending beyond them by connecting with scores of other churches and ministries that are actively engaged in ministering to Hindus all over the world. We hope these authors (and many others) will embark on further research, dialogue continually to glean fresh insights, and develop new resources to equip Christians everywhere to address the rapidly growing need for authentic Christian witness among Hindus worldwide.

Witness in the Bible

The term *witness* generally refers to one who bears testimony about a person, place, or event. In contemporary English, the notion of witness is associated with an eyewitness, one who has seen or observed, or one who is an onlooker or a bystander. However, throughout the Bible, this term is employed in forensic contexts to indicate one who can explain what has happened based upon their personal experience of the event or issues related to the event being investigated. This is a legal or forensic term to establish the veracity of truth claims and reject deceit and falsehood. The purpose of seeking testimonials of witnesses is to establish truth such that appropriate judgment may be determined. Two or more independent witnesses are generally sought to arrive at the correct judgment.

In the Old Testament, the act of bearing witness is closely related to legal proceedings and ethical accountability. The Ten Commandments forbid bearing false witness against others (Exod 20:16). The Deuteronomic law necessitates the witness of two or more people (Deut 19:15), and all false witnessing is a punishable offense (Deut 19:16–21). The law of Moses demanded the evidence of several witnesses to convict a person of a capital crime (Deut 17:6–7; Num 35:30). They certify facts (Jer 32:10, 12; Ruth 4:9–11; Isa 8:2) but could also prove to be a false or malicious witness.

In ancient times, this was a legal term designating the testimony given for or against someone on trial before a court of law. A witness is intended to verify events and provide truth claims in legal matters. God's relationship with the chosen people of Israel is seen as covenantal, in which God's actions on behalf of Israel are presented as acts of witness to the covenant, and Israel's response and obedience are their testimony to the commitment to the covenant. The prophetic witness entailed speaking God's messages and warnings to the chosen people containing both the message of hope and restoration as well as judgment for their disobedience (e.g., Isaiah, Hosea, or Jeremiah). Psalms also portrays the created natural order as a witness to God's power and sovereignty (Ps 19:1–4).

In the New Testament, Jesus instructed his disciples to be his witnesses by sharing the message of salvation and his teaching with others. Over two hundred times, *witness* is used in the New Testament in some form in Greek, and most appear in the Johannine Gospel, where seventy-five instances appear. Acts has thirty-nine, and the Pauline writings have thirty-five. Jesus commanded his disciples to go and make disciples of all nations, baptizing them and teaching them to observe all his teachings with assurance to be with them till the end of the age (Matt 28:19–20). Later Jesus promised them the empowerment of the Holy Spirit to be his witness to the ends of the Earth (Acts 1:8). In this post-resurrection appearance of Christ, Luke records the fulfillment of Jesus' promise of the Spirit and the final charge to his followers to have the power to bear witness. The *power* (δύναμιν) refers to a supernatural spiritual enablement of the disciples to bear witness and proclaim the message of Christ (Luke 2:14–20; 4:31, 33; 14:3; cf. 6:10; Rom 1:16–17).[1] As the story of Christianity unfolds in the book of Acts, we see that this promise of the Spirit is available to all believers as well, not just the Twelve (Acts 6:3, 5; 9:31; 11:24, 28; 13:52; 15:28; 21:4, 11).[2]

For the early apostles, this witness meant being an eyewitness of the resurrection, earthly life, and ministry of Jesus. It refers to individuals who had direct experience with Jesus, particularly those who witnessed his ministry, crucifixion, and resurrection. They were considered as authoritative sources of information about Jesus' life and teaching. Throughout Acts, the apostles and early Christians are shown to actively engage in sharing and giving their testimony of Jesus as their Messiah, emphasizing his resurrection and calling people to repentance and faith.

---
1 Bock, *Acts*, 63; Fitzmyer, *Acts of the Apostles*, 205.
2 Schnabel, *Early Christian Mission*, Vol 1:392–93.

Luke also uses the noun *witness* to Stephen (22:20) and Paul (22:15; 26:16), besides the Old Testament prophets (10:43; cf. 26:22), the Holy Spirit (5:32), and God the Father himself (14:3; 15:8; cf. 14:17)—all who "bear witness" of Christ. Thus, the concept of *witness* in Acts refers to "witnesses who bear a divine message" and, importantly, the original messenger.[3] From this, we draw the concept of "ambassador," as meaning to represent someone else, who in authority has sent you on a mission to carry the message in person. The Apostle Paul claims that "we are ambassadors for Christ, God making his appeal through us" (2 Cor 5:20). Consequently, an ambassador embodies the message of the messenger, and it is conveyed to another in person.

Furthermore, the root word for *witness* in the Acts of the Apostles is μάρτυς (*martys*) or μαρτυρία (*martyria*), which is translated as "testimony." From this root word, we derive the English words *martyr* and *martyrdom*. In early Christianity, as well as in many parts of the world today, Christian witnessing is closely linked to suffering and persecution. Thus, *witness* refers to one who suffers and is even ready to die rather than give up his or her faith in Christ. They are so convinced about Jesus and his message of salvation that they are willing to suffer even to the point of death. In Acts 6:13, the witnesses who charged Stephen with blasphemy against the Temple and the Law are described as false witnesses. Later, Stephen (Acts 7) and James the son of Zebedee (Acts 12) were martyred for their faith. Their willingness to endure persecution and death was seen as the ultimate testimony of their faith in Jesus.

There is nothing that can shake off the deep-abiding trust of the early followers of Christ in the saving power of Jesus and the incredible transformation they have experienced such that witnessing came naturally to them. Oftentimes, it includes both verbal proclamations as well as a radical lifestyle in obedience to the risen Christ that produced a transformational impact on people and societies. The concept of *witness* in Acts underscored the importance of personal testimony and the role of individuals in sharing the message of Jesus Christ, meaning the whole church took the whole message to (their) whole world, and the mission was not confined to a few highly trained religious professionals doing one a week for an hour or so. Thus, mission as witness highlights the transformative power of encounters with the risen Christ for every Christian and the work of the Holy Spirit in equipping believers for this task.

---

3 BAGD, *Greek-English Lexicon of the New Testament*, 2nd ed., 494.

In 2022, one in seven Christian believers around the world have suffered persecution for their faith. An average of 16 believers were killed for following Jesus, which comes to close to 6,000 total martyrs, a 24 percent increase in Christians killed for the faith from the previous year.[4] There has been unprecedented levels of persecution against Christians by radical Hindus in India in the last few years. Since the current Bhartiya Janata Party (BJP) came to power, Christians and other minorities in India have suffered more in the hands of majority Hindus than ever in the history of Independent India. The anti-conversion laws are in place in many states of India where Hindus are ruling, and the media barrage of hate messages against minorities continues unabated in an attempt to make India a *Hindu Rashtra* (Hindu Nation), which actually is contrary to its constitutional framework. Many cases of assault, disruption of church services, rape, murder, burning of churches, etc. have been reported all over the country.

At the point of writing this conclusion, horrific and deadly violence has broken out against Christians in the northeastern Indian state of Manipur, which has drawn the widespread condemnation of many national and global leaders, as well as numerous Christian institutions worldwide. Some Diaspora Hindus have been emboldened by the Hindutva agenda and are contributing to it by supporting and funding some proponents of the radical Hindu ideology. The Gospel of Jesus Christ reached the shores of India in AD 52 through the witness of the Apostle Thomas who was martyred for his faith after two decades of ministry in India. Thus, Christians have lived and been bearing witness to Jesus in India before the gospel reached Western Europe or the Americas were even "discovered." Contrary to the popular caricature that Christianity is a Western religion, we must not forget that Christianity is more native to India than the West.

Christian Witness in Pluralistic Contexts

India is a pluralistic nation with a great amount of diversity of every imaginable form, and their global dispersion has transformed many host nations into pluralistic societies. Christian witness in a pluralistic context refers to the practice of sharing about Jesus and the Christian faith in multiethnic, multicultural, and multireligious settings where people of diverse origins, faith backgrounds, and philosophical worldviews live in

---

4 Annual report on persecution against Christians in World Watch List. Accessed Aug 15, 2023. https://www.opendoorsus.org/en-US/persecution/countries/.

close proximity. Any mission engagement in pluralistic contexts requires navigating the complexities of diversity, patient listening, fostering dialogue, and sustained engagements, while firmly upholding their convictions about Jesus and his values, without being obnoxious and counterproductive. As diversity and pluralism become a new reality in many parts of the world, the Christian ministry of reaching out to others who are unlike ourselves will become the foundational mission paradigm in the twenty-first century.[5]

Here are ten practical suggestions, not in any preferred sequence or importance, that have emerged repeatedly in these preceding essays: *First*, showing respect and sensitivity to the beliefs and practices of others is of utmost critical importance when engaging in witnessing to Hindus anywhere. *Second*, empathetic listening is crucial to develop mutual understanding and earn the right to show and share our way of life and faith in Jesus Christ. *Third*, find a common ground of shared values and concerns which builds bridges across the chasms of the religio-cultural divide. *Fourth*, aim to establish relationships by offering true friendships rather than viewing the other solely as a project for conversion or as a trophy to be won. *Fifth*, Christians should engage in dialogue with humility and authenticity, acknowledging the legitimacy of different views and sharing our faith sincerely and genuinely, without coercion or manipulation.

Sixth, learn and become good at the art of storytelling by sharing personal testimonies of divine intervention in our life or how God granted peace and guided us through a difficult life situation. This creates trust and deeper connection while showing the power of a living God and God's love for us. *Seventh*, ethical living must back up our witnessing. Demonstration of love, compassion, and integrity impacts how others view our faith. *Eighth*, learn about various Hindu religious beliefs, practices, and sects, as it will generate more informed interaction and respectful conversations. *Ninth*, be patient in witnessing to Hindus, and do not feel rushed to see any immediate results. Any witness to Hindus will require a long-term engagement that may span many years and multiple engagements from many witnesses. We must not abandon one's current circle of friends so as to engage with others which can produce faster results. *Tenth*, and finally, avoid any triumphalist attitude in Christian witnessing. We must not view our faith as superior or treat alternative belief systems as heathen or inferior but engage people of

---

5 Bosch, "Mission as Witness," 474–88. Also, Eiko and Lim, *Christian Mission in Religious Pluralistic Society*; George, *Holy Spirit and Christian Mission in a Pluralistic Context*.

other religious and spiritual backgrounds in humility and the spirit of Christ. This is not a conclusive list, and readers and other scholars would add several other helpful pointers in this regard.

Christian witnessing in pluralistic Hindu contexts must also overcome numerous baggage and preconceived ideas associated with Christianity generally held among some Hindus. First of all, Christianity is often viewed wrongly by Hindus as a Western religion. It is associated with the former colonial masters who exploited the people and resources of India, and some view that after gaining independence from colonial rule, all Indian subcontient Indians must detach from Western religious affiliations as well. However, we must be reminded that Jesus was an Asian (West Asian to be precise), and the Christian faith originated in Asia and spread to other parts of Asia and Africa before it ever reached the West. Showing Jesus with blue eyes or blonde hair (as done in some paintings and films) does not make Jesus a Westerner. India is mentioned in the Bible, and Christianity reached India through one of his devoted disciples, Thomas, who traveled from Jerusalem to the southwestern shores of India (the modern state of Kerala) in AD 52. Apostle Thomas bore witness to the risen Christ to the people of India in the first century AD and established Christian communities and was eventually martyred for his faith in the southern city of Chennai (formerly known as Madras and in the modern state of Tamil Nadu).

Another notable hurdle to overcome is that all Christians are assumed to be from lower caste or people belonging to outcaste communities of India and they should be kept at a distance socially and not permitted into the homes or temples of the Hindus. It is true that much of the Christian mission work in the past few decades has focused more on lower castes (overlooking the middle class, educated intelligentsia, and the priestly class) who were low-hanging fruits and more than eager to break out of their socioreligious bondage to embrace the Christian faith for the sake of social and economic upward mobility. It is true that a large number of Christians in India at the present time have risen from the lower castes, although there are many from higher castes also now. After their conversion to Christianity, many were able to gain a good education, secure well-paying jobs, improve economically, be apprised of their sociopolitical rights, and fight against caste and social discrimination meted out against them. In recent years, many of them have migrated to foreign lands, seeking freedom from discrimination, shame, and injustice.

Another common hurdle would be how Christianity is portrayed in Indian cinemas and literature, where Christians are depicted as meat-eating and alcohol-drinking people with loose morality and anti-national views. The Indian popular media has painted a negative picture of Christianity and overlooked the good deeds or upright living of Indian Christians. It might have risen out of the tendency of Christians to wear Western clothes or embrace new habits that are contrary to traditional Indian values like respecting elders and being obedient to parents. The emphasis on abandoning the old ways of life among new Christians and their disassociation of family members in the face of social pressures are generally interpreted incorrectly. Since the Indian culture and religion are so intricately intertwined that any rejection of a certain cultural expression is often interpreted as anti-Hindu and by extension considered that the loyalty of Christians lies elsewhere, not to their family or the native land. Any religious switching in a deeply communitarian culture is difficult, and some even fear misfortune or retaliation by the spirits of the land. Most new Christians from Hindu backgrounds will suffer rejection from their family, some form of prejudice, scandalous gossip in the community, face isolation and lose the support of communal and religious establishments. Some tend to react against such predicaments to further accentuate common misunderstandings among Hindus about Christians and are unable to fit into or find alternate Christian communities that can fully grasp where the new Christians are coming from or provide appropriate support and necessary care.

Final Words

Christians throughout all ages have borne witness to the life, message, and saving power of Jesus to people all around them. The Christian faith is a faith to be shared with others. It is a giveaway faith, not something to be consumed and held for ourselves. It is only when we share our life in Christ and observe the transformation it produces in others that we fully grasp what we believe about this faith in the first place. Being a follower of Jesus does not mean going through a set of rituals or signing up for membership in an organization. Neither does it require granting any intellectual consent to a set of beliefs or regularly going through some religious motions. Being a Christian is being in a relationship with a living God, and when we live a life that flows out of our vibrant, intimate relationship with Jesus, witnessing occurs naturally. That does not mean I do not have to learn or equip myself to understand people and get better at engaging people of different cultures and religious backgrounds. That is precisely why Ashok and I worked on this book, to glean wisdom from a select group of global Indian Christian leaders, several of whom have had Hindu upbringings and are now followers of Jesus Christ.

Acknowledgments

Sam George and Ashok Kumar

Every book has a backstory and many labor tirelessly to bring it out. This book is no exception. The idea for the book was birthed in 2017 at the Hethne (HETH-nay) conference in Chiang Mai, Thailand—a gathering of Christian workers and missionaries who minister among Hindu peoples, some from India and Nepal, but most came from diaspora communities around the world. Ashok was one of the primary organizers of the conference, and Sam was one of the plenary speakers.

Besides the stimulating conversations and content provided throughout that week, the conference represented a time of intense fellowship and togetherness. On the sidelines of the conference, at one of those dinner conversations, someone shared their wishful thinking about how wonderful it would be to compile the collective wisdom of the group and others who were not there as a resource for those who were unable to come to the conference but were ardently serving the Lord in reaching Hindus in different parts of the world.

Dreaming about such a resource is one thing and working on it to make it a reality is an entirely different matter. We both were extremely busy with workloads spanning several projects at that time. The idea got submerged only to surface again in 2020 as Ashok planned to host another Hethne conference. We gave some initial thoughts and consulted several mission leaders in India and elsewhere for this project and in order to identify voices and perspectives that need to be included in this resource. Upon contacting potential contributors, some were eager to be part of the project and others declined, requiring us to expand our list of contributors. However, the convening of a global event had to be rescinded on account of the COVID-19 pandemic, and this project was pushed to the backburner as several contributors fell sick and the project was nearly scrapped. Then a few of the contributors and well-wishers to Hindu Diaspora ministries revived the project and we worked toward the next Hethne conference in 2024.

Many groups of people made this book project a reality. First of all, we would like to acknowledge God's supernatural work in our lives and the divine guidance and provisions we experienced during this project, despite countless roadblocks. Many have silently prayed and wished to bring this book to see the light of day, as this far exceeds all human abilities and planning. So we praise God and pray it will be a blessing to Christians worldwide.

We appreciate all the contributors for writing their chapters and distilling their thoughts and years (decades in several cases) of ministry experience working among Hindu peoples in diverse contexts. Thanks for working with us and tolerating our persistent follow-ups, chats, and requests for your chapter. Your patience and burden for sharing the gospel of Jesus with Hindus are unmatched, especially many of you who come from Hindu backgrounds, and most may never fully grasp the cost of following Jesus you faced. Your reflection and passion is a huge blessing to this project.

We place on record the patience of the publishers of this book, as they waited for many years while this project took numerous convoluted detours and delays. Thank you to an exceptional team at William Carey Publishers, especially Vivian, Melissa, and others who toiled to lay out, copyedit, proofread, cover design, and market this resource widely. We value the kind words of all endorsers, and we sincerely thank each one of them. Many others whom we had approached for contributions to this volume were unable to provide them but encouraged us to produce this volume. We gratefully acknowledge our colleagues at Lausanne Movement and World Evangelical Alliance Global Witness who supported our various efforts in ministries.

I (Ashok) would like to thank my wife and two adult children for allowing me to travel and serve globally to reach Hethne communities everywhere. I am grateful to Sudan Interior Mission (SIM, East Asia) for their ongoing cooperation for all Hethne initiatives that I currently lead. Likewise, I'm thankful for the support and encouragement I received earlier from Operation Mobilization (OM) Singapore for Hethne ministries.

I (Sam) am grateful for the support of my wife and our two boys as I took up a major role with the Lausanne Movement that required me to be "gone" so frequently to faraway places. Th anks much for your prayers and encouragement.

Soli Deo Gloria (Christmas 2023)

Bibliography

Aghamkar, Atul Y. "Family Coherence and Evangelization of Urban India." In *God So Loves the City*, edited by Charles Van Engen and Jude Tiersma. Monrovia, CA: MARC, 1995.

Agnihotri, R. K. *Crisis of Identity: The Sikhs in England*. New Delhi: Bahri Publications, 1987.

Akin, Daniel L. "Axioms for a Great Commission Resurgence." In *The Great Commission Resurgence: Fulfilling God's Mandate in Our Time*. Nashville: B&H Academic, 2010.

Allen, Roland. *Missionary Methods: St. Paul's or Ours?* Grand Rapids: Eerdmans Publishing, 1962.

Allen, Roland. *The Spontaneous Expansion of the Church*. Grand Rapids: Eerdmans Publishing, 1962.

Ambedkar, B. R. *The Untouchables: Who Were They and Why They Became Untouchables?* New Delhi: Amrit Books, 1948.

Anderson, Alan B., and James S. Frideres. *Ethnicity in Canada: Theoretical Perspectives*. Toronto: Butterworths, 1981.

Anderson, Benedict. *Imagined Communities*. London: Verso, 1983.

Appasamy, A. J. *Christianity as Bhakti Marga*. Madras: Christian Literature Society, 1991.

Ariarajah, Wesley. *Hindus and Christians: A Century of Protestant Ecumenical Thought*. Grand Rapids: Eerdmans Publishing, 1991.

Arrow. "De Caribbean Man." Accessed July 14, 2023. https://www.jiosaavn.com/lyrics/caribbean-man-lyrics/AF8ICUZbXAE.

Australian Government Department of Education. International Education Data and Research. Accessed March 25, 2024. https://www.education.gov.au/international-education-data-and-research/international-student-numbers-country-state-and-territory.

Ayrookuzhiel, M. Abraham. *The Sacred in Popular Hinduism*. Madras: Christian Literature Society, 1983.

Ballard, Roger. "The Growth and Changing Character of the Sikh Presence in Britain." In *The South Asian Religious Diaspora in Britain, Canada, and the United States*, edited by Harold Coward, John R. Hinnells, and Raymond Brady Williams, 127–44. Albany: State University of New York Press, 2000.

Banks, Robert. *Paul's Idea of Community*. Peabody, MA: Hendrickson Publishers, 1994.

Banks, Robert, and Julia Banks. *The Church Comes Home: A New Base for Community and Mission*. Claremont, CA: Albatross Books, 1986.

Barrett, Lois. *Building the House Church*. Kitchener, Ontario: Herald Press, 1986.

Barth, F. *Ethnic Groups and Boundaries*. Oslo: Jhansen and Nielsen, 1969.

Barua, Ankur. *Debating "Conversion" in Hinduism and Christianity*. New York: Routledge, 2015.

Baudhayana Sutra, II.1.2.2. Accessed August 1, 2023. https://www.wisdomlib.org/hinduism/book/baudhayana-dharmasutra/d/doc116416.html.

Bauer, Walter. *A Greek-English Lexicon of the New Testament*. Translated by William F. Arndt and F. Wilbur Gingrich. 4th ed. London: University of Chicago Press, 1957.

Bauman, Zygmunt. *Globalization: The Human Consequence*. New York: Columbia University Press, 1998.

Baumann, Martin. "Conceptualizing Diaspora." *Temenos* 31 (1995): 19–35.

Baumann, Martin. "The Hindu Diaspora in Europe." In *Religious Communities in the Diaspora*, edited by Gerrie ter Haar, 87–88, 95. Nairobi: Acton Publishers, 2001.

Baumann, Martin. "Sustaining 'Little Indias': Hindu Diasporas in Europe." In *Strangers and Sojourners: Religious Communities in the Diasporas*, edited by Gerrie ter Haar. Leuven, 95–132. Belgium: Peters Publishers, 1998.

Belle, C. V. *Indians in Malaysia*. Singapore: Institute of SE Asian Studies, 2015.

Bender, Harold S. "The Anabaptist Vision." In *The Recovery of the Anabaptist Vision*, edited by Guy F. Hershberger, 29–52. Scottdale, PA: Herald Press, 1972.

Bharati, Agehandanda. "Ritualistic Tolerance and Ideological Rigour: The Paradigm of the Expatriate Hindus in East Africa." *Contributions to Indian Sociology* 10 (1976): 317–39.

Bharati, Dayanand. *Understanding Hinduism*. New Delhi: Munshiram Manoharlal, 2005.

Bhattacharya, Sabyasachi. "When Vivekananda Reconstructed Hinduism." *Frontline*, October 18, 2018. https://frontline.thehindu.com/columns/sabyasachi-bhattacharya/when-vivekanandareconstructed-hinduism/article25298170.ece.

Bilimoria, Purushottama. "Hindu-Christian Dialogue in the Making in Australia." *Journal of Hindu-Christian Studies* 7 (1994): 32–33, 37.

Bock, Darrell L. *Acts: Baker Exegetical Commentary on the New Testament*. Grand Rapids: Baker Academic, 2007.

Bosch, David. *Transforming Mission: Paradigm Shifts in Theology of Mission*. Maryknoll, NY: Orbis Books, 1991.

Brack, La Bruce. *The Sikhs of Northern California*. New York: AMS Press, 1988.

Brain, Joy B. *Christian Indians in Natal 1860–1911: An Historical and Statistical Study*. Cape Town: Oxford University Press, 1983.

Breton, Raymond. "Institutional Completeness of Ethnic Communities and Personal Relations to Immigrants." *American Journal of Sociology* 70, no. 2 (1964): 193–205.

Britannica. "*Ashramas*: The Four Stages of Life." Accessed August 1, 2023. https://www.britannica.com/topic/Hinduism/Karma-samsara-and-moksha#ref50468.

Canadian Bureau of International Education, "Infographics 2023." Accessed March 25, 2024. https://cbie.ca/infographic/.

Carter, Marina. *Coolitude: An Anthology of the Indian Labour Diaspora*. Anthem Press, 2002.

Castagne, Patrick. "Forged from the Love of Liberty." Words of the National Anthem of Trinidad and Tobago.

Chappell, Frank R. "Negotiating Contemporary Hindu Beliefs and Practices in the United States." In *Religions of South Asia* 12.1 (2018): 82, 85, 89–92.

Che Soh, Roslina. "The Cultural and Legal Perspectives on Wife Battering in Malaysia." *The Law Review* 4 (2010): 613–22.

Chesterton, G. K. *Orthodoxy*. New York: John Lane Co., 1908.

Chhetri, Rajendra. "Strategies for Effective Christian Witness among Hindus." In *South Asian Journal of Missions Research*. Accessed August 1, 2023. https://www.sajomr.org/index.php/sajomr/article/view/238/208.

Chinn, Leiton Edward. "Making Room at Your Table for International Students." *Christianity Today*, November 2018.

Clifford, James. "Traveling Cultures." In *Cultural Studies*, edited by L. Grossberg, C. Nelson, and P. A. Treiehler, 96–116. New York: Routledge, 1992.

Cohen, Robin. *Global Diaspora: An Introduction*. London: UCL Press, 1997.

Coleman, Robert E. *The Master Plan of Discipleship*. Grand Rapids: Baker, 1998.

Coleman, Robert E., Bobby Harrington, and Josh Patrick. *Revisiting the Master Plan of Evangelism*. USA: Exponential Resources, 2014.

Coward, Harold. "Hinduism in Canada." In *The South Asian Religious Diaspora in Britain, Canada, and the United States*, edited by Harold Coward, John R. Hinnells, and Raymond B. Williams, 151–72. Albany: State University of New York Press, 2000.

Dale, Tony, and Felicity Dale. *The Rabbit and The Elephant: Why Small Is the New Big for Today's Church*. New York: Barna Books, 2009.

Danker, Frederick W., et al. *Greek-English Lexicon of the New Testament and Other Early Christian Literature*, 23rd ed. Chicago: University of Chicago Press, 2000.

Dessai, Elizabeth. *Hindus in Deutschland*. Moers, Germany: Aragon, 1994.

Dhand, Arti. "Hinduism to Hindus in the Western Diaspora." *Method and Theory in the Study of Religion* 17.3 (2005): 274.

Dickson, John. *The Best Kept Secret of Christian Mission: Promoting the Gospel with More Than Our Lips*. Grand Rapids: Zondervan, 2010.

Dijk, Alphons van. "Hinduismus in Suriname und den Niederlanden." *Zeitschrift fur Missionswissenschaft und Religionswissenschaft* 80.3 (1996): 193.

D'Mello, John. "Letting the Converted Speak … Towards an Emic Approach to Conversion." *Jnanadeepa Pune Journal of Religious Studies* 3/1 (January 2000): 5–22.

Doniger, Wendy. *The Hindus: An Alternative History*. New York: Penguin Press, 2009.

Doniger, Wendy. *The Laws of Manu*, translated by Wendy Doniger. New York: Penguin Classics, 1991.

Eck, Diana L. "Negotiating Hindu Identities in the US." In *The South Asian Religious Diaspora in Britain, Canada, and the United States*, edited by Harold Coward, John R. Hinnells, and Raymond B. Williams. Albany: State University of New York Press, 2000.

The Economist. "India's diaspora is bigger and more influential than any in history." *The Economist*, June 12, 2023. https://www.economist.com/international/2023/06/12/indias-diaspora-is-bigger-and-more-influential-than-any-in-history.

Eickelman, Dale F., and James Piscatori. "Social Theory in the Study of Muslim Societies." In *Muslim Travellers, Pilgrimage, Migration and the Religious Imagination*, edited by Dale F. Eickelman and James Piscatori, 3–28. London: Routledge, 1990.

Elazar, Daniel J. "The Jewish People as the Classical Diaspora: A Political Analysis." In *Modern Diasporas in International Politics*, edited by Gabriel Sheffer. New York: St. Martin's Press, 1986.

Embassy of India in Manila, Philippines. "Bilateral Political Relations." Accessed March 20, 2024. https://www.eoimanila.gov.in/page/bilateral-political-and-cultural-relations/.

Embassy of India in Manila, Philippines. "Bilateral Trade." 2023. Accessed August 1, 2023. www.eoimanila.gov.in/eoi.php?id=bilateral-trade-and-economic-relations.

Fitzmyer, Joseph A. *The Acts of the Apostles: A New Translation with Introduction and Commentary*. London: Bloomsbury Publishing, 1998.

Francis, T. Dayanand, ed., *The Christian Bhakti of A. J. Appasamy*, 94–100. Madras: CLS, 1992. Originally appeared in the *National Council of Churches Review*, 1948: 23–26.

Gandhi, M. K. *The Story of My Experiments with Truth*. New York: Penguin Random House, 2018.

Gareis, Elisabeth. "Intercultural Friendship: Effects of Home and Host Region." *Journal of International and Intercultural Communication* 5, no. 4: 309–28.

Garrison, David. *Church Planting Movements*. Bangalore: WIGTake Resources, 2004.

George, Roji T. *Holy Spirit and Christian Mission in a Pluralistic Context*. Bengaluru: SAIACS Press, 2017.

George, Sam. "Crossing *Kala Pani*: Overcoming Religious Barriers to Migration." In *Diaspora Christianities: Global Scattering and Gathering of South Asian Christians*, edited by Sam George, 69–83. Minneapolis: Fortress Press, 2018.

George, Sam, ed. *Desi Diaspora: Ministry to Scattered Global Indian Christians*. Bengaluru: SAIACS Press, 2019.

George, Sam. "Motus Dei (The Move of God): A Theology and Missiology for a Moving World." In *Reflections of Asian Diaspora*, Volume 3 of *Asian Diaspora Christianity*, edited by Sam George, 95–122. Minneapolis: Fortress Press, 2022.

George, Sam. "Shaming the Shame: Healing Inner Wounds Through Loving Relationships." In *Caring for the South Asian Soul: Counseling South Asians in the Western World*, edited by T. V. Thomas and Thomas Kulanjiyil, 171–88. Bangalore: Primalogue, 2010.

George, Sam, and Steve S. Chang interview. *Journeys of the Asian Diaspora and Indian Christians: A Conversation with Sam George*. Accessed July 16, 2023. https://sola.network/article/journeys-of-the-asian-diaspora-and-indian-christians/.

George, Sam, and T. V. Thomas. Series editors of "Indian Diaspora Series," which includes *Malayali Diaspora* (2014), *Tamil Diaspora* (2020), and *Telugu Diaspora* (forthcoming). New Delhi: Serials Publications.

Georges, Jayson, and Mark D. Baker. *Ministering in Honor-Shame Cultures: Biblical Foundations and Practical Essentials*. Downers Grove, IL: IVP, 2017.

Glasser, Arthur. "The Apostle Paul and the Missionary Task: A Study in Perspective." In *Crucial Dimensions in World Evangelization*, edited by Arthur Glasser, Paul Hiebert, C. Peter Wagner, and Ralph Winter, 27. Pasadena, CA: William Carey Library, 1976.

Gopalakrishnan, V. S. "Crossing the Oceans." *Hinduism Today Magazine*. August–September 2008. Accessed March 23, 2024. https://www.hinduismtoday.com/magazine/july-august-september-2008/2008-07-crossing-the-ocean/.

Gopinath, A. *Footsteps in the Sands of Time*. Kuala Lumpur: Akrib Negara Malaysia, 2007.

Green, Michael. *Evangelism in the Early Church*, 207. London: Hodder and Stoughton, 1970.

Greenway, Roger, and Timothy Monsma. *Cities: Missions' New Frontier*. Grand Rapids: Baker, 1989.

Grudem, Wayne. *Systematic Theology*. Grand Rapids: Zondervan, 1994.

Harr, Gerrie Ter, ed. *Religious Communities in the Diaspora*. Nairobi: Action Publishers, 2001.

Hawley, John Stratton. "Hinduism: Household Religious Practice," *JRank Articles*, 2014. https://family.jrank.org/pages/769/Hinduism-Household-Religious-Practice.html.

Hedlund, Roger E. *Christianity Made in India: From Apostle Thomas to Mother Teresa*. Fortress Press, 2017.

Hedlund, Roger E. *Christianity Is Indian: The Emergence of an Indigenous Community*, MIIS, New Delhi: ISPCK, 2000.

Hedlund, Roger E. *Quest for Identity: India's Churches of Indigenous Origin*. New Delhi: ISPCK, 2000.

Hiebert, Paul G. *Transforming Worldviews*. Grand Rapids: Baker Academic, 2008.

"Higher Education Student Statistics: UK, 2018/19." Higher Education Statistics Agency website. Accessed August 1, 2023. https://www.hesa.ac.uk/news/16-01-2020/sb255-higher-education-student-statistics.

Hodge, David R. "Working with Hindu Clients in a Spiritually Sensitive Manner." *Social Work: A Journal of the National Association of Social Workers* 49, no. 1 (January 2004): 27–38.

Hoefer, Herbert. "Gospel Proclamation of the Ascended Lord." *Journal of Biblical Literature* 128, no. 2 (2009): 325–45.

Hutheesing, M. O. L. K. "The Thirate Kalyanam Ceremony among South Indian Hindu Communities of Malaysia." *Eastern Anthropologist* 36 (1983): 131–47.

Ingram, Chip. *The Invisible War*. Grand Rapids: Baker Books, 2006.

Institute of International Education website. *Open Doors*. New York. Accessed March 25, 2024. https://opendoorsdata.org/fact_sheets/student-mobility/.

IS/IVCF. "To Know Christ and to Make Him Known." Accessed July 15, 2023. https://isivcftt.com/about/.

Isaiah, G. "Post-Conversion Pastoral Care." In *Conversion in a Pluralistic Context: Perspectives and Perceptions*, edited by Krickwin C. Mark and Plamthodathil S. Jacob, 209–17. Delhi: Indian Society for the Promotion of Christian Knowledge (ISPCK), 2000.

Jackson, Robert, and Eleanor Nesbitt. *Hindu Children in Britain*. Stoke-on-Trent: Trentham Books Ltd., 1993.

Jaffrelot, Christophe, and Ingrid Therwath. "The Sangh Parivar and Hindu Diaspora in the West: What Kind of Long-Distance Nationalism?" *International Political Sociology* 1 (2007): 278–95.

Johnson, Marcus Peter. *One with Christ: An Evangelical Theology of Salvation*. Wheaton: Crossway Books, 2013.

Kalpana, Hiralal. *Global Hindu Diaspora: Historical and Contemporary Perspectives*. New York: Routledge, 2018.

Kappen, S. "The Church as the Bearer of New Values." In *Seeking Christ in India Today*, edited by Mathai Zachariah, 55–64. Nagpur, India: NCC, 1979.

Karpat, Kemal H. "The *hijra* from Russia and the Balkans: The Process of Self-definition in the Late Ottoman State." In *Muslim Travellers, Pilgrimage, Migration and the Religious Imagination*, edited by D. F. Eickelman and J. Piscatori, 131–52. London: Routledge, 1990.

Kauai's Hindu Monastery website. "Nine Beliefs of Hinduism." Accessed Aug 1, 2023. https://www.himalayanacademy.com/readlearn/basics/nine-beliefs.

Kaur, A. "HINDRAF and the Malaysian Indian Minority after the 2018 General Elections in Malaysia." *Sage Journal*, 2019: 9–11.

Kemp, Simon. "Digital 2024: India." February 21, 2024. Accessed March 25, 2024. https://datareportal.com/reports/digital-2024-india#.

Kim, Hanna. "Public Engagement and Personal Desires: BAPS Swaminarayan Temples and Their Contribution to the Discourses on Religion." *International Journal of Hindu Studies* (2009): 15–17, 21.

Kitagawa, Joseph M. *The Christian Tradition: Beyond Its European Captivity*. Philadelphia: Trinity Press, 1992.

Knott, Kim. "Bound to Change? The Religions of South Asians in Britain." In *Aspects of South Asian Diaspora*, edited by Steven Vertovec, 86–111. New Delhi: Oxford University Press, 1991.

Knott, Kim. *Hinduism in Leeds: A Study of Religious Practice in the Indian Hindu Community and Hindu-Related Groups*. Leeds: University of Leeds, 1986.

Knott, Kim, and Sadja Khokher. "Religious and Ethnic Identity among Young Muslim Women in Bradford." *New Community* 19 (1993): 593–610.

Koshy, T. E. *Bakht Singh of India: The Incredible Account of a Modern-Day Apostle*. Downers Grove, IL: IVP Books, 2008.

Kruger, Rene. "Das Biblische Paradigma der Diaspora. Die solidarische und missionarische Gemeinschaft der Glaubigen." *Die evangelische Diaspora* 63 (1994): 98–99.

Kuhatschek, Jack. *Evangelism: Reaching Out through Relationships*. Grand Rapids: Our Daily Bread Ministries, 2017.

Kumar, Ashutosh. *Coolies of the Empire: Indentured Indians in Sugar Colonies 1830–1920*. Cambridge: Cambridge University Press, 2017.

Kumar, P. Pratap. "Tamils in South Africa: Quest for Identity." In *Tamil Diaspora: Intersectionality of Migration, Religion, Language and Culture*, edited by Peter Vethanayagamony, 191–210. New Delhi: Serials Publications, 2020.

Kurien, Prema. *A Place at the Multicultural Table: The Development of an American Hinduism*. New Brunswick, NJ: Rutgers University Press, 2007.

Lalvani, Kartar. *The Making of India: The Untold Story of British Enterprise*. London: Bloomsbury, 2016.

Larson, Gerald James. "Hinduism in India and in America." In *World Religions in America*, edited by Jacob Neusner, 4th ed., 179–98. Louisville: John Knox Press, 2009.

Leonard, Karen. *Locating Home: India's Hyderabadis Abroad*. Palo Alto, CA: Stanford University Press, 2007.

Leoni, Zeno. *American Grand Strategy from Obama to Trump: Imperialism After Bush and China's Hegemonic Challenge*. London: Palgrave Macmillan, 2021.

Lessinger, Joanna. *From the Ganges to the Hudson: Indian Immigrants in New York City*. Boston: Allyn and Bacon, 1995.

Levitt, Peggy. "Local-Level Global Religion: The Case of US-Dominican Migration." *Journal for the Scientific Study of Religion* 37, no. 1 (1998): 75.

Lewis, C. S. *The Screwtape Letters*. London: Geoffrey Bles, 1961.

Logan, Penny. "Practicing Hinduism: The Experience of Gujarati Adults and Children in Britain." Unpublished report. Thomas Coram Research Unit, University of London Institute of Education. 1988.

Louis, Prakash. "Conversion and Cultural Alienation from the Perspective of the Converted." *Third Millennium Indian Journal of Evangelization* 3, no. 3 (July–September 2000): 68–80.

Love, Richard D. "Conversion." *Evangelical Dictionary of World Missions*, edited by A. Scott Moreau, 231–32. Grand Rapids: Baker Books, 2000.

Maharaj, Brij. "Challenges Facing Hindus and Hinduism in Post-Apartheid South Africa." *Journal of Sociology and Social Anthropology* 4, no. 1–2 (2013): 93–103.

Manjaly, Thomas. *Collaborative Ministry: An Exegetical and Theological Study of Synergos in Paul*. Bangalore: Asia Trading Corporation, 2001.

Map Global. "What Is the 4–14 Window?" April 15, 2018. Accessed July 16, 2023. https://www.mapglobal.org/blog/2018/4/15/what-is-the-4-14-window.

Marie, Rowanne Sarojini. "Across the *Kala Pani*: Untold Stories of Indentured Indian Women of Christian Origin in South Africa." In *Oral History Journal of South Africa* 2, no. 1 (2014): 89–101.

Mathew, Joseph. *Contemporary Religious Conversions*. New Delhi: AuthorsPress, 2013.

Mattam, Joseph, and Joseph Valiamangalam, eds. *Emerging Indian Missiology—Context and Concept*. New Delhi: FOIM/ISPCK, 2006.

McGavran, Donald A. *Understanding Church Growth*. Grand Rapids: Eerdmans Publishing, 1982.

Media to Movements. www.MediaToMovements.org and www.VisualStory.org/mtmsurvey. Accessed August 1, 2023.

Mehta, Brinda. *Diasporic (Dis)location: Indo-Caribbean Women Writers Negotiate the Kala Pani*. Jamaica: University of the West Indies Press, 2004.

Meiring, P. G. J. "Truth and Reconciliation in South Africa: The Role of the Faith Communities." *Verbum et Ecclesia* 26, no. 1 (2005): 146–73.

Michaelson, Maureen. "Domestic Hinduism in a Gujarati Trading Caste." In *Hinduism in Great Britain*, edited by R. Burghart, 32–49. London: Tavistock, 1987.

Miller, J. G. "Cultural Diversity in the Morality of Caring: Individually-Oriented versus Duty-based Interpersonal Moral Codes." *Cross-Cultural Research* 28 (1): 3–19.

Mohan, Rohini. "Surge in Indians adopting foreign citizenship, highest numbers in more than a decade." *The Strait Times*, August 10, 2023. https://www.straitstimes.com/asia/south-asia/surge-in-indians-adopting-foreign-citizenship-highest-numbers-in-more-than-a-decade.

Mortuza, Shamsad. "Beyond '*Kalapani*' and Tagore's Search for a Shared Regional Identity." *Journal of Indian Ocean*, September 2017. London: Taylor & Francis.

Moxnes, Malvor. "Honor and Shame." In *The Social Sciences and New Testament Interpretation*, edited by Richard Rohrbaugh. Peabody, MA: Hendrickson Publishers, 1996.

Naidu, Janet. "Retention and Transculturation of Hinduism in the Caribbean." *Guyana Journal*, March 2007. Accessed July 14, 2023. http://guyanajournal.com/hinduism_caribbean.html.

Nair, G. K., and Gabriel Naidoo, eds. *Celebrate Indian Christians in South Africa 1860–2010*. Durban, South Africa: Legacy Literacy, 2010.

Nameeta. "When Being Christian Means Losing Everything You Love—For Jesus' Sake." *Vidyajyothi Journal of Theological Reflection* 67, no. 6 (June 2003): 427–41.

Ndaliso, Chris. "Hindu Bodies Sue Durban Church for R1Million over 'Hate Speech.'" *IOL* Accessed June 30, 2022. https://www.iol.co.za/dailynews/news/kwazulu-natal/hindu-bodies-sue-durban-church-for-r1m-over-hate-speech-50585592.

Ndaliso, Chris. "Hindu Body Opens Case of Crimen Injuria against Two Durban Pastors for 'Attacks.'" *IOL* Accessed June 30, 2022. https://www.iol.co.za/dailynews/news/kwazulu-natal/hindu-body-opens-case-of-crimen-injuria-against-two-durban-pastors-for-attacks-50344174.

Ndaliso, Chris. "Hindu Organisation Launches Equality Court Action against Chatsworth Pastors for 'Denigrating and Insulting' Their Religion." *IOL* Accessed June 30, 2022. https://www.iol.co.za/dailynews/news/hindu-organisation-launches-equality-court-action-against-chatsworth-pastors-for-denigrating-and-insulting-their-religion-94646d37-9d97-4688-ae43-53df9232a481.

Neill, Stephen. *Bhakti: Hindu and Christian*. Christian Literature Society, 1974.

Nichols, Bruce J. "A Living Theology for Asian Churches: Some Reflections on the Contextualization-Syncretism Debate." In *The Bible & Theology in Asian Contexts: An Evangelical Perspective on Asian Theology*, edited by Bong Rin Ro and Ruth Eshenaur, 19–37. Manila: Asia Theological Association, 1984.

Niebuhr, Richard H. *Christ and Culture*. New York: Harper Torchbooks, 1956.

Nxumalo, Mphathi. "Outcry over Durban Pastor's Views on Hinduism and His Parents' Conversion to Christianity." *IOL* Accessed June 30, 2022. https://www.iol.co.za/dailynews/news/kwazulu-natal/outcry-over-durban-pastors-views-on-hinduism-and-his-parents-conversion-to-christianity-49546878.

Nye, Malory. *A Place for Our Gods: The Construction of an Edinburgh Hindu Temple Community*. Richmond, UK: Curzon, 1995.

O'Callaghan, Marion. "Hinduism in the Indian Diaspora in Trinidad." *Journal of Hindu-Christian Studies* 11 (1998): 4–5, 9.

Office for National Statistics (UK). "Religion and Participation in England and Wales." Accessed August 1, 2023. https://www.ons.gov.uk/peoplepopulationandcommunity/culturalidentity/religion#.

Ojong, Vivian Besem. "Indianness and Christianity: Negotiating Identity/Cultural Values in the Context of Religious Conversion Among South African Indians Living in Chatsworth, South Africa." *The Oriental Anthropologist* 12, no. 2 (2012): 431–44.

Open Doors US. World Watch List of Christian Persecution. Accessed August 15, 2023. https://www.opendoorsus.org/en-US/persecution/countries/.

Pallatino, Chelsea L. "Factors Contributing to Domestic Violence among Hindu Asian Indian Immigrants in Allegheny County." *Journal of Health Disparities Research and Practice*, 2011.

Panikkar, K. M. *A Survey of Indian History.* Bombay: National Information and Publication, 1947.

Pappu, S. S. Rama Rao. "Hindu Ethics." In *Contemporary Hinduism, Ritual, Culture, and Practice*, edited by Robin Rinehart, 155–78. Santa Barbara, CA: ABC-CLIO Inc., 2004.

Partridge, Christopher, ed. *Introduction to World Religions.* Minneapolis: Fortress Press, 2013.

Patole, James. "Towards an Understanding of the New Middle Classes in India: Missiological Perspective and Implications." *The Asbury Journal* 74, no. 2 (2019): 427–44. https://place.asburyseminary.edu/asburyjournal/vol74/iss2/11.

Pattison, Stephen. *Shame: Theory, Therapy and Theology.* Cambridge: Cambridge University Press, 2000.

Paul, Timothy. "Impacting the Hindu Diaspora in North America." *International Journal of Frontier Missiology*, Fall (2009): 129–33.

Pennington, Paul J. *Christian Barriers to Jesus: Conversations and Questions from the Indian Context.* Pasadena, CA: William Carey Library, 2017.

Petty, Richard E., and John T. Cacioppo. *Communication and Persuasion: Central and Peripheral Routes to Attitude Change.* New York: Springer-Verlag, 1986.

Pew Research Center. "Asian Americans: A Mosaic of Faiths," 2012. Accessed July 1, 2023. https://www.pewresearch.org/religion/2012/07/19/asian-americans-a-mosaic-of-faiths-overview/.

Pinto, J. Prasad. "Mission in the North American Context." In *Emerging Indian Missiology: Context and Concept*, eds. Joseph Mattam and Joseph Valiamangalam, 130–31. New Delhi: Fellowship of Indian Missiologists/Indian Society For Promotion Of Christian Knowledge (FOIM/ISPCK), 2006.

Pocock, David F. "Preservation of the Religious Life: Hindu Immigrants in England." *Contributions to Indian Sociology* 10 (1976): 357–62.

Pohl, Christine D. "Responding to Strangers: Insights from the Christian Tradition." *Studies in Christian Ethics*, 2006, 81–101. https://doi.org/10.1177/0953946806062287.

Post. "Religious Tolerance Is a Two-Way Street." *IOL* Accessed July 15, 2022. https://www.iol.co.za/thepost/opinion/religious-tolerance-is-a-two-way-street-bae94076-9153-47ad-a403-4411b92719de.

Promise Church. "What Is 4/14 Window Movement?" Accessed July 16, 2023. https://promise414.com/4-14-winddow/?lang=en.

Rai, Sarita. "How Big Tech Is Importing India's Caste Legacy to Silicon Valley." *Bloomberg Business Week*, March 11, 2021.

Rainer, Thom S., and Eric Geiger. *Simple Church*. Nashville: B&H Publishing Group, 2006.

Rajan, S. Irudaya, and Rakesh Ranjan Kumar. "India's Great Student Out-Migration." *World Bank Blogs*. September 14, 2023. https://blogs.worldbank.org/peoplemove/indias-great-student-out-migration-0#.

Rajapaksa, Mahinda. "Mahinda Chinthana: A Commentary on Policy Options," in Sri Lanka, 2007. https://www.ips.lk/wp-content/uploads/2017/01/Mahindachinthana-2007.pdf.

Raman, M. J. *The Malaysian Indian Dilemma*. Kuala Lumpur: Manickam Janakey Raman, 2000.

Raman, P. "Ambassadors of Hindutva: How Saffron Has Seeped into Our Diplomatic Space." *The Wire*, July 26, 2022. https://thewire.in/government/ambassadors-of-hindutva-how-saffron-has-seeped-into-our-diplomatic-space.

Ramaswamy, Krishnan. "The Diaspora Press: *India Abroad* Encourages Debate." In *Invading the Sacred: An Analysis of Hinduism Studies in America*, edited by Krishnan Ramaswamy, Antonio de Nicolas, and Aditi Banerjee, 397–404. Delhi: Rupa & Co., 2007.

Ramji, Hasmita. "British Indians 'Returning Home': An Exploration of Transnational Belongings." *Sociology* 40, no. 4 (August 2006): 645–62. Sage Publications.

Rao, Jaitirtha. "*The Indian Conservative: A History of Indian Right-Wing Thought*." New Delhi: Juggernaut, 2019.

Rao, Ramesh. "Hindu God, Must Indeed Be Heathen." *India Abroad*, November 28, 2003.

Reddy, I., and F. J. Hanna. "The Lifestyle of the Hindu Women: Conceptualizing Female Clients from Indian Origin." *Journal of Individual Psychology* (54): 384–98.

Regala-Angangco, Ofelia. "The Indian Community in the Philippines." *Philippines Sociological Review* 6, no. 2 (April 1958): 10.

Richard, H. L. *Following Jesus in the Hindu Context*. Pasadena, CA: William Carey Library, 1998.

Richard, H. L. "Hinduism: A Brief Overview." In *Rethinking Hindu Ministry: Papers from the Rethinking Forum*, 3–9. Pasadena, CA: William Carey Library, 2011.

Rogozinski, Jan. *A Brief History of the Caribbean from the Arawak and the Carib to the Present*. New York: Penguin Books, 1992.

Rothenberg, F. S. *Diaspora, Zerstreuung*.

Rukmani, T. S. *Hindu Diaspora Global Perspectives*. New Delhi: Munshiram Manohar Lal Publishers Pvt. Ltd., 2001.

Rye, Ajit Singh. "The Indian Community in the Philippines." In *Indian Communities in Southeast Asia*, edited by K. S. Sandhu and A. Mani, 707–73. Singapore: Institute of Southeast Asian Studies, 2006.

Safrai, Shemuel, and Menahem Stern, eds. *The Jewish People in the First Century*, 2 vols. Assen, Netherlands: Van Gorcum & Co., 1974–76.

Safran, William. "Diasporas in Modern Societies: Myths of Homeland and Return." *Diaspora* 1 (1991): 83–99.

Sathyadass, Daniel. "A Study of the Process of Discipling Listeners through Radio Homes of Trans World Radio–India (TWR), and Its Implications for House Church Planting in India." DMin Dissertation, South Asian Institute for Advanced Christian Studies (SAIACS), Bangalore, 2016.

Schnabel, Eckhard J. *Early Christian Mission: Jesus and the Twelve*. Vol. 1. Downers Grove, IL: IVP, 2004.

Schnabel, Eckhard J. *Early Christian Mission: Paul and the Early Church*. Vol. 2. Downers Grove, IL: IVP, 2004.

Sethi, Suresh, and Kamlesh Jain. "Indian Family Systems, Collectivistic Society and Psychotherapy." *Psychiatry in India* 38, no. 2 (1989): 107–16.

Shaye, J. D. Cohen, and Ernst S. Frerichs. "Preface." In *Diasporas in Antiquity*, edited by J. D. C. Shaye and E. S. Frerichs. Atlanta: Scholars Press, 1993.

Sheffer, Gabriel. "A New Field of Study: Modern Diasporas in International Politics." In *Modern Diasporas in International Politics*, edited by Gabriel Sheffer, 1–15. London: Croom Helm Publishers, 1986.

Shultz, Timothy. *Disciple Making among Hindus: Making Authentic Relationships Grow*. Pasadena, CA: William Carey Library, 2016.

Simson, Wolfgang, and George Barna. *The House Church Book: Rediscover the Dynamic, Organic, Relational, Viral Community Jesus Started*. New York: Barna Books, 2009.

Sittser, Gerald. *Resilient Faith: How the Early Christian "Third Way" Changed the World*. Grand Rapids: Brazos Press, 2019.

Smart, Ninian. "The Importance of Diaspora." In *Migration, Diaspora and Transnationalism*, edited by Steven Vertovec and Robin Cohen, 421–24. Aldershot, UK: Edward Elgar Publishing, 1999.

Smart, Ninian. "The Importance of Diasporas." In *Gilgul: Essays on Transformation, Revolution, and Permanence in the History of Religions*, edited by S. Shaked, D. Shulman, and G. G. Stroumsa, 288–97. Leiden, Netherlands: Brill, 1987.

Smith, Huston. *The World's Religions*. New York: Harper Collins, 1991.

Snyder, Howard. *New Wineskins: Changing the Man-Made Structures of the Church*. London: Marshall, Morgan and Scott, 1975.

Soon, I. "50 Years of Women's Activism." *The Star Malaysia*, August 29, 2013.

Staffner, Hans. *Jesus Christ and the Hindu Community*. Anand: GSP, 1988.

Subrahmanyan, P. T. "The Conversion from Hinduism to Christianity: A Christian Response with Specific Reference to the Issues of Individual Brahmin Converts." BD thesis, Senate of Serampore College, 2004.

Subramanian, Ajantha. *The Caste of Merit: Engineering Education in India*. Cambridge, MA: Harvard University Press, 2019.

Sylvester, Jerome. *Khristbhakta Movement: Hermeneutics of a Religio-Cultural Phenomenon*. ISPCK, 2013.

Tagore, Rabindranath. *Letters from Java*. Translated by Indrani Chaudhurani and Supriya Roy. Kolkata: Visva Bharati, 2010.

Takamizawa, Eiko, and David S. Lim. *Christian Mission in Religious Pluralistic Society*. Seoul: East-West Center for Mission Research and Development, 2019.

Tate, M. D. *The Malaysian History, Problems and Future*. Selangor, Malaysia: Vinlin Press, 2008.

Tatla, D. S. *The Sikh Diaspora: The Search for Statehood*. London: UCL Press Ltd., 1999.

Teja, Gary, and John Wagenveld. *A World of Gods: Planting Churches in a Pluralistic World*. Sauk Village, IL: Multiplication Network Ministries, 2022.

Tharoor, Shashi. "*Pax Indica: India and the World of the 21st Century.*" New Delhi: Penguin Random House India, 2013.

Thayer, Joseph. Thayer's Greek: 1248, 2409. Διακονία (Diakonia)–Service, Ministry. Ἱερεύς (Hiereus)–a Priest. Accessed April 26, 2021. http://biblehub.com/thayers/1248.htm; http://biblehub.com/thayers/2409.htm.

Thomas, M. M. "The Church in India—Witness to the Meaning of the Cross Today." In *The Future of the Church in India*, edited by Aruna Gnanadasan, 1–11. Nagpur, India: NCC, 1990.

Thomas, Terence. "Hindu Dharma in Dispersion." In *The Growth of Religious Diversity: Britain from 1945, Vol. I: Traditions*, edited by Gerald Parsons, London: Routledge, 1993.

US Census Bureau. "2020 Census Quick Facts: Indian Americans." 2021. https://www.census.gov/library/stories/2023/09/2020-census-dhc-a-asian-population.html.

US Census Bureau. "American Community Survey, Table DP05," 2020. https://data.census.gov/table?q=DP05.

Van Hoogen, E. Joel, with Charles A. Cook. *Pathway to the Soul: Reaching People through Spirit-Led Dialogue*. Camp Hill, PA: WingSpread Publishers, 2014.

Vertovec, Steven. *The Hindu Diaspora Comparative Patterns*. London: Routledge, 2000.

Vertovec, Steven. *Hindu Trinidad: Religion, Ethnicity and Socio-Economic Change*. London: Macmillan, 1992.

Vertovec, Steven. "Religion and Diaspora." Conference on "New Landscapes of Religion in the West." School of Geography and the Environment, University of Oxford, September 27–29, 2000, 1–45.

Vertovec, Steven. "Three Meanings of 'Diaspora,' Exemplified among South Asian Religions." *Diaspora* 6, no. 3 (1997): 19.

Viola, Frank, and George Barna. *Pagan Christianity*. Wheaton: Tyndale House, 2008.

Vivekananda. *Swami Vivekananda and His Guru: Letters from Prominent Americans on the Alleged Progress of Vedantism in the United States*. London and Madras: Christian Literature Society, 1897. Accessed January 20, 2021. www.vivekananda.net/NewspaperReports/17July97.html.

Warner, R. Stephen. "Immigration and Religious Communities in the United States." In *Gatherings in Diaspora: Religious Communities and the New Immigration*, edited by R. S. Warner and J. G. Wittner, 3–34. Philadelphia: Temple University Press, 1998.

Watson, David, and Paul Watson. *Contagious Disciple Making: Leading Others on a Journey of Discovery*. Nashville: Thomas Nelson, 2014.

Werbner, Pnina. *Imagined Diaspora among the Manchester Muslims: The Public Performances of Pakistani Transnational Identity Politics*. Oxford: James Curry Ltd., 2002.

White, R. E. O. "Salvation." In *Evangelical Dictionary of Theology*, edited by Walter Elwell. Grand Rapids: Baker Books, 1984.

Whitman, Sarah M. "Pain and Suffering as Viewed by the Hindu Religion." *The Journal of Pain* 8, no. 8 (August), 2007: 607–13. http://www.uphs.upenn.edu/pastoral/events/Hindu_painsuffering.pdf.

Wilford, Andrew C. *Cage of Freedom: Tamil Identity and the Ethnic Fetish in Malaysia*. Singapore: National University of Singapore, 2007.

Williams, Eric. *From Columbus to Castro: The History of the Caribbean*. New York: Vintage Books, 1984.

Williams, Raymond B. "Asian Indian and Pakistani Religions in the United States." In *The Annals of the American Academy of Political and Social Science*, edited by A. W. Heston, 178–95. Vol. 558.

Williams, Raymond B. "Immigrants from India in North America and Hindu-Christian Study and Dialogue." *Journal of Hindu-Christian Studies*, vol. 11 (1998): 23–24.

Williams, Raymond B. *An Introduction to Swaminarayan Hinduism*. Cambridge: Cambridge University Press, 2001.

Williams, Raymond B. *A New Face of Hinduism: The Swaminarayan Religion*. Cambridge: Cambridge University Press, 1984.

Williams, Raymond B. *Religions of Immigrants from India and Pakistan: New Threads in the American Tapestry*. Cambridge: Cambridge University Press, 1988.

Wilson, Kevon. "The Caribbean Is One of the Most Religious Places in the World." *Exceptional Caribbean* website. Accessed July 14, 2023. https://exceptionalcaribbean.com/2021/12/09/the-caribbean-is-one-of-the-most-religious-places-in-the-world/.

Wolf, Thomas. "The Wrinkled Wired Elephant: Firsts, Facts and Facets of India." Paper presented at The Bakke Graduate University DMin. Cohort. New Delhi. February 23, 2005.

Women's Aid Organization Malaysia. Accessed March 22, 2024. See https://wao.org.my/wp-content/uploads/2021/02/Annual-Statistics-2019.pdf.

Younger, Paul. *New Homelands: Hindu Communities in Mauritius, Guyana, Trinidad, South Africa, Fiji, and East Africa*. Oxford: Oxford University Press, 2010.

Author Profiles

Sam George, PhD, serves as director of the Global Diaspora Institute at the Wheaton College Billy Graham Center and as a Catalyst of the Lausanne Movement. He holds degrees in Mechanical Engineering, Business Management, and Theology. He researches and teaches around the world about global migration, diaspora missions, and World Christianity. Sam is the author/editor of a dozen books, including three volumes on *Asian Diaspora Christianity*.

Ashok Kumar, DMin, was born and brought up in India, living as a practicing Hindu for the first twenty years of his life. He then became a follower of Jesus in the early 1980s. Ashok has been involved in missions for more than thirty-five years. He spent most of this time with OM India, OM Singapore, and onboard an OM ship. He is currently part of the SIM East Asia team, leading the *Hethne* Initiative, and serves on the global leadership of the Mission Commission of the World Evangelical Alliance. He obtained a Master of Theology degree from Trinity Theological College, Singapore, and a Doctor of Ministry degree from Gordon-Conwell Theological Seminary in Boston.

Atul Y. Aghamkar, PhD, served as a professor and the head of the department of Missiology at two prominent theological institutions in India for over two decades. He currently serves as the Director of the National Center for Urban Transformation in Bangalore, India. His interest and research in diaspora studies led him to produce Building Bridges with Hindus in Diaspora, a video series that is accessible at www.ncutprojects.com.

Wilson Paluri, PhD, serves as a professor of religion and cultural studies at New Theological College (India) and is an ordained priest of the Church of North India. He is associated with national and international organizations that are reaching out to Hindus with the gospel. His passion is to teach and train young leaders and God's servants to be effective witnesses of Christ to people of other faiths, especially Hindus. His areas of interest include Indic studies, social philosophy, interreligious relations, and mission studies.

Martin Alphonse, PhD, is a retired Methodist pastor of an Indian community church in Portland, Oregon, and a professor at Multnomah Seminary and University. He completed his doctoral research at Fuller Theological Seminary and has served as a pastor and professor in Chennai, India, and Singapore. As an itinerant preacher, Martin travels worldwide regularly. He and his wife live in the suburbs of Portland and are the parents of three adult children.

Rahil Patel is a tutor at The Oxford Centre for Christian Apologetics (OCCA) in Oxford, UK. His work revolves around Hinduism (a group of multiple religions) and how the Christian faith can build bridges into that Eastern worldview and offer the beauty of the Gospels. Rahil is also an independent consultant to the

UK Government on India and human rights, as well as freedom of religion and belief. Earlier, Rahil was a Hindu monk for twenty years with one of the influential Hindu traditions. He was also the head of Hindu efforts in Europe and Russia before he had a powerful encounter with Jesus Christ. Rahil's autobiography (*Found by Love*) is available in several languages.

Daniel Sathyadass, DMin, is currently based out of Dallas and serves with Citylight/TMS Global, which seeks to spark home-church movements across the world. Earlier he, along with family and friends, pioneered Radiance, a home-church network in Bangalore, until 2005. From 2012 to 2018, Daniel also served as chaplain of the South Asian Institute of Advanced Christian Studies in Bangalore. He is married to Sayanora and has three grown sons and a daughter-in-law.

P. T. Subrahmanyan, PhD, obtained his BD and MTh (in Religion) degrees from the Senate of Serampore. He completed his MA (Philosophy) with rank in the University of Kerala and received his PhD from Mahatma Gandhi University. He is the national director of *Bharat Veda Abdhyayan* and on the faculty of the religion, philosophy, and culture department of India Bible College and Seminary in Kerala, India. He studied and conducted research at Free University in the Netherlands and Fuller Seminary in the US. He serves as a visiting professor at several institutions in India and abroad in the fields of religion and philosophy, besides being an associate pastor of a local church and a resource person for several mission efforts in India.

Kamesh Sankaran, PhD, is a professor and the Chair of Engineering Physics at Whitworth University, and he also heads the university's capstone core course, Worldviews in Policy. He is an aerospace engineer with over twenty years of experience as a researcher on advanced spacecraft propulsion systems. Kamesh teaches and preaches at his local church, where he serves as an elder. He grew up a devout Hindu in India and came to Christ when he was an international student at Princeton University. Kamesh served for many years as the chairman of Partners International, an eighty-year-old missions organization that equips and empowers indigenous Christian ministries in forty of the least-reached nations in the world. Kamesh is married to Angela, who works as a nurse practitioner. Angela grew up in Canada and Ecuador in a multigenerational missionary family and did her graduate studies in the US.

Anil Yesudas is an interfaith activist and a housing-rights activist. He studied Pharmacy, MBA, MA in Health Law, and MA in Community Development. After working for ten years in the pharmaceutical industry, he transitioned to serve as a Brethren Assembly worker and lived in homeless shelters voluntarily, from July 2007 to July 2008, to understand homelessness. He develops contextualized rituals, conserving biblical theology while being culturally relevant to the Hindu world. Anil lives in Chicago, with his wife Christina, and their two children.

Author Profiles

Ashwin Ramani comes from the southern part of India and is the first in his entire family lineage to become a follower of Jesus. Ashwin came to faith in Christ at the age of eighteen from an upper-caste Hindu family. Ashwin and his wife, Aboli, pastored a church in northwest India before coming to Canada for his higher theological studies. After graduating with a Masters in Divinity (MDiv), Ashwin has been on the pastoral staff at Centre Street Church in Calgary since 2012. He is currently doing doctoral studies.

Srinivasa Moorthy has been married to Valar for the last fifteen years, and they have two amazing sons and lives in Chennai, India. Srinivasa is an IT Engineer turned into a Family Life Educator. He earned an MA in Family Life Education from Martin Luther Christian University, in India. His passion is to develop holistic disciples who live a balanced and abundant life. Srinivasa and Valar have been on Christian television channels speaking on marriage enrichment through their weekly programs—more than two hundred episodes so far. Their family has lived in multiple cities in India, plus the UK, and has traveled to more than ten countries in South Asia, Southeast Asia, Europe, and the US in the last decade.

Mark Edward Sudhir is the lead pastor of the Fil-Indian Fellowship and Emmanuel Masihi Punjabi Fellowship. He is a missionary and church planter among the Hindu and Sikh diaspora, discipling indigenous leaders from different backgrounds. He serves as an executive member of the Lausanne Sikh Working Group and as a Facilitator of the International Sindhi Partnership. He earned an MDiv from a school in India, a ThM from a school in South Korea, and currently doing a doctorate in Intercultural Studies from a school in the Philippines. Mark is also a Christian musician and has several albums to his credit.

Anita Lazarus is a teacher and counselor and is involved in the governance of two international schools in South India. Currently, she is also leading a small team of experienced teachers, scattered across India, who are assembling a resource for middle-school teachers that will help them see their role and their subjects through the lens of a biblical worldview. As a counselor registered with the CCAI in India and the NACC in Malaysia, she has had varied experience in cross-cultural counseling with people of different faiths. During a fourteen-year stay in Melaka, Malaysia, she has also taught three modules in the Lay Counsellor's Course for the Malaysian Baptist Theological Seminary in Penang. Her husband is a decorated fighter pilot from the Indian Air Force. They have two sons and two grandchildren.

Chandra was born in Los Angeles, California, in 1956 and felt God's calling to identify with people of other cultures at a young age. After attending university, she and her husband joined the staff of a large Christian organization in 1978, then moved their young family to Kenya in 1981, where they worked as Bible teachers among the African and Asian peoples of Kenya. After they returned to the States in 2002, Chandra continued her Bible teaching among people of various cultures, both in-person and over the Internet. She helps believers share the love and hope of Christ effectively with their neighbors. Chandra and her husband now make their home in Texas. They have four children—two of whom live abroad—and four grandchildren.

Naveen is based in Australia and serves with a multinational team of digital missionaries, in which he combines over forty years of Information Technology experience, including six years of research on sharing the gospel online. Naveen is developing new software tools and researching digital ministry strategies.

Krishna (Kris) Ramsundar, DMin, is an adjunct professor at the Pentecostal Theological Seminary in Cleveland, Tennessee, and pastor of the Manantial de Vida Church of God in Grand Rapids, Michigan. Kris served as the president of the Mexican Bible Seminary in Hermosillo, Sonora, Mexico, for six years, and was also a member and vice-president of the Alliance for Education in Latin America (ALEAL). Originally from Trinidad and Tobago, he came to faith in Christ from Hinduism as a teenager. After finishing his studies at Lee University (BA) and the Pentecostal Theological Seminary (MA), Kris and his family moved to New Haven, Connecticut, where he completed an MDiv from Yale University and a Clinical Pastoral Education (CPE) residency at Yale-New Haven Hospital. He eventually completed a DMin program from the Pentecostal Theological Seminary in the United States. Kris is married to Dr. Michelle Carattini de Ramsundar, and they have two daughters.

Rev. Louie Naidoo is the senior pastor of the Queensburgh Evangelical Bible Church in Durban, South Africa. He has been in Christian leadership for over forty years while serving in churches and parachurch leadership positions. Currently, Louie also serves as head of the BTh program for the South African Theological Seminary. He is passionate about diaspora missions, church planting, and preparing God's people to be salt and light in the world. Louie is married to Sybil, and they have two adult children, one of whom is married.

Rethinking Hindu Ministry:
Papers from the Rethinking Forum | H. L. Richard

Hindu traditions are diverse and complex. Simple summaries of Hindu beliefs and practices aren't adequate to explain their captivating allure for Hindus. This collection of papers from seasoned practitioners observes Hindu traditions and Hindu ministry from new angles, introducing new perspectives on ministry in Christ's name that are relevant far beyond the Hindu world. Broad conceptual pictures and detailed practical advice is presented. Also highlighted are some remarkable Hindus who surrendered to Christ—and wrestled with the meaning of following Him in their Hindu families. This is the first book to turn to for pointers on sharing Christ with Hindus.

Disciple Making among Hindus:
Making Authentic Relationships Grow | Timothy Shultz

Drawing on thirty years' experience among Hindus, Timothy Shultz writes this book as a testimony of the kingdom of God growing in a non-Christian environment. *Disciple Making among Hindus* describes how Hindu people experience and respond to Jesus Christ. What are the core values and rhythms of their cultural world? What are the patterns of community and discipleship that help them draw closer to Jesus? Through moving personal stories, biblical reflection, and practical wisdom, Shultz introduces us to the centrality of family, the covenantal relationships that make up Hindu social life, and the yearning for authentic spiritual experience.

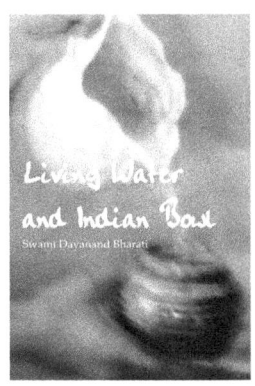

Living Water and Indian Bowl | Dayanand Bharati

This is an insightful analysis based on personal experience of Christian work among Hindus and the error and inadequacy of Western Christianity in the Hindu world. Numerous anecdotes are the greatest strength of this important book.

> "Bharati presents the transcultural Good News
> in culturally understandable ways for the India
> of the 21st century."
>
> —H. Stanley Wood, Center for New Church Development,
> Columbia Theological Seminary

visit us at missionbooks.org

www.ingramcontent.com/pod-product-compliance
Lightning Source LLC
Chambersburg PA
CBHW052136070526
44585CB00017B/1846